ARTHUR OSVER

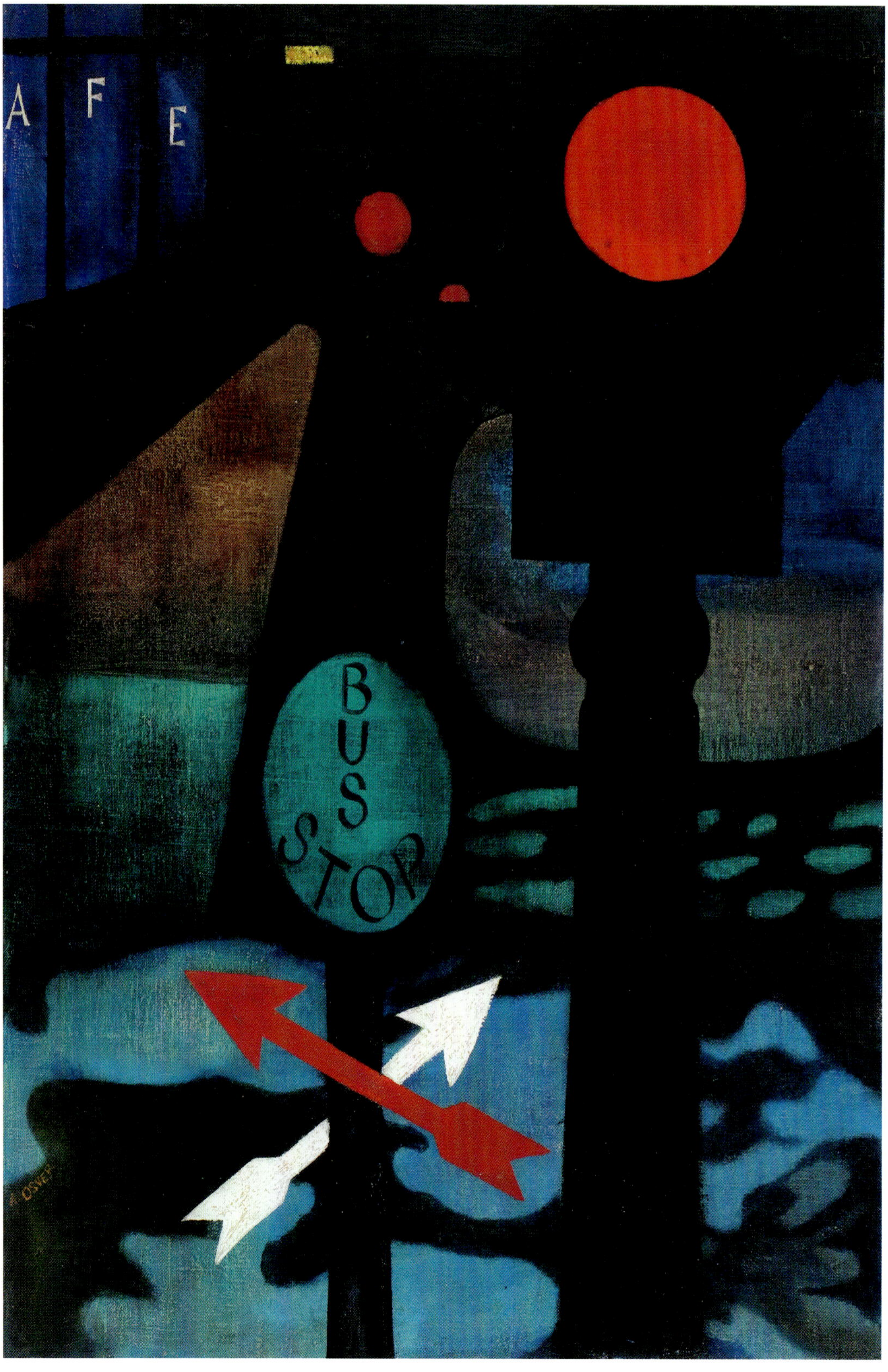
AFE
BUS
STOP

ARTHUR OSVER

Urban Landscape, Abstraction, and the Mystique of Place

EDITED BY

Angela Miller

WITH CONTRIBUTIONS BY

Matthew Bailey

Richard Gaugert

Angela Miller

Arthur Osver

Jennifer Padgett

MILDRED LANE KEMPER ART MUSEUM

SAM FOX SCHOOL OF DESIGN & VISUAL ARTS

WASHINGTON UNIVERSITY IN ST. LOUIS

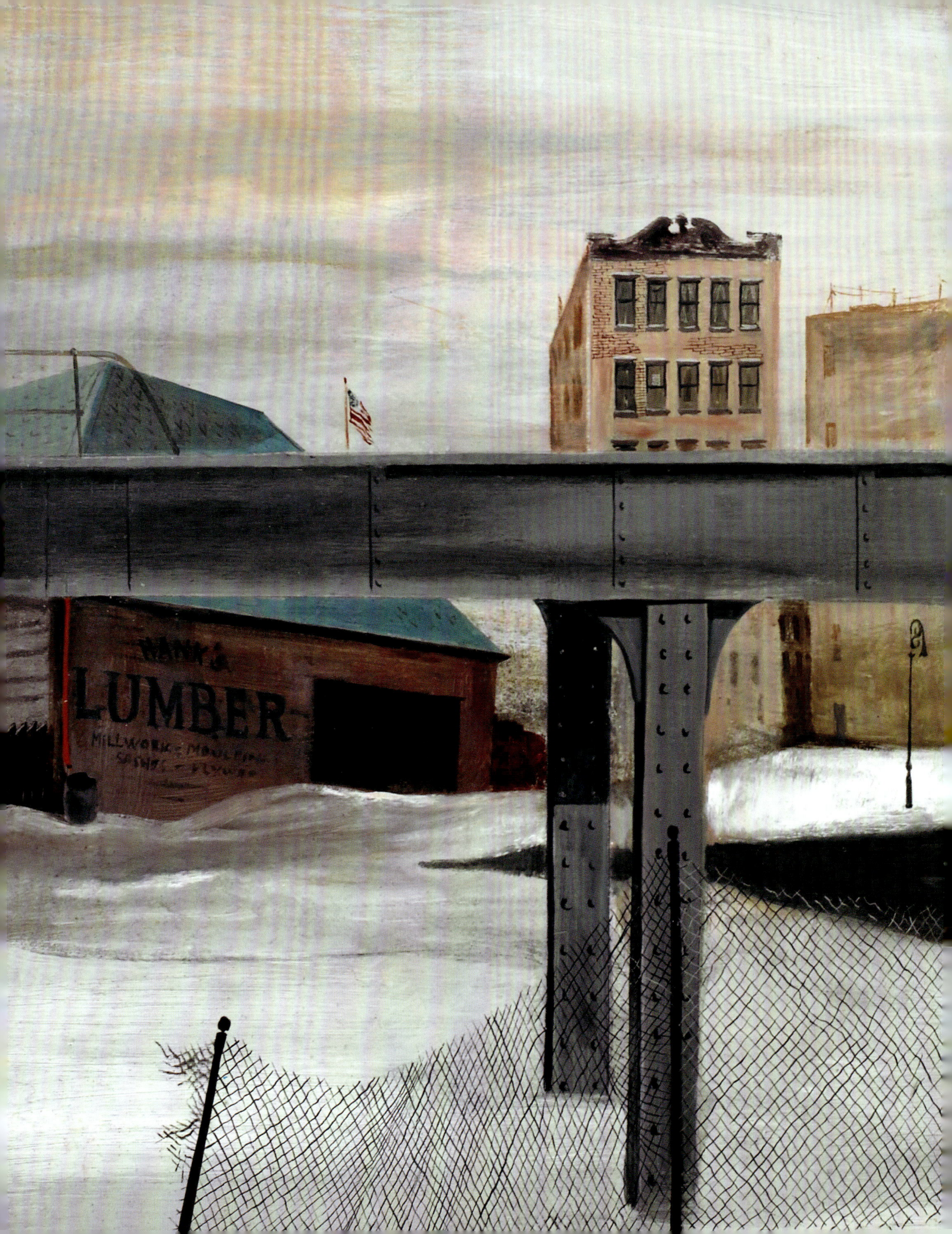
LUMBER

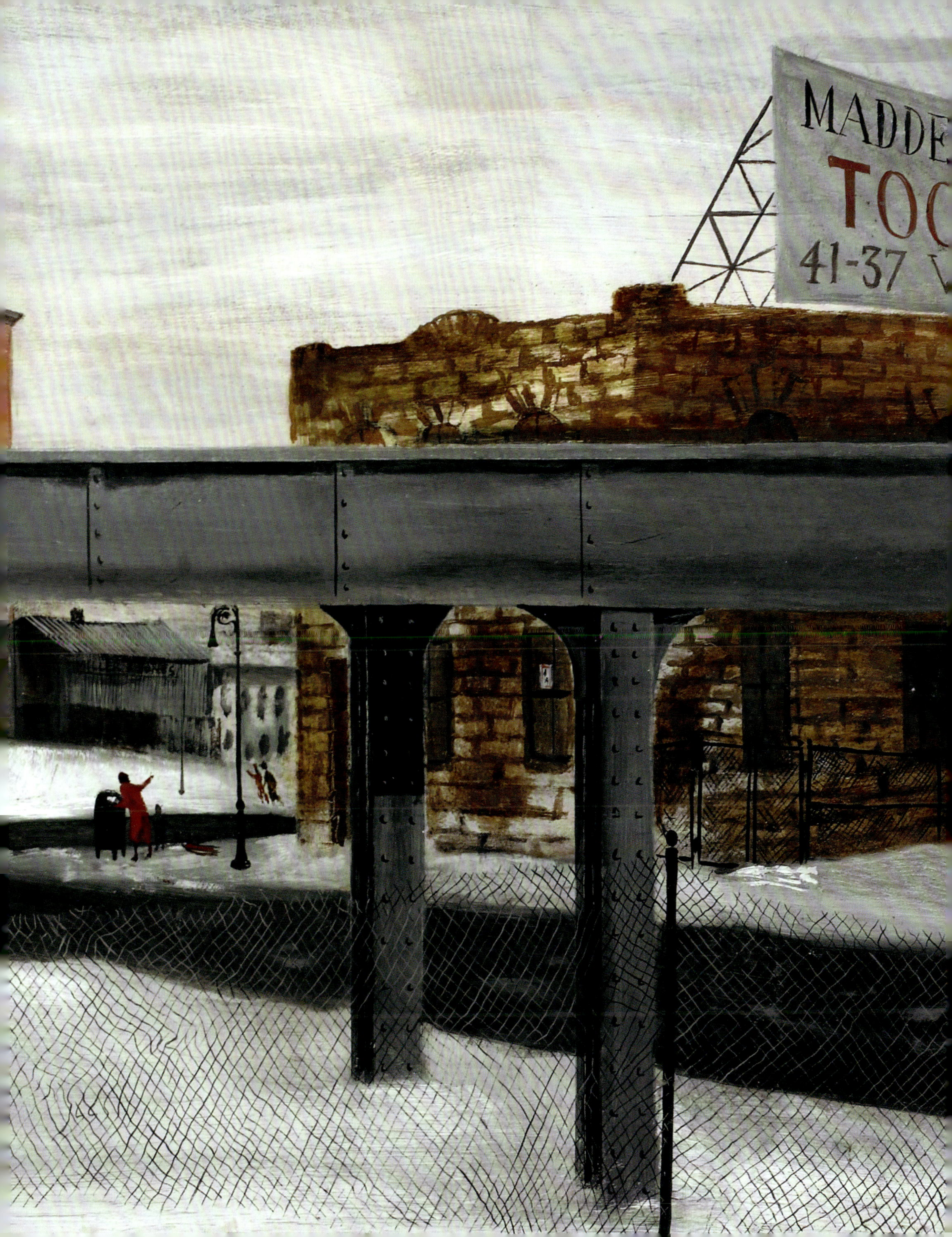
MADDE
TOC
41-37

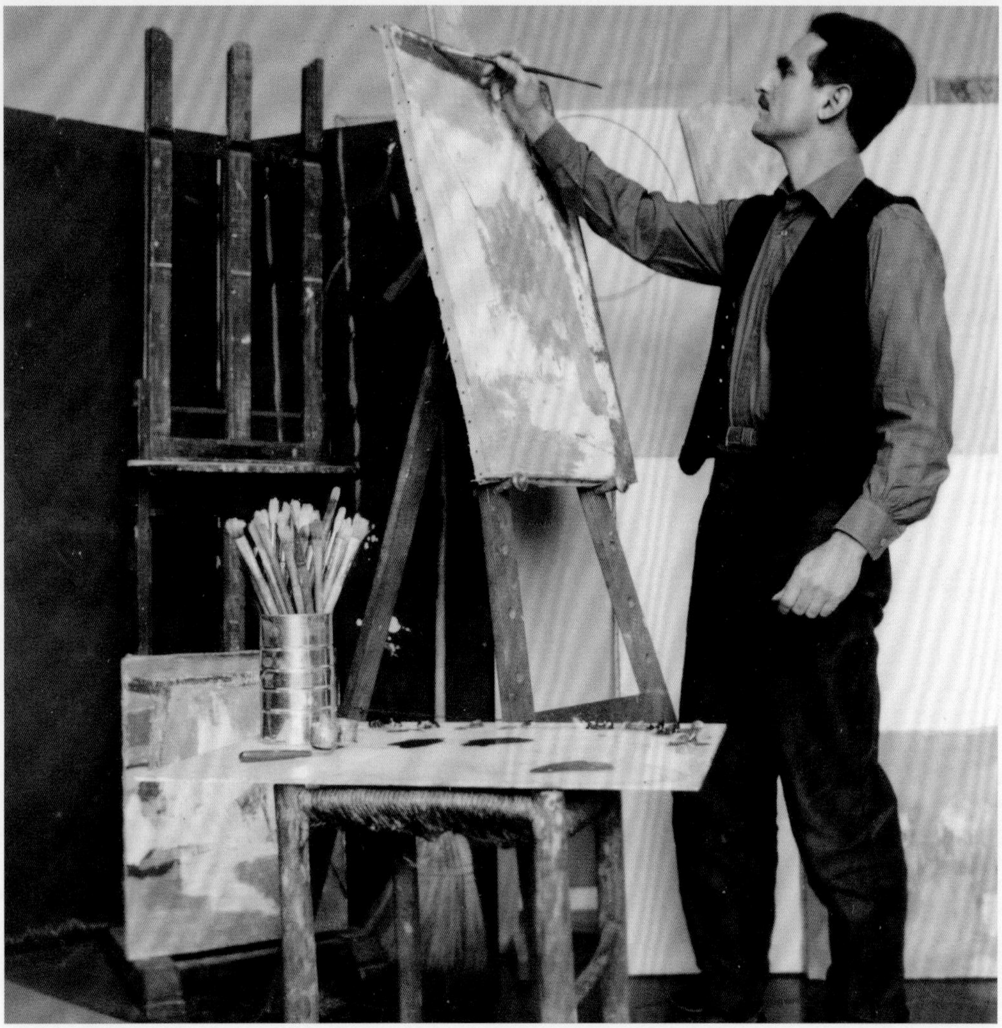

CONTENTS

FOREWORD

Arthur Osver's artistic practice spanned more than seventy-five years, taking shape in two distinct periods: his early years in Chicago and New York, and his Midwestern years from his move to St. Louis in 1960 until his death in 2006. When Osver arrived to teach at Washington University in St. Louis, he was forty-eight years old. At that point he had already achieved significant success as a painter. He had received such notable awards as a Guggenheim Fellowship and a Prix de Rome, he had served as a member of the International Fulbright Commission, and his work had been exhibited and collected by the Metropolitan Museum of Art, the Whitney Museum of American Art, and the Art Institute of Chicago, among others. Osver had also developed a distinctive style, amassing a compelling body of work exploring urban industrialized landscapes.

While Osver's early work captures the visceral realities of the environment around him, surrealist tendencies filter into his urban realism, endowing his images of ventilators, cranes, and pipes—set against signature dramatic skies—with uncanny animation. Although he had traveled abroad, spending a significant amount of time in Rome and Paris, his work during this period was deeply rooted in the American urban scene.

Encouraged by his friend Philip Guston and convinced by the persistence of Kenneth Hudson, dean of what was then called the School of Fine Arts at Washington University, Osver moved to St. Louis to teach. Hudson, a painter himself, may in fact be best known for the great artists who joined the faculty during his tenure, including Guston, followed by Werner Drewes and Max Beckmann in the late 1940s.

While Beckmann and Guston had left St. Louis more than a decade earlier, Osver arrived at an important moment in the life of the University's School of Art. Prior to Osver's arrival, the patron and collector Etta Steinberg had funded the commission of a young faculty member in the School of Architecture, Fumihiko Maki (who went on to win a Pritzker Prize in 1993), to design Steinberg Hall to house the University's art collection, which opened in 1960.

The collection, which had been transformed with the acquisition of significant modernist works during H. W. Janson's tenure as curator from 1944 to 1948, further expanded in the 1960s under the directorship of William N. Eisendrath Jr. The newly named Gallery of Art (now the Mildred Lane Kemper Art Museum) was completed the year Osver arrived on campus. Soon a hub of activity, the galleries in Steinberg Hall featured a robust program of exhibitions throughout the 1960s, including works by Alexander Calder, Jean Dubuffet, Max Ernst, Wassily Kandinsky, and Paul Klee, all of which are represented in the collection. These must have stimulated the discourse and conversations in the classroom, as did exhibitions of Abstract Expressionism with works in the Museum's collection by such major artists as Sam Francis, Guston, Franz Kline, Willem de Kooning, Robert Motherwell, and Jackson Pollock.

Osver's arrival at Washington University marked a pivotal period in his own career. He and his wife, Ernestine Betsberg, who was also an accomplished painter, quickly became deeply engaged in the St. Louis art community as well as around the School. The change of location and his professorship allowed Osver time and space for greater experimentation as he moved further toward large-scale abstraction. However, Osver had been skeptical of the prevailing developments of Abstract Expressionism and remained committed to investigating the relationship of painting to the immediate physical environment rather than to nonobjective painting. In the late 1960s the architecture of the Grand Palais in Paris offered him a motif that grounded his explorations of line and abstract form in an urban landscape, and, over time, color, light, and pattern became as central to his work as gesture, line, surface, and atmosphere. It is clear from his lecture notes, unpublished writings, and interviews that Osver continued to challenge himself in new directions both in his studio and in the classroom, and his intense artistic searching remained with him throughout his years in St. Louis.

As an art professor Osver was an exemplar for and mentor to his students, who benefited from his deep commitment, real world experience, and generosity as a teacher. From 1960 until his retirement in 1981, Osver had a profound impact on a large number of successful alumni. While I unfortunately never met him, first impressions of Osver as a teacher came to me from the artist Judy Pfaff, a personal friend of mine as well as an alumna of the School (BFA 1971). She has told me how, after a short period of study at Southern Illinois University in nearby Alton, she reached out as a young artist to Osver, having been impressed with his paintings, which she first saw exhibited in Steinberg Hall. Osver agreed to meet with her, recognized her potential, and proceeded to make it possible for her not only to study at Washington University, but also to attend Yale University's summer art program at Norfolk in 1970. She went on to study at Yale for her MFA, and she credits Osver with giving her the opportunities and space to do what she needed to do as an artist (including working with Betsberg in the couple's home garden). Another of Osver's students, John Moore (BFA 1966), an accomplished painter and the former chair of the Department of Fine Art at the University of Pennsylvania (who also went on to Yale for his MFA), described Osver in a recent conversation as "a beautiful painter who was supportive of a wide variety of stylistic approaches as a teacher."

The essays in this volume by Angela Miller, professor in the Department of Art History & Archaeology in Arts & Sciences at Washington University, and Matthew Bailey, an art historian who received his PhD in the same department, make abundantly clear that Arthur Osver's career was substantial and distinctive. He sustained a remarkably consistent high level of production throughout his life, and the intensity of his work never abated. As the current dean of the School, I am proud to be part of this first in-depth study of Osver's oeuvre and artistic influences. I extend my thanks to the authors, as well as to the editorial department and its team at the Mildred Lane Kemper Art Museum. I also am honored to thank William H. Danforth, who served as chancellor of Washington University from 1971 to 1995, for his impassioned contribution. And finally, I am deeply grateful for the fundamental support of two outstanding artists and alumni, Peter Shank and Paul Shank, trustees of the Estate of Arthur Osver and Ernestine Betsberg. Without their deep passion and commitment to Osver's work, coupled with their persistence and energy, this monograph would not have been realized. Together with their brother, Stephen Shank—also an artist and alumnus—and his wife, Julia Golden, they have devoted innumerable hours to this project, sifting through boxes and boxes of correspondence and personal papers, archiving and caring for a great number of Osver's paintings, tracking down those in private and public collections, and perhaps most importantly applying their vast and intimate knowledge of his life and work to the complex process of researching this history so it could be told. Simply put, without them this book would not exist. I congratulate them, along with Thomas Martin, also a trustee of the Estate of Arthur Osver and Ernestine Betsberg, for this fine achievement. And I would be remiss if I did not take this opportunity also to thank them for their continued support of the School through their roles as trustees of the Estate. Their dedication to both art and education ensures that the legacy of Osver lives on.

CARMON COLANGELO
Ralph J. Nagel Dean, Sam Fox School of Design & Visual Arts
E. Desmond Lee Professor for Collaboration in the Arts
Washington University in St. Louis

INTRODUCTION AND ACKNOWLEDGMENTS

I am pleased to present the first comprehensive study of Arthur Osver's long and productive career, which was characterized by a consistently distinguished oeuvre, a rigorous work ethic, and a questioning attitude toward the technical and formal aspects of painting. Osver continued to paint until the end of his life, adopting new collage techniques and incorporating language into his works in the final phase. When he was in his nineties, two weeks after major surgery he was asking his friend and former student Paul Shank to help him stretch canvases. A man of considerable modesty, Osver remained restless in his own evolving relationship to his work. This entry in his "painting journal" from October 6, 1942, is typical in its expression of self-doubt: "Today I got myself into a nervous, confused state by working and not thinking clearly as to what I wanted to achieve. Every performance of this kind by me must be considered a defeat, a retrogression and I must strive hard to master myself so that I can unleash all the good work that I am confident lies within me."[1] In 1945, after suppressing the impulse to tone down the red in one of his paintings, he wrote, "I thought of how in painting, experience had a tendency to make one overcautious, how the accumulation of skills instead of freeing the mind and hand often hampered it. That what should be the springboard for new experimentation turned out to be the mill-stone around one's neck. That is what I must fight."[2] Osver's earnest pursuit of continual reinvention was an enduring trait.

Even though he did not repeat himself or settle into any singular style, we still know an Osver when we see one: some quality of the tentative, some resistance to the facile body memory that occasionally substitutes for thought in the work of those who have painted over a lifetime. He wrote of the "muscular tactile involvement" that was required for good painting.[3] His figurative and referential work—rooted in urban landscape—contains abstract elements, a certain melancholy or muted palette, a play between two-dimensional form and allusions to depth and spatial recession. An example of his play of contradictions between flatness and recession is *Monday Morning* (1946; pl. 11), in which rectangular shapes of sheets and towels assert their abstract patterns while the receding line of a roof pulls the viewer back toward a more perspectival space. And the abstract work—with its mottled textures and elegant tracery of lines—frequently carries sentiments of familiar derelict industrial forms, long lived with and roughened by time. Never doctrinaire about any purported boundary between figuration and abstraction, Osver oscillated between the two, "grubbing about" with paint until a subject emerged;[4] achieving an endless range of color and palette variation, painting with splotchy but never purely gestural freedom, calculating mass in relation to implied space or ground in ways that might achieve maximum emotional resonance. He remained grounded in process, repudiating the idea of a preconceived end: "I have always had to go through this process of getting an initial image, manipulating it, perhaps losing it and rediscovering it, until all of a sudden it jells for me."[5]

Above all, what anchored Osver always in some form of landscape was his responsiveness both to his interior mood and to the exterior world in which he lived and worked. While his works, in his words, "conveyed a landscape sensation,"[6] he felt no fidelity to "direct perception of the subject."[7] His works—to borrow the title of one of them—were a *diary* of his subjective states, which he connected to his world of relations, ideas, words, buildings, and things. The art both mirrored and shaped the man. The facture of his work is never slick or assured; each stroke is considered, taking its own measure. Unlike the work of his New York School contemporaries, which remained a force he reckoned with, both questioning and learning from it, Osver's rarely displays any sense of urgency or speed, but rather a slow, meditative engagement with paint and color and shape in their emotive consequences. About an Amedeo Modigliani show he saw at the Museum of Modern Art in 1951, he commented, "Critics say he always paints the same picture with variations, *but what variations!*"[8] And about a similar comment regarding the work of Paul Cézanne—that he was "standing still"—Osver wrote, "May I be permitted to stand still like Paul Cézanne!"[9]

If Osver used his art to explore his relation to the world, teaching became one further arena in which to do that. From 1947, when he first began teaching at the Brooklyn Museum Art School and Columbia University, up to his retirement in 1981, Osver would integrate teaching into his life as an artist. In 1960 he accepted a position at Washington University while continuing to be nationally active as a Guggenheim Foundation and American Academy in Rome jurist. At what was then known as the School of Fine Arts, Osver offered guidance and support to generations of young artists, who are quick to acknowledge his critical role in their formation.[10] Osver's legacy therefore remains not only his paintings but also his impact on the next generation of painters.

* * * *

This sustained tribute to Osver's work and life as an artist would not have been possible without the dedication and passion of the artists Peter, Paul, and Stephen Shank (the latter two students of Osver) and Thomas Martin, a trustee, along with Peter and Paul Shank, of the Estate of Arthur Osver and Ernestine Betsberg. We are grateful for their generosity in allowing us access to the archives and for their personal assistance based on their friendship with Osver.

Deep gratitude is also due to the many individuals and organizations who contributed to this project. Among those who provided images of, information about, and access to Osver's paintings, specific thanks go to the archivists and librarians at the Library of Congress, the St. Louis County Library, and the Smithsonian Archives of American Art; Philip Slein Gallery, St. Louis, Missouri, and Winfield Gallery, Carmel, California, both of which represent the Estate of Arthur Osver; and Jean-Paul Torno, who photographed many of the works reproduced in this publication.

It was an honor to be part of the team that brought this project to fruition. My thanks to Matthew Bailey for our many conversations about Osver's work and for his scholarly essay in this volume, and to former chancellor William H. Danforth, whose remembrance helps bring to light the intellectual vibrancy of Osver's years at Washington University. Leading the project from start to finish was Jane Neidhardt, head of publications at the Kemper Art Museum; her vision helped shape this publication, and I thank her for our collegial collaboration. Also essential was Holly Tasker, publications and communications assistant, who extensively researched both photos and paintings and provided editorial assistance with every aspect of this project. Jennifer Padgett, then a PhD candidate in the Department of Art History & Archaeology at Washington University in St. Louis, served a key role as research assistant, helping organize archival materials and compiling the chronology for this book. I am also deeply grateful to Karen Jacobson, Los Angeles, for her editorial expertise, and to Michael Worthington, also of Los Angeles, for his sensitive design of this beautiful publication.

Last but far from least, I extend my gratitude to the leadership at Washington University. Especially significant for this project is the support of Carmon Colangelo, Ralph J. Nagel Dean of the Sam Fox School of Design & Visual Arts. His thoughtful foreword highlights the importance of Osver's influence as both an artist and an educator during his many years at the School. I am also grateful to Sabine Eckmann, William T. Kemper Director and Chief Curator at the Mildred Lane Kemper Art Museum, for her rigorous commitment to scholarship and to her vision as a director, and to Chancellor Mark S. Wrighton, whose continued support of the arts and humanities is essential for all major undertakings such as this.

ANGELA MILLER, PHD
Professor of Art History & Archaeology
Arts & Sciences
Washington University in St. Louis

NOTES

1. Arthur Osver, "My Painting Journal," October 6, 1942, Arthur Osver Papers, Estate of Arthur Osver and Ernestine Betsberg, St. Louis; hereafter cited as Osver Papers, St. Louis.
2. Osver, "My Painting Journal," November 1, 1945, Osver Papers, St. Louis.
3. Arthur Osver to Henry A. (Al) Leindecker, September 13, 1962, correspondence between Henry A. (Al) Leindecker and Arthur Osver, 1949–63, microfilm reel 3948, Arthur Osver Papers 1943–1975, Archives of American Art, Smithsonian Institution, Washington, DC; hereafter cited as Osver Papers, AAA.
4. Arthur Osver, "Overlapping & Linkages," Osver Papers, St. Louis.
5. Arthur Osver, in *Arthur Osver: The Saint Louis Years* (St. Louis: Saint Louis Art Museum, 2000), unpaged.
6. Arthur Osver, "St. Loup," Osver Papers, St. Louis.
7. Arthur Osver, "Notes on 'Ernestine' and 'St. Loup,'" Osver Papers, St. Louis.
8. Osver to Leindecker, May 2, 1951, Osver Papers, AAA.
9. Osver to Leindecker, May 8, 1952, Osver Papers, AAA.
10. Several of Osver's former students spoke eloquently about this at Osver's memorial service, held at Washington University's Graham Chapel on October 22, 2007. Audiotape, Osver Papers, St. Louis.

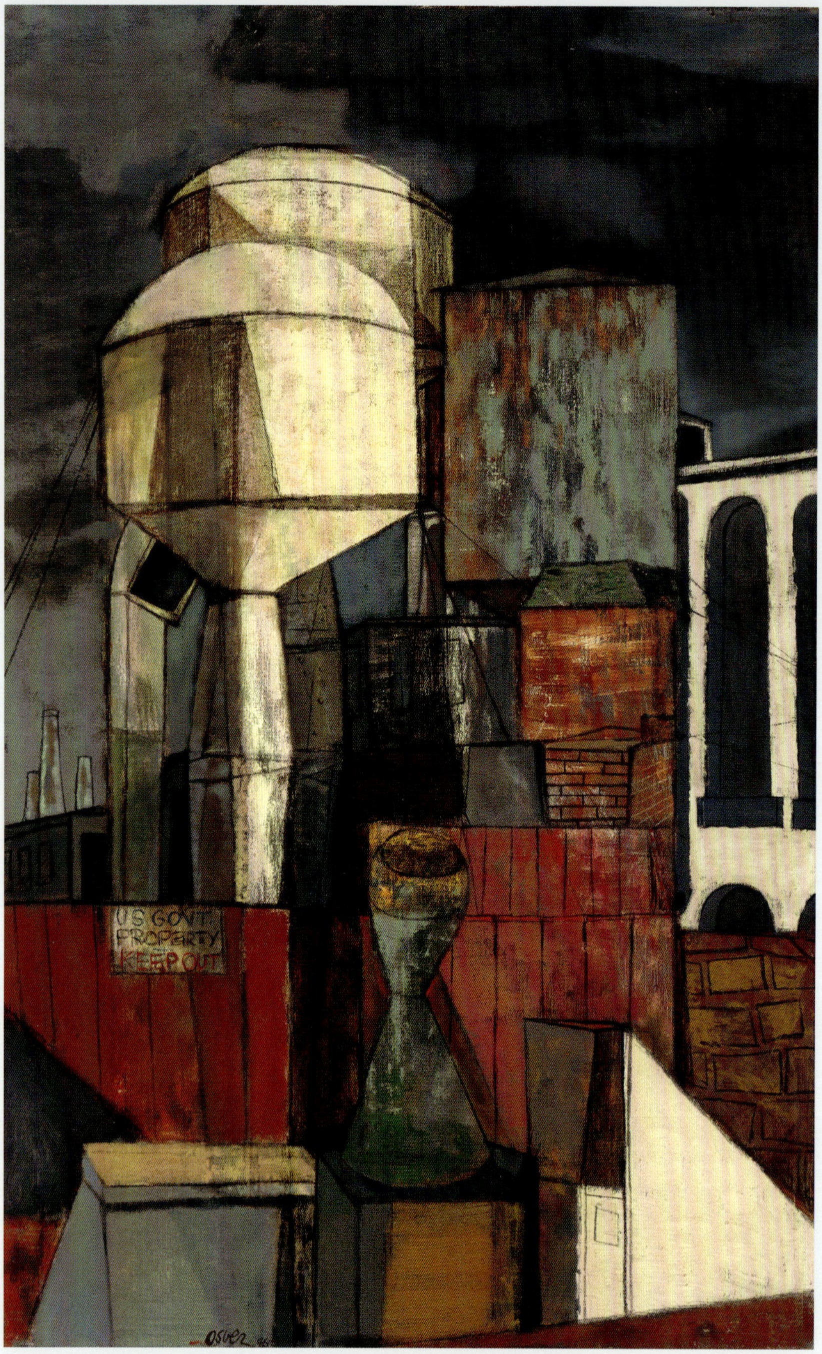

Fig. 1

***The Tanks,* 1946–47**

Oil on canvas, 44 1/8 × 27 7/8"

The Museum of Fine Arts, Houston, Museum purchase

Creased by Time: Arthur Osver's "Memory Haunted" Urban Landscapes of the 1930s and 1940s

Angela Miller

I remember as a child peering out of our fifth-floor apartment window at the strange world of rooftops below me; a world of strange shapes and sizes and colors; of grotesque chimneys, wires, and wash hanging on the line. From then on I began to shake off the "plein air" type of painting that I had found so ill-suited to the Chicago scene. I began to paint the city as I experienced it directly.
ARTHUR OSVER

There is a mystique in places and things; I see it clearer myself now than I did then....
I once labeled myself essentially a landscapist. In a way I still am. Only, the landscape is becoming more and more an inner personal one.
ARTHUR OSVER

These two statements by Arthur Osver indicate the two contrary paths of his work: in one direction, toward the externals of experience—the imprint of the world on the artist—and in another, toward the inner landscape of mind and imagination. In his early career these two opposing impulses wove together in a manner that would come to characterize much of the subjectively charged painting that took shape in the wake of 1930s Social Realism, as "experience" shifted its register from social immediacy toward more private meanings inflected by histories of personal and national loss. Subjective mood intertwined with the chastened spirit of a nation beset by the Great Depression, unemployment, dreams deferred or derailed.[1] Faced with these challenges, the nation turned inward, away from Europe.

Throughout the many phases of his development as an artist, Osver was—as he claimed—always a landscapist. His juvenile paintings from his childhood in suburban Chicago drew on a standard repertoire of "crags, forests, and water leaping over falls, and rapids, and perhaps tiny little figures gazing at the immensity of nature," the expressions of a dreamy boy keen

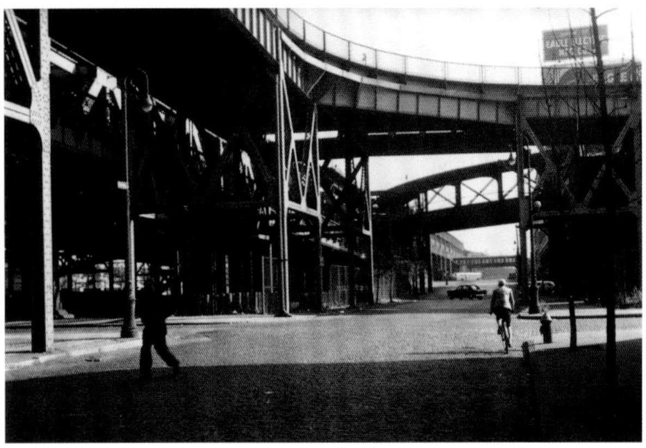

Fig. 2
Undated photograph by Arthur Osver of Long Island City, Queens
Arthur Osver Papers, Estate of Arthur Osver and Ernestine Betsberg, St. Louis

to become an artist.[2] He would eventually define himself as an urban painter, his focus happening to be—as he put it—"on this world of wires and chimneys and tar paper and all the rest of it."[3] He painted his industrial landscapes in Long Island City, where he and his wife, the artist Ernestine Betsberg, moved in 1943, leaving behind Greenwich Village. Osver described Long Island City as "a conglomerate industrial and residential section of Queens."[4] It was abandoned during the weekends, and in Osver's work of these years the industrial infrastructure of the neighborhood—water tanks, ventilators, chimneys, and older commercial buildings—seems to take on an almost human sense of presence in the absence of people themselves (fig. 1). He had first become familiar with the area while working at a factory making water purification tablets. "I liked the neighborhood," he said later about the landscape of Queens, likening it to his midwestern roots. "Somehow it sort of materialized, began to be like Chicago—commercial buildings, bridges, strange structures that turned me on as an artist. It was visually wonderful material for me. So we decided to move to Queens" (fig. 2).[5] Osver and Betsberg rode bikes throughout the metropolitan region, from Queens to Brooklyn, to Staten Island on the ferry, to Coney Island, and back to Long Island City, sometimes traveling forty miles in a day.

Osver's paintings, however, were not portraits of place but condensations of his impressions. "There was nothing that was specifically this bridge or that building or that roof top; but they were a composite of all of the bridges and roof tops and buildings that I had seen."[6] His early movement away from plein air naturalism—painting on the spot and out of doors—happened in this moment of both embracing the place and responding to it through a filter of memory. He later commented that these works were related "to the idea of delayed reaction.... Painting is getting yourself into a frame of mind. I remember those week-end bike-trips during the war and all that looking. I never painted what I saw. I painted from the excitement and incitement of what I saw."[7]

This habit of retrospect would remain with him throughout his career, but its origins may have been in the somber climate of Osver's childhood, shadowed by emotional loss. His streak of sadness seems to have had its origins in the death of his mother, with whom he was very close, when he was fifteen, after which his family life came unraveled. His brother was sent to a military academy, and he went to live with friends who had children, seeing little of his father after that. The sense of absence to which he responded so strongly in the deserted landscapes of Long Island City and elsewhere may have been an echo of this deeper feeling of desolation, now softened into the subdued moodiness of the adult work. But melancholy pervades the work of others of this generation as well, from Louis Guglielmi to Edward Hopper, a sense that people within these deserted American spaces seem dispossessed, mute witnesses to a landscape that they occupy without inhabiting. Osver's urban landscapes carry the imprint of the human, even in its absence. The marginal urban landscapes to which he was so deeply attracted resonated not only with his own melancholic mood of these years but also with a generation touched by national depression and withdrawal from the brash confidence of an earlier generation. In Europe a mood of emotional reserve, psychological enigma, and uncanny animation of the inanimate had already taken shape by the 1920s, in the years after World War I.

Osver lived in Long Island City for nine years, which he later claimed were among the most productive of his career. During this period he was awarded a Guggenheim Fellowship (1949) and numerous other honors, including the Rome Prize Fellowship (known colloquially as the Prix de Rome), awarded by the American Academy in Rome (1952–53). The combination of work in the factories of Long Island and time spent painting in his studio proved very fruitful. The inspiration behind the body of work he produced in Long Island City was Osver's attraction to America's "industrial look"[8]—but an industry already worn and creased by history. His interest in industrial themes took shape in his Guggenheim proposal to tour the "great industrial cities like Pittsburgh, Youngstown, Gary, and Chicago," where he would "paint, sketch, and strengthen my perceptions."[9] Rejecting the search for "the specific, novel, or picturesque," Osver proposed to explore his industrial subject "plastically" to use form to express from within the "urban and industrial civilization" by which he felt so strongly affected. He also recorded his attraction to "old tenements, billboards, factories, warehouses, giant smokestacks, and river-front coal

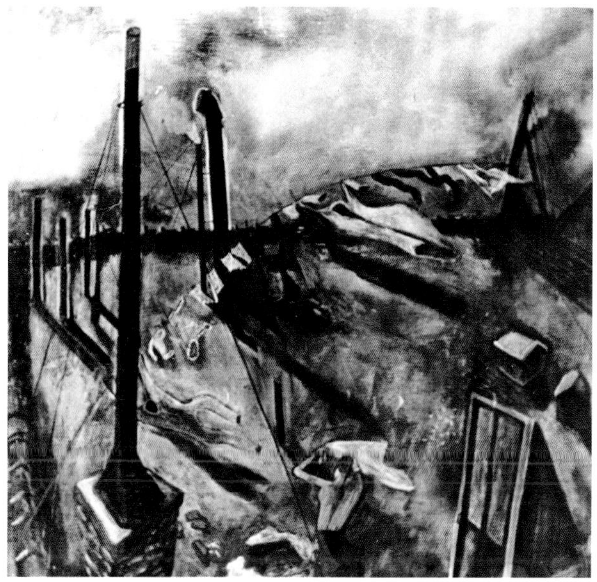

Fig. 3
***High Wind*, 1939**
Oil on canvas, dimensions unknown
Location unknown

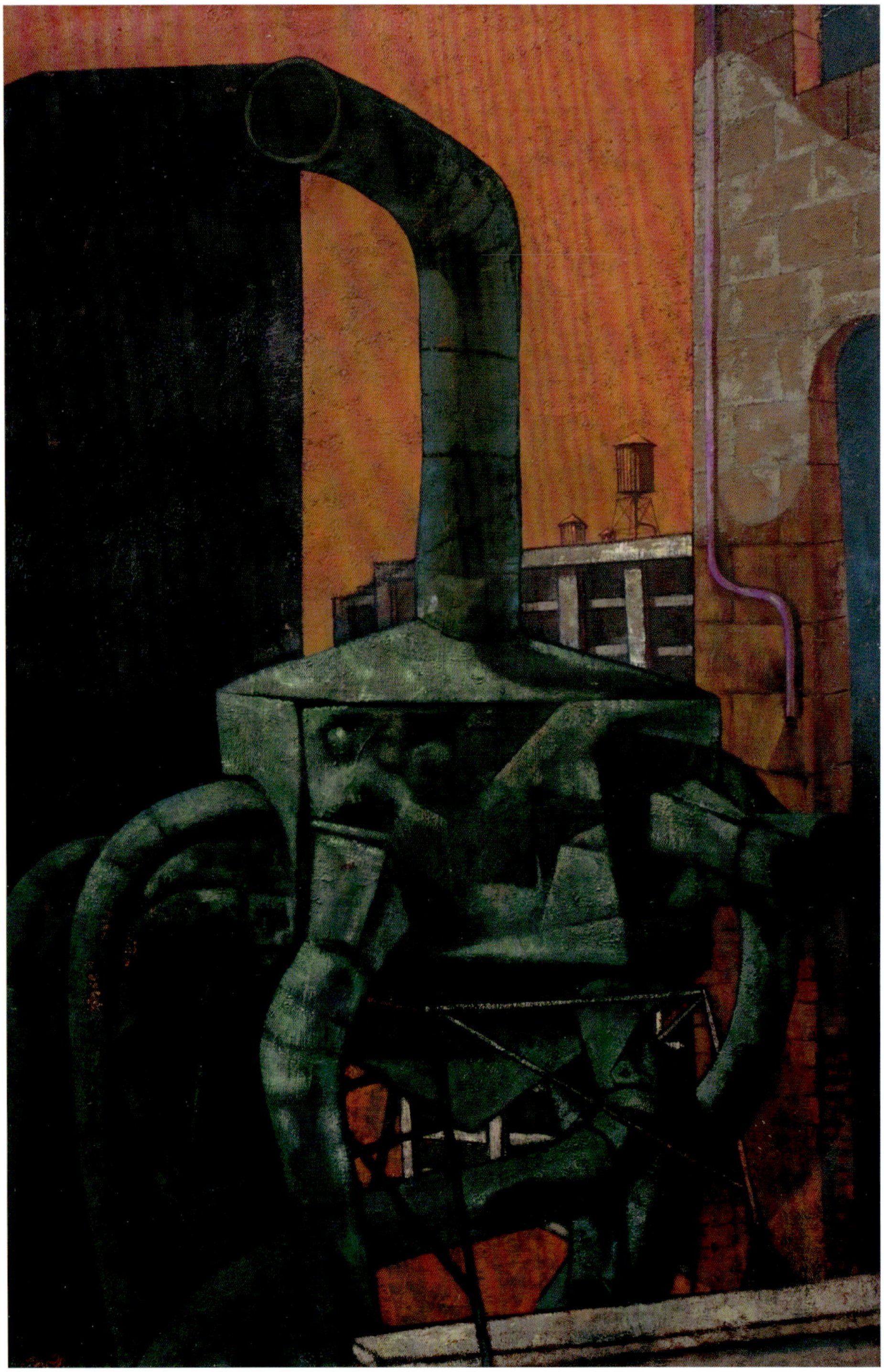

Fig. 4
***Green Ventilator*, 1946**
Oil on canvas, 40 x 27"
Estate of Arthur Osver and Ernestine Betsberg

yards."[10] These raw materials of the industrial landscape became the instruments through which he expressed his own sense of place, his personal experience of the lived landscape. "I wasn't seeing them with a tourist's eye but with the eye of an actual denizen of this lair of strange creatures that we call habitations and factories and bridges and everything else that goes to make up the American industrial scene."[11]

The "strange creatures" that populate Osver's urban world do indeed exude an uncanny animation.[12] In his *High Wind* (1939; fig. 3), clothes being whipped by the wind have, in his words, "a certain surreal quality by looking as if the person who had worn the clothes was still in them."[13] The displacement of the human onto things and objects in the urban environment was a persistent feature of Osver's form of Magic Realism, a loose nationwide movement to explore the moody, time-creased landscapes that existed on the margins of Henry Luce's "American Century."[14] Rooftop ventilators populate Osver's canvases of the late 1930s and 1940s like characters in a play, with their vacant black faces, awkward shapes, and sinuous arms snaking their way through the compositions. But what, after all, are ventilators, those curious fixtures that are everywhere visible and yet most often unseen, unnoted? They are the connectors between interior spaces—industrial in nature—and the world beyond the building, gyroscopes that transmit industrial exhalations from the inside to the outside. Situated at some midway point between industrial and organic shapes, they are like the lungs of the building, allowing it to breathe. In a talk at the Saint Louis Art Museum many years later, in 1973, Osver called them "almost humans."[15] For a young artist searching for a subject, ventilators perhaps carried some maternal suggestion, with their swelling bellies, pivoting around as if surveying the landscape or standing like imposing sentinels atop their buildings. Osver's ventilators are also often worn, old, slightly sagging from the weight of time, quasi-anthropomorphic in their mortal attire of poignant dereliction. His *Red Ventilator* (1945; pl. 9) seems like a body limp and weighted down with age, supported from below only by a frail armature of wood.[16] Sitting atop a roof, the ventilator threatens to slide into our space, the perspective tilted up at a precipitous angle against a vacant sky. Osver frequently used such off-kilter perspectives to create a sense of unease or

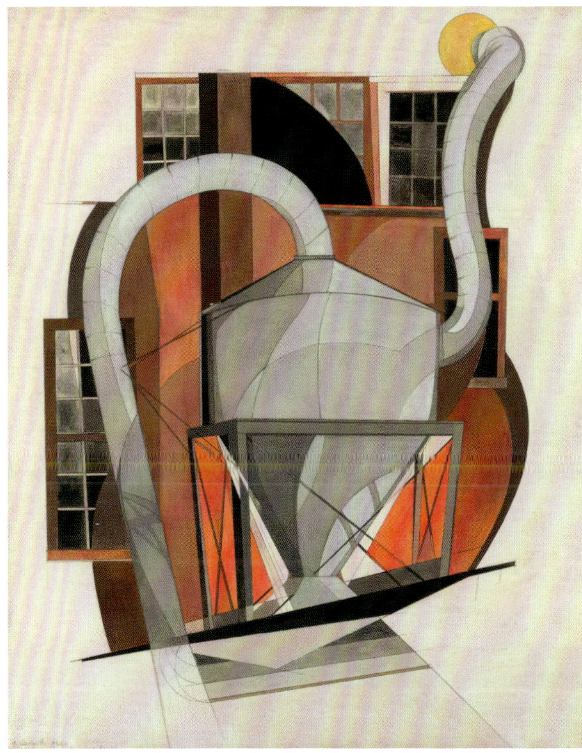

Fig. 5
Charles Demuth (American, 1883–1935)
***Machinery*, 1920**
Gouache and graphite on paperboard, 24 x 19 7/8"
The Metropolitan Museum of Art, New York, Alfred Stieglitz Collection, 1949

precariousness that physically evoked the uncertainty of the historical moment. A 1947 review called the subject of *Green Ventilator* (1946; fig. 4) "an overpowering, malevolent monster," identifying "surreal overtones" in Osver's recent works while also, paradoxically, noting the poise and impersonality of their forms.[17]

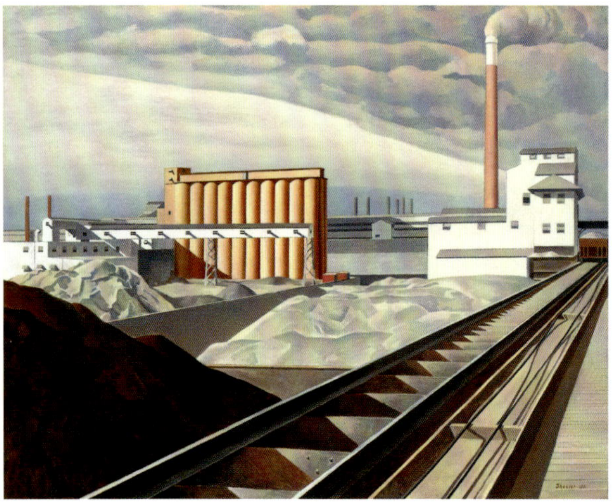

Fig. 6
Charles Sheeler (American, 1883–1965)
***Classic Landscape*, 1931**
Oil on canvas, 25 x 32 1/4"
National Gallery of Art, Washington, DC,
Collection of Barney A. Ebsworth

This oscillation of meaning—between organic and mechanical, maternal and threatening, anthropomorphic and impersonal—characterized Magic Realism as it transformed the languages of Social Realism in the later 1930s with anti-naturalistic, uncanny, and absurd elements: blank red skies, spatial ambiguities, and interruptions in narrative logic. *Green Ventilator*—shown at the annual Contemporary American Painting exhibition at the Whitney Museum of American Art, New York, in 1946—is one of Osver's most successful works from this period. With its richly mottled surfaces the color of oxidized copper and its octopus-like arms, the ventilator seems on the verge of subsiding into a condition of organic decrepitude that carries its own strange beauty. The sky behind it is a flat rusty red, which gives an ominous presence to the empty spaces. These industrial forms—with their dense, abraded surfaces—seem to anticipate their own dereliction rather than looking proudly toward the future. The American painter Charles Demuth had already by the 1920s captured the mood of the aging industrial landscape in his own paintings of ventilators, in Lancaster, Pennsylvania (fig. 5). Demuth, suffering from diabetes, may have transferred his sense of physical frailty to his scenes of his hometown, where he returned to live in the 1920s.

Such melancholic treatment of aging industrial forms differs strikingly from the incisive profiles and glistening surfaces of much "machine art" between the wars. In these years Precisionism—the tightly painted geometric rendering of urban landscapes, largely devoid of human presence, airless and unatmospheric—was the language of urban modernity. A hard-edged, pristine style, Precisionism—in works such as Charles Sheeler's *Classic Landscape* (1931; fig. 6)—seemed to turn deliberately away from all indications of human presence. Favoring an impersonal and coolly remote geometry of the built environment, it drained away any signs of motion—of the brush, of feeling, indeed of time itself—and locked the

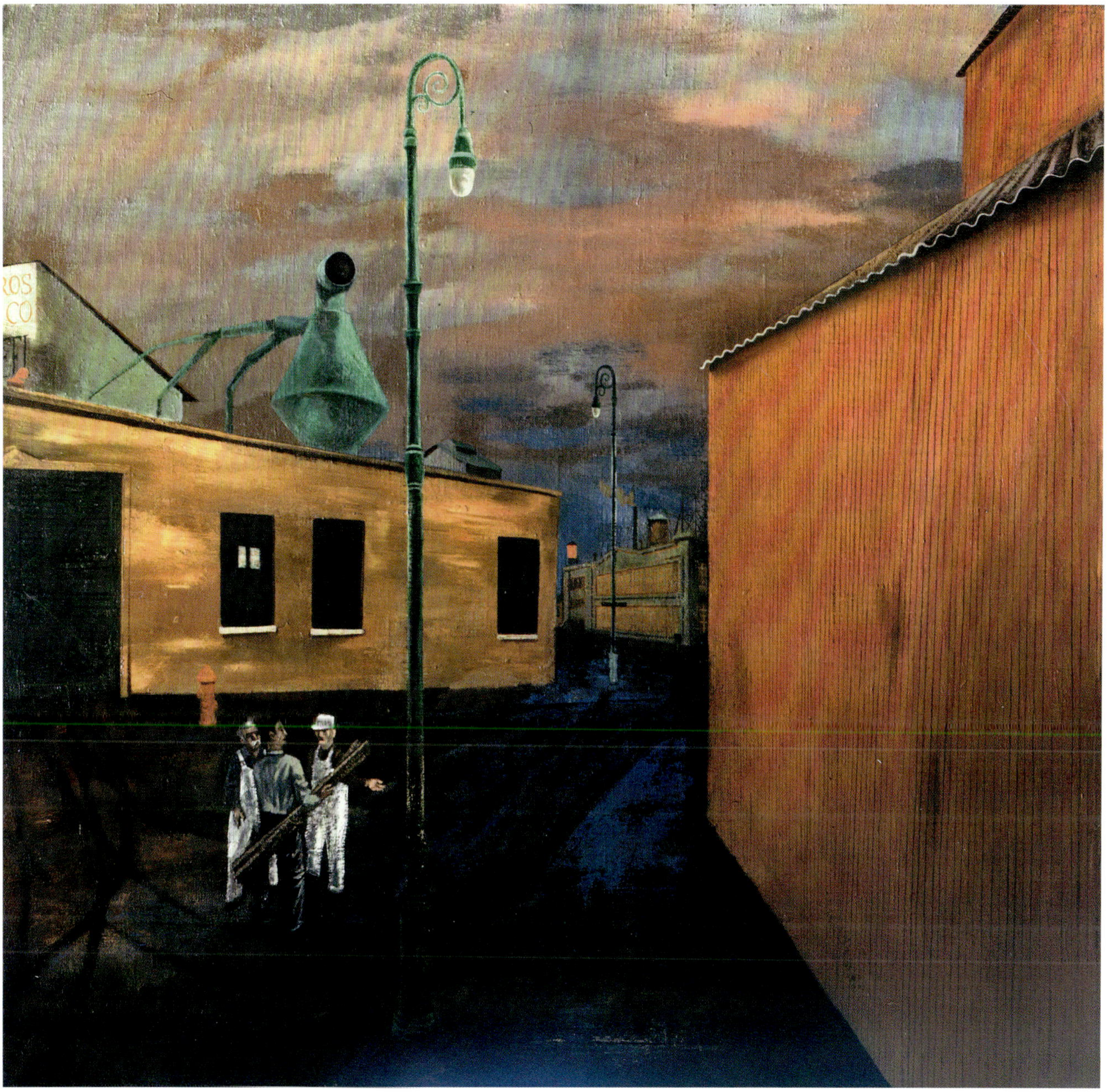

Fig. 7
***After the Rain*, c. 1945**
Oil on canvas, 32 x 30"
Location unknown

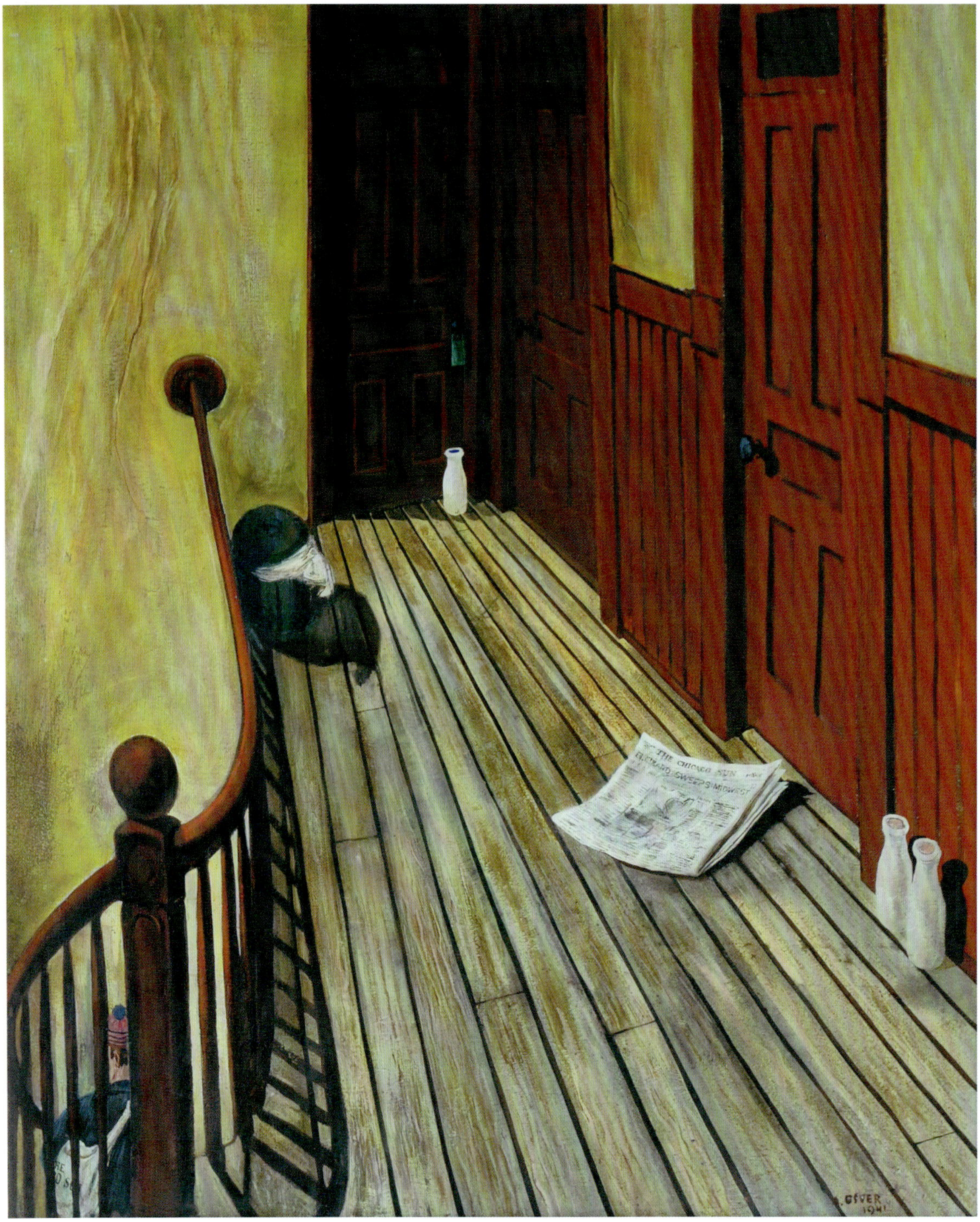

Fig. 8
***Hallway*, 1941**
Oil on canvas, 30 x 36"
Estate of Arthur Osver and Ernestine Betsberg

unstable and dynamic energies of industry and modern cities into a taut equilibrium of grid-like horizontals and verticals.[18] Osver's industrial landscapes of the early 1940s, by contrast, are dense, labyrinthine, and packed with skewed buildings, as if torqued by some outside force that deflects them from their right angles (fig. 7). And unlike the smooth, uninflected surfaces of Precisionist works, Osver's buildings and streets seem corroded by time. Even his more intimate domestic scenes, such as *Hallway* (1941; fig. 8), offer only glimpses of retreating figures. James Thrall Soby, director of the department of paintings and sculpture at the Museum of Modern Art in New York, explicitly contrasted Sheeler's work with that of Osver, whose portrayal of the underside of modern industry pointedly departed from Sheeler's precisely calibrated and empty industrial landscapes.[19] Osver's urban scenes seem ramshackle; the relations among their elements the result of happenstance rather than human planning. Their temporal location seems ambiguous, neither clearly of the present moment nor situated in the past. With its somber hues, uptilted streetscapes, and deserted urban space, *Greenpoint Windows* (1945; pl. 8), for example, offers a variant mood on a recurrent theme of haunted cities in the art of these years. Its rows of blank windows, its rough facades, its play between surface plane and recessional depth suggest—as do many of Osver's works from these years—the distance from the older interwar language of machine-age geometries, and an atmosphere of alienation identified with Magic Realism.

Years of depression had taken a toll on the nation, transforming clarity into suggestively shadowed density. *Stamford Gas Works* (1933; fig. 9), by Osver's contemporary Alexander Brook, embodies similar themes of industrial ruin, uncertainty, and loss.[20] Osver's work balances the elegiac with the place-specific; his gentle attachment to the curious mechanical landscape of his neighborhood remains primary. The sense of forlorn intimacy that these works exude is characterized by a familiarity born of long exposure to a particular place. Osver was referred to as the "Utrillo for Brooklyn."[21] Yet for all the familiarity and Sunday domesticity this implies, Osver's industrial spaces—full of blocked vistas, walls at odd angles, and curtailed prospects—also evoke discontinuity, a world in "fragments" (a word he used), as if one is arriving at a scene drained of productive energies,

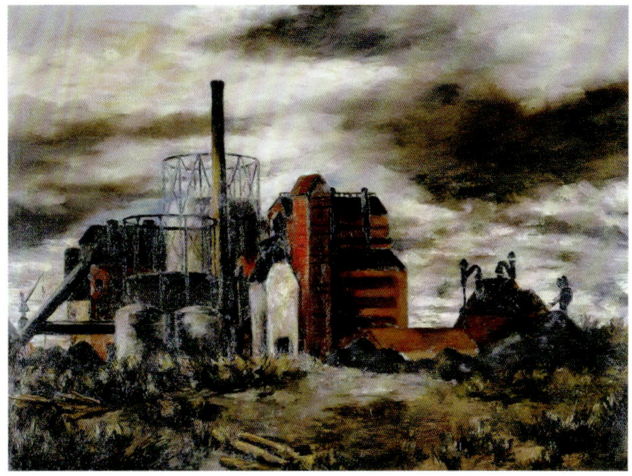

Fig. 9
Alexander Brook (American, 1898–1980)
***Stamford Gas Works*, 1933**
Oil on canvas, 26 x 36 1/4"
Georgia Museum of Art, University of Georgia, Extended loan from the Jason Schoen Collection, Miami

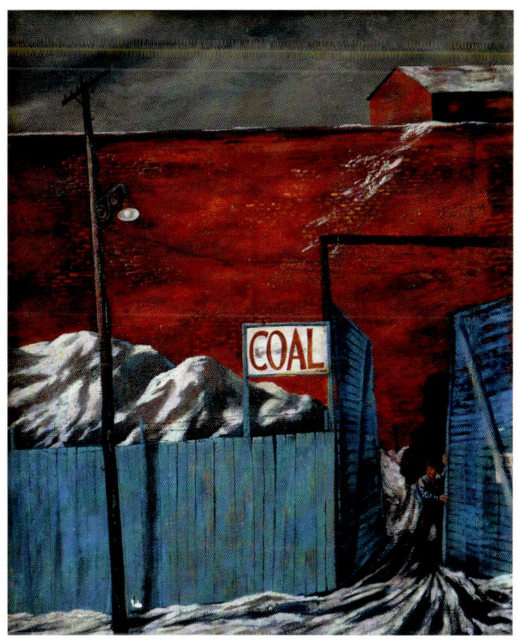

Fig. 10
***Coal Yard*, 1942**
Oil on Masonite, 29 x 24"
Private collection

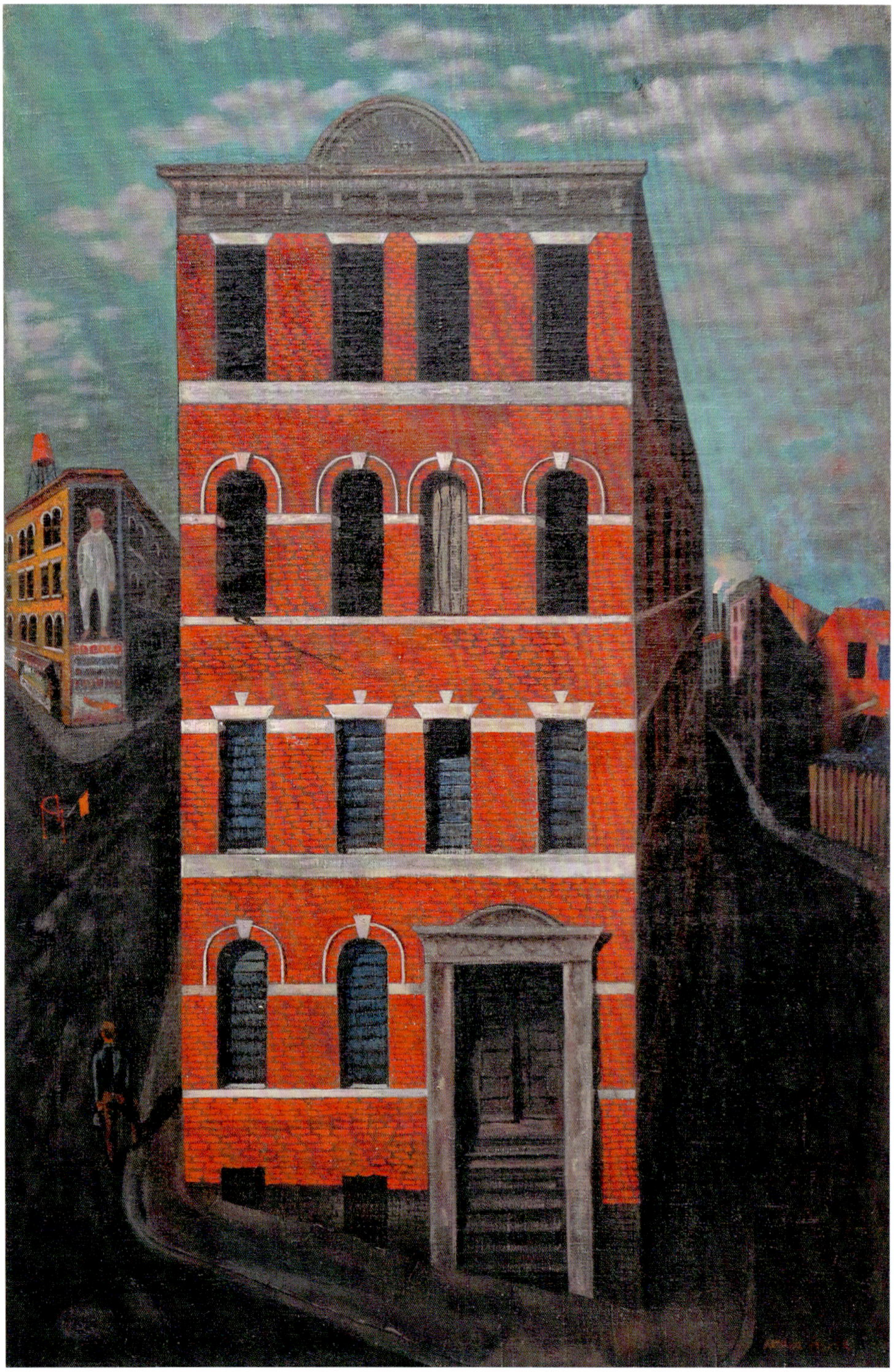

Fig. 11
***The John Hoyes Building,* 1941**
Oil on canvas, 40 x 30"
Estate of Arthur Osver and Ernestine Betsberg

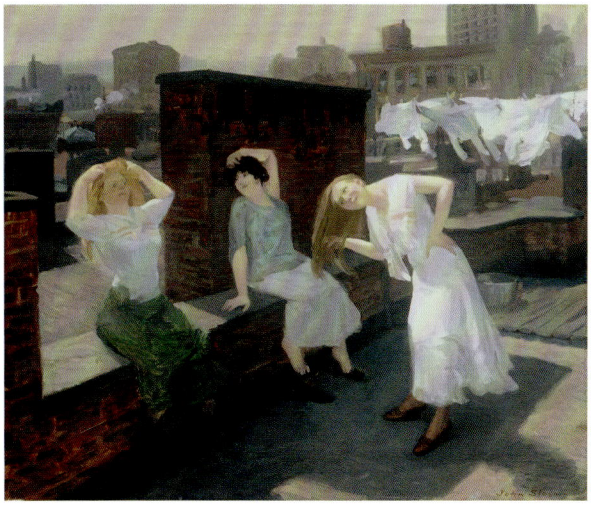

Fig. 12
John Sloan (American, 1871–1951)
***Sunday, Women Drying Their Hair,* 1912**
Oil on canvas, 26 1/8 x 32 1/8"
Addison Gallery of American Art, Phillips Academy, Andover, Massachusetts, Museum purchase

even as cotton-puff clouds of smoke signal that the factories are still operating. Blocked horizons are evident in works such as *Coal Yard* (1942; fig. 10). The effect at times is a sense of compositional awkwardness. Osver's urban spaces often seem to end nowhere. Dark windows beckon one into unreadable interiors; the boarded-up windows and closed doors of nineteenth-century industrial buildings suggest that access to the past has been closed off, as in *The John Hoyes Building* (1941; fig. 11). If Precisionism, in its reification of the unstable energies of industry and capitalism, represented a denial of time and process, Osver's works express the corrosions of history and the condition of rupture from the wholeness of the past. His contracted urban scenes press the viewer into close encounters with overscaled motifs such as chimneys or dangle us over rooftops. Using forced perspective and other spatial distortions increased the sense of precariousness, as if the ground plane is sliding downward. Elsewhere his urban spaces seem illogical and impossible to map, with multiple ground planes and plunging sight lines, a world of spatial discontinuities that suggest psychological fragmentation.

And then there are the rooftops. "Somewhere along the line I had become interested in the world some stories up.... We had always lived way up, usually on the top floor.... And being up on the top floor, one of the things that interested me tremendously was rooftops."[22] Osver's rooftops evoke a world that is not liberating or intimate, in the way that rooftops often were in the art of the Ash Can painters of the 1910s and 1920s (fig. 12)—the place where one kept pigeons or went to meet a lover, a space oriented to the city and yet free of its obstructions. Osver's rooftops seem abstracted and agoraphobic. Space does not leave one free but instead disrupts one's sense of orientation to the ground plane. Other roofs seem to trap their tiny lost figures in worlds that are both bounded and vertiginously open, seeming to block vision with obtruding clouds. In Osver's *Melancholy in the Sun* (1938; fig. 13), a solitary young man sits in a pose of wistful introversion, eyes closed.[23]

The precarious or ruinous state of Osver's industrial landscapes also finds its echo in Edward Hopper's psychologically charged and silent urban worlds and in the themes of dereliction and age that characterize the work of Aaron Bohrod, Charles

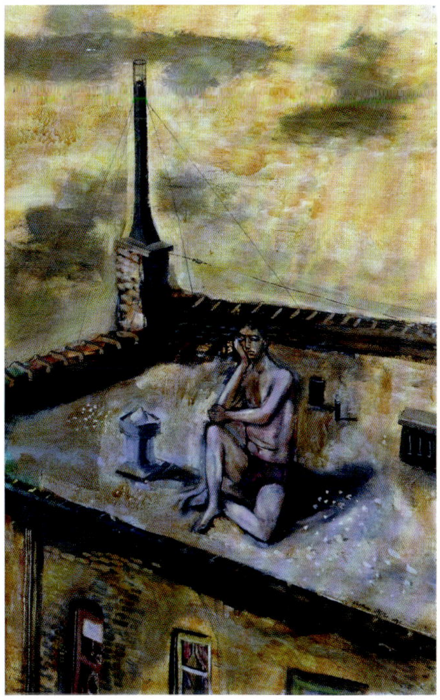

Fig. 13
***Melancholy in the Sun,* 1938**
Oil on canvas, 32 x 21"
Private collection

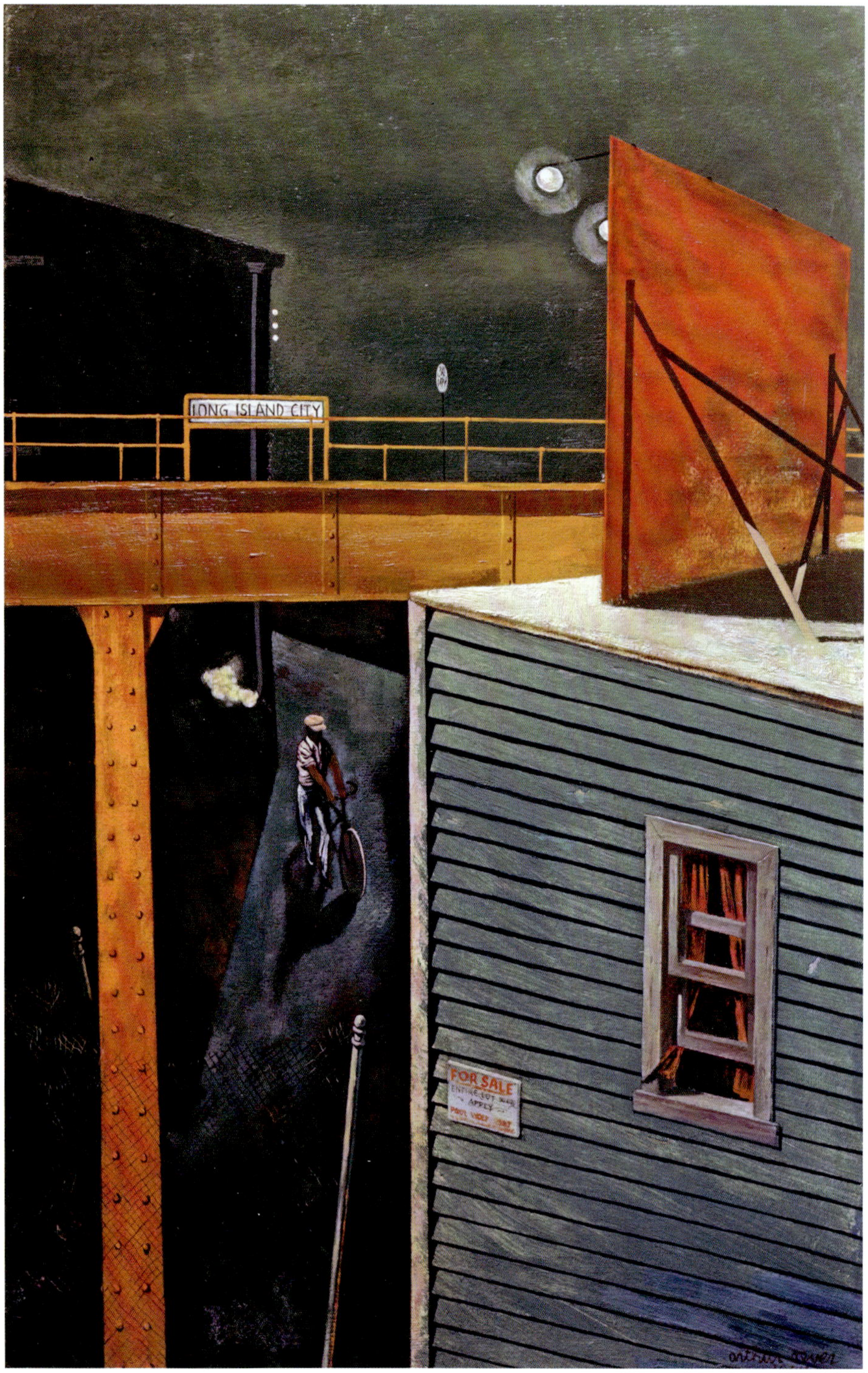

Fig. 14

***Coming Home*, c. 1944**

Oil on canvas, dimensions unknown

Location unknown

Burchfield, Morris Kantor, John Pellew, and other artists who had their start in the interwar decades and whose work Dorothy C. Miller included in her 1943 exhibition *Romantic Painting in America* at the Museum of Modern Art. Modern industry in the 1920s was commonly linked to the pioneering energies of the nineteenth century. But it would also soon come to be associated with environmental devastation and blamed for a dispirited and listless culture devoid of aesthetic beauty. Riddled with age, these Neo-Romantic works were saturated with a sense of loss and disappointment that suggests a powerful counterpoint to the official rhetoric of strength and unity surrounding the industrial buildup toward war in the years around Pearl Harbor. Yet, unlike many works in which the balance of external world and imagination tilted definitively toward inner landscapes, as in the more overtly Surrealist paintings of these years, these works were still grounded in a specific landscape, filtered through a melancholic sense of loss.

Like many other artists during the Depression, Osver adopted an inward-turning frame of reference, focusing on the local and regional scene. Nonetheless his work suggests affinities with *Neue Sachlichkeit* (New Objectivity) and with artists directly linked to Magic Realism. By the early 1940s, while other New York artists had begun to turn to myth-based abstraction, Osver continued to wrest a sense of emotional alienation and absence out of the materials of the urban landscape itself. He responded to a form of American Cubism, rethinking pictorial realism by playing with the ambiguity of flatness and perspectival depth; and—similar to 1920s New Objectivity—his use of tilted or exaggerated recession and plunging perspectives radically contracts space within his urban landscapes, which often lack any orienting foreground (fig. 14), while his use of deep, saturated colors of similar value minimizes the sense of spatial depth, as do his chalky and flat textures.

Along with these modernist elements, Osver's work of the late 1930s drew on the Social Realism of artists such as Nicolai Cikovsky, who painted the Brooklyn waterfront, and the narrative enigmas of his contemporary O. Louis Guglielmi, who created similar desolate streetscapes inspired by Brooklyn (fig. 15). Osver, however, generally avoided the more explicit social and political content of Guglielmi and other artists working in

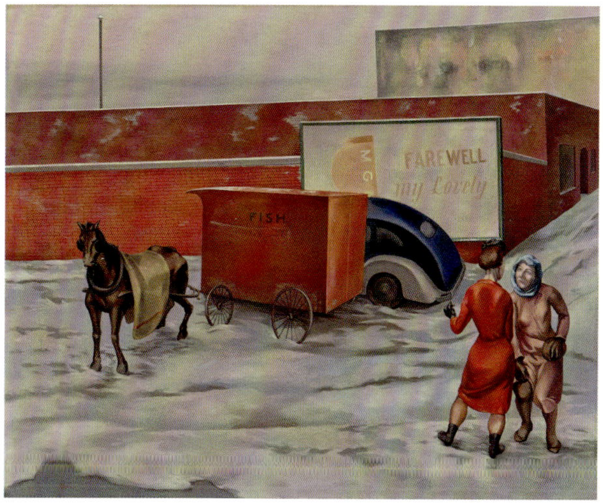

Fig. 15
O. Louis Guglielmi (American, b. Egypt, 1906–1956)
***Recurrent Theme in Red*, 1943**
Oil on canvas, 24 x 30"
Walker Art Center, Minneapolis, Gift of the T. B. Walker Foundation, Gilbert M. Walker Fund, 1944

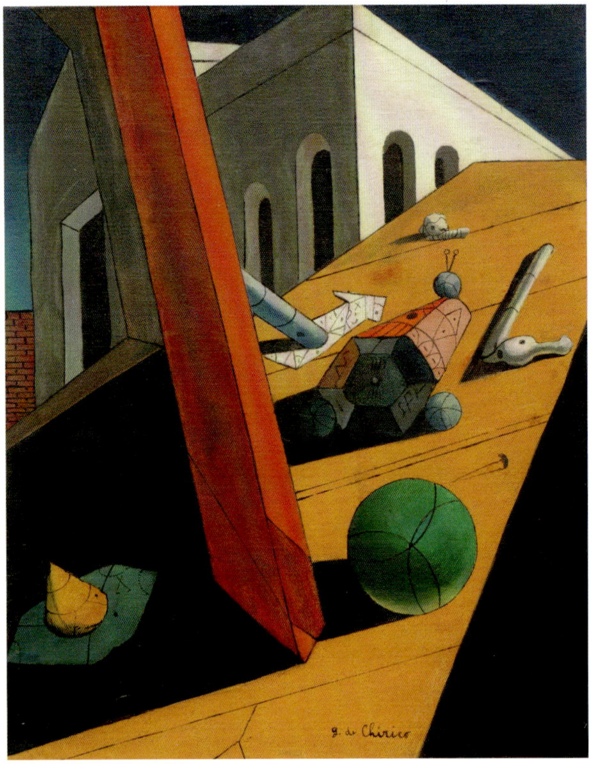

Fig. 16
Giorgio de Chirico (Italian, b. Greece, 1888–1978)
***The Evil Genius of a King*, 1914–15**
Oil on canvas, 24 x 19 3/4"
The Museum of Modern Art, New York, Purchase

the orbit of socially minded Surrealism—artists whose narrative absurdities spoke of the broader illogicality of a capitalist system of gross inequities and wasted lives.[24] But if Osver's work lacked specific social or topical comment or commitments, it did prompt audiences and critics to conjure more elusive feelings that transcended the time and place. He shared with others in the late 1930s an intuitive sense of how objects in the urban landscape, scarred by use and time, might radiate a significance beyond their immediate location, becoming imaginatively freighted symbols, as the critic Howard Devree noted in 1951: "he has commented on the environment with which man has webbed himself 'round, this urban anatomy becoming a symbol instead of remaining a mere picturesque fact."[25] Contemporary critics linked Osver's work to that of the Italian Metaphysical painter Giorgio de Chirico (1888–1978; fig. 16), who was such a foundational figure for the haunted, dreamlike art of the European figurative Surrealists and Magic Realists in the 1920s and 1930s. Osver's industrial scenes—such as *Melancholy of a Rooftop* (1942; pl. 3), exhibited in *Romantic Painting in America*—did indeed occasionally tilt toward a "wider Surrealist orbit," in the words of Soby.[26]

For Osver the object's significance was emotional. Only loosely suggesting any specific social content, his landscapes occupied instead an environment of belatedness and absence, as if he had arrived on the scene after the defining events and actions had already passed. In 1947 the critic John D. Morse commented of Osver: "Industry and industrial forms fascinate him, but he is not at all interested in the social problems brought about by the industrial revolution. He is an artist with convictions but without a 'message'.... The human figures were only props, added to give an accent of color or tone.... In a world of growing tension between the haves and the have-nots it is refreshing to find this kind of painting."[27] Morse's uneasiness with social content exposes a certain fatigue that critics and audiences felt with the language of Social Realism, beginning in the late 1930s. Osver's depopulated landscapes shifted "American scene painting" from social observation to a more reflective and introspective expression. The mottled surfaces of his paintings above all convey the human expression that seems so absent in the subjects themselves. He reflected on his process, noting that he built up his paintings slowly; they required "ample time" for "their proper realization," an element of time and temporal unfolding that is evident in their accreted and dense quality.[28] Reviewing a show of Osver's work at Grand Central Art Galleries in New York, Devree recognized his skill in transforming such "unpromising" subject matter as "roof tops along the Astoria waterfront" into "semi-abstract subjects of poetic beauty.... Like the true poet, [he] makes us wonder where our eyes have been."[29] Osver himself explicitly repudiated "mere technical brilliance and dexterity," an impulse that drew him away from the picturesque in favor of the awkward composition and homely lack of finish in his works of these years.[30]

Another review, illustrated by Osver's *Pipes and Chimneys* (1944–45; fig. 17), further defined a change of direction for the artist. Covering the artist's third solo exhibition at Grand Central in 1947, Renée Arb noted his shift from a concern with subject to artistic "means":

> Gone are the haunted urban vistas; by focusing right on his imagery, Osver becomes less literary, more abstract. A Brooklyn rooftop, with its perpendicular clutter of pipes and shafts, becomes less an evocation of Chirico-like nostalgia and more a site of balance and tension between plane and surface, volume and shape.... In the thick complex movement of *Pipes and Chimneys*, Osver hovers near the realm of cubist invention. Other works with their taut line and tilting towers suggest Feininger. But there is a new breadth in Osver's vision; he should make good his promise of a valid modern idiom.[31]

The passage suggests a period-specific understanding of abstraction that illuminates Osver's own movement into abstraction in the 1940s (fig. 18). Morse, for example, described *The Majestic Tenement* (1946; fig. 19) as "a superb abstraction in its literal sense": "instead of non-objective lines, colors, and forms, is an epitomization of the many brief moments of visual awareness that every city dweller knows. They are abstracted into a satisfying harmony of brick-tans, blues, whites, and darks that *are* the landscape of a city."[32] Pulling the view away from its

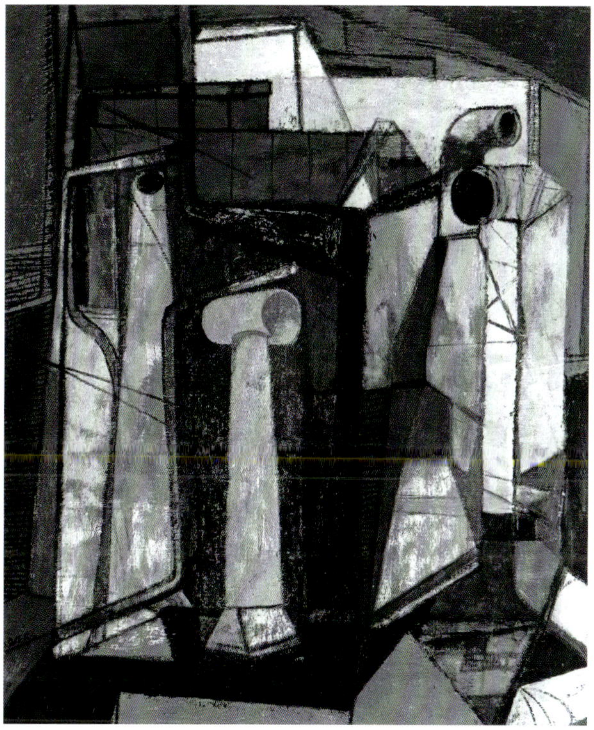

Fig. 17
***Pipes and Chimneys*, 1944–45**
Oil on canvas, 28 x 23"
Location unknown

illusion of depth, Osver also turned away from his technique of building up glazes to create a sense of depth. Instead he now used white lead paint to create an impermeable ground that did not reflect colors but left them "flat," thus isolating the outline and shape of the forms rather than their three-dimensional effects. And yet he continued to tether these shapes to their real-world referents, both through the associative properties of color and through the rhythm of forms alternating with silhouetted space that suggested the urban outline. In Osver's works the voids are as expressive as the solids.

Critics at the time were also quick to distinguish Osver's increasingly abstract works from nonobjective painting. The difference lay in the process of abstraction from nature, in contrast to the formal invention of artists engaged in the 1930s and 1940s with the Abstract American Artists group, which severed all ties to nature in creating purely ideal or mental geometries. Osver as an artist remained tied to the world of buildings and urban landscapes, even at his most abstract. Unlike the work of the Abstract Expressionist artists of the New York School, which would come to dominate the practice of abstraction in the 1950s, Osver's work remained rooted in explorations of place and motif. But his time working in Rome in 1952–53 would signal a fundamental shift in his work, severing the close, emotionally laden connections he felt with the industrial world of the United States in the late 1930s and early 1940s and drawing him in a very different direction.

Osver was throughout his life an alert and curious reader, someone who thought deeply about his process and questioned the sources of his art. He and his wife, Ernestine, had as friends writers such as Ralph Ellison and William Styron, dancers and choreographers, and painters such as Philip Guston.[33] In a revealing reflection many years later, in 1976, Osver explained that the growing interest in abstract form, or what he called "formal awareness," that he experienced during his years in Rome came from his sense of "not feeling as deeply into my material" while working there. This Roman exile from the urban landscapes he loved produced paintings that were structured around a more self-conscious "language of form, … color, shape, mass, line, everything that goes to make up the abstract elements of a painting."

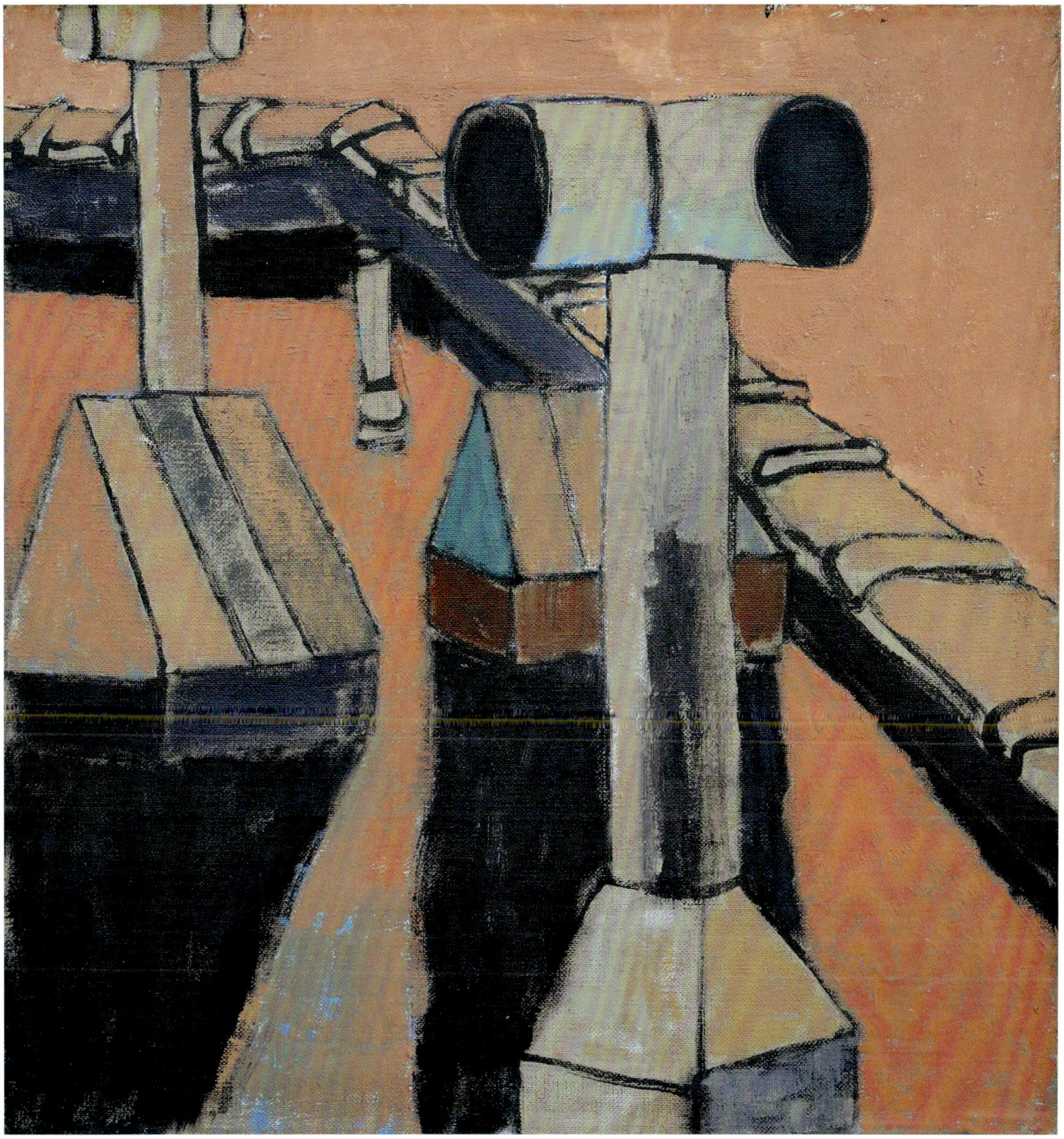

Fig. 18
***Rooftop II*, 1940s**
Oil on canvas, 21 x 20"
Private collection

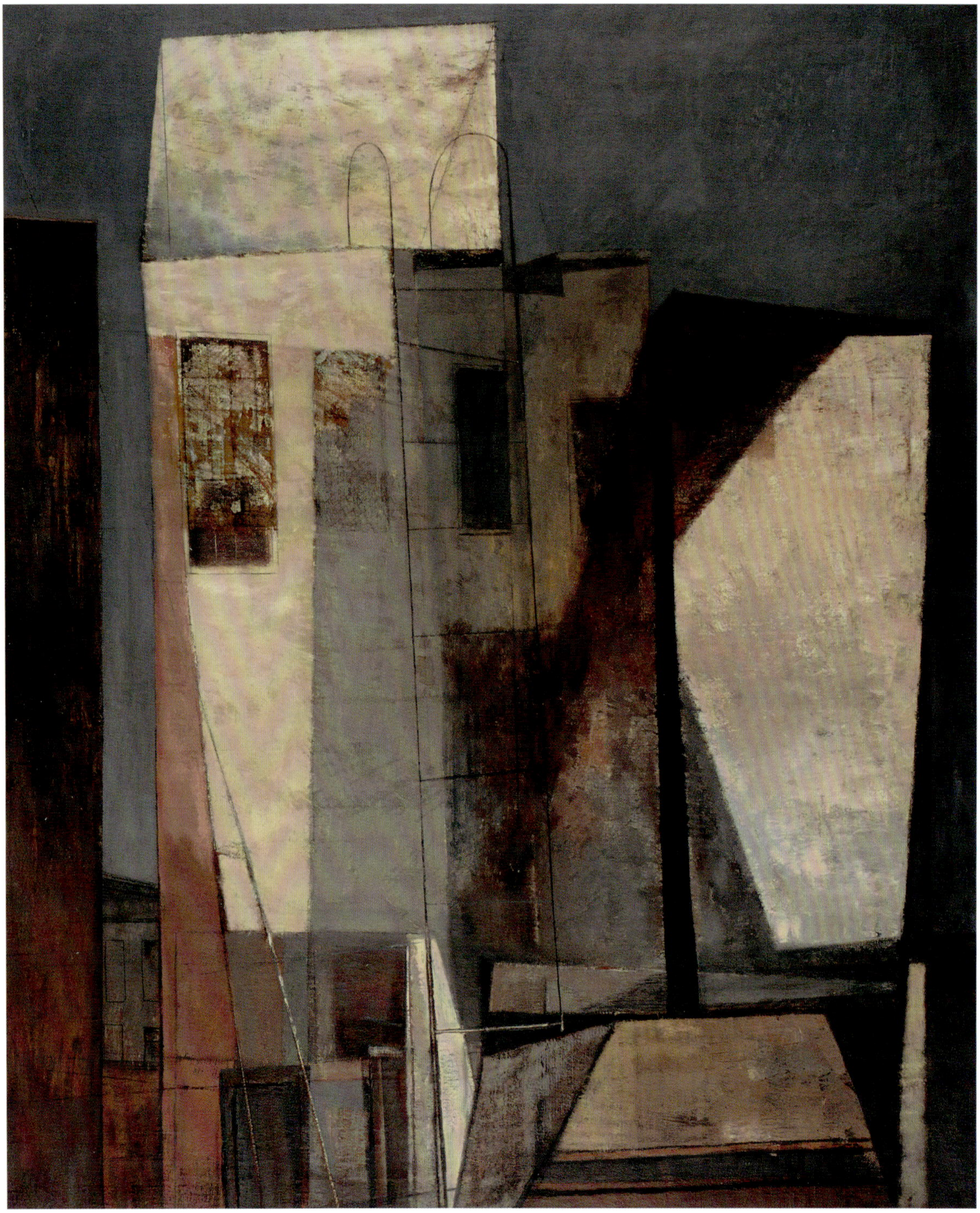

Fig. 19
The Majestic Tenement, 1946
Oil on canvas, 46 1/4 x 38 3/4"
Pennsylvania Academy of the Fine Arts, Philadelphia,
Joseph E. Temple Fund

In the absence of the kind of personal and emotive connection he had felt with the melancholic industrial landscapes of Long Island City, his Roman paintings seemed to him to lack "intensity": "I didn't have quite the involvement in that subject matter that I had with the American city.... It was a little for me like being on top of it instead of under it and within it."[34]

The process of abstraction, in other words, was for Osver related to an experience of emotional distancing or disengagement from his sources. This was not a negative development but simply a different stage in his growth as an artist, "the beginning of something in the Rome experience that hadn't happened there before."[35] Of his shift toward abstraction, Osver reflected that he could not return to his earlier way of painting, despite the emotional connection he continued to have with his American subjects. His "fall" into abstraction moved him from a certain innocence—a direct emotional connection with his subject—into a self-consciousness of form. As he put it in 1976, "Perhaps I know more—and I hate to say this—but feel less.... I wasn't as skillful ... or educated a painter as I am today.... Now I have much more knowledge, much more experience."[36]

Osver's reflection on the relationship between abstraction, feeling, and experience offers a glimpse of a much broader transition in American art, a movement away from an expressive paradigm of art as capturing something of the emotional texture of an artist's world—and the imbrication of imagination with place and memory—and a movement toward art as a primarily formal language governed by aesthetic elements abstracted from experience. While these two need not be mutually exclusive, Osver's shift away from an emotively and personally satisfying urban environment, as well as his growing involvement with themes less tied to his personal history, put him in league with others increasingly involved with problems of abstraction remote from the place-centered and memory-haunted concerns of the later 1930s. In the postwar moment much American art would move away from the expression of place toward mythic narratives and universals, which largely—if not entirely—rejected the grounding of self in experience, memory, and history, pursuing instead the challenges of self-enactment in the moment. In Abstract Expressionism, Osver would find both inspiration and defining difference.

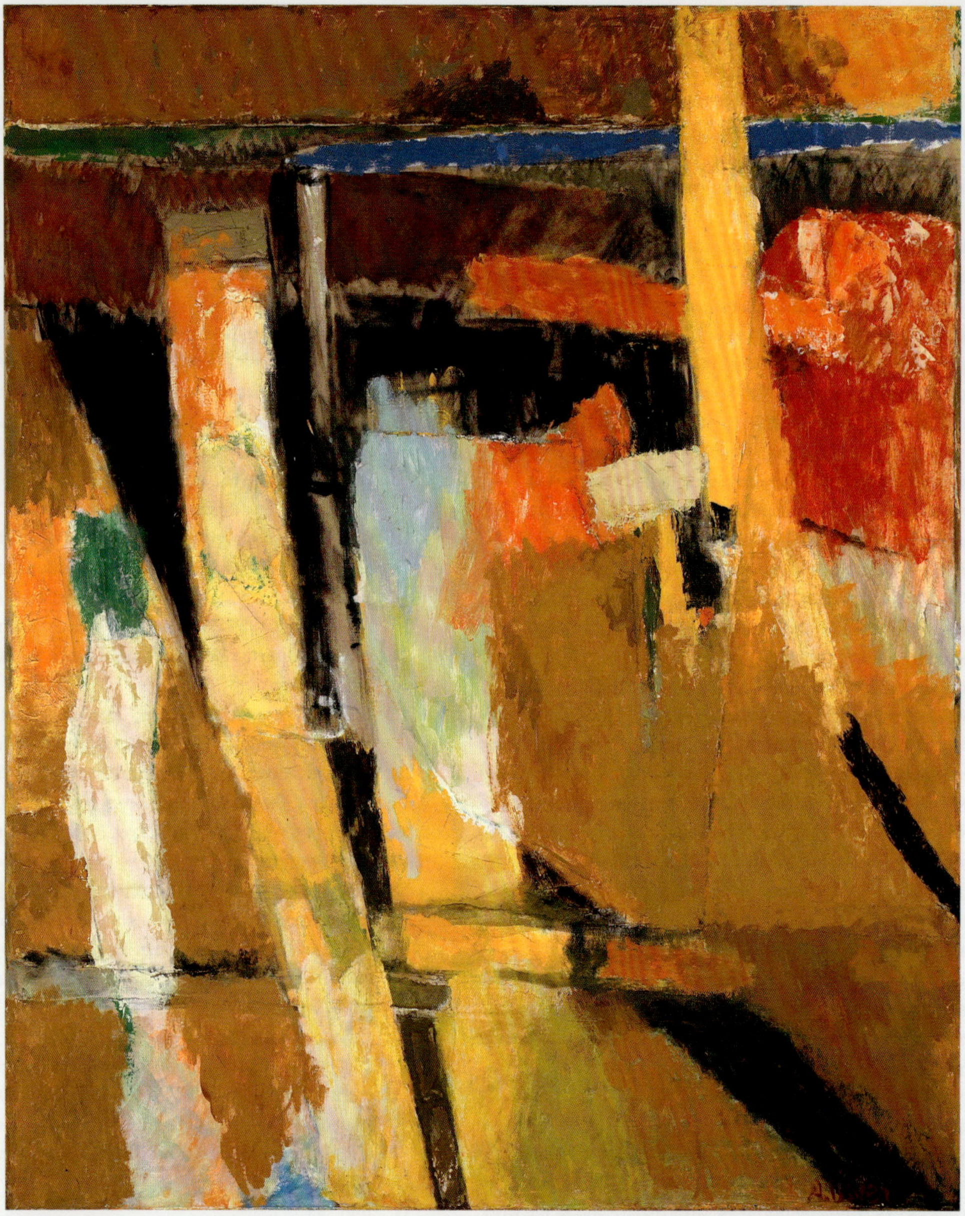

Fig. 20

***The Voyage*, 1961**

Oil and paper on canvas, 63 x 51 3/4"

Smithsonian American Art Museum, Gift of S. C. Johnson & Son, Inc.

From Story to Form: Arthur Osver's Abstractions

Matthew Bailey

Arthur Osver's art underwent transformations in the 1950s, part of a broader shift in the languages of art in these postwar years. In place of smokestacks, parapets, water towers, ventilators, and other industrial elements rendered in muted hues, the artist began painting with looser brushwork, distorted forms, and vivid colors, demonstrating a turn toward abstraction that he would explore for the rest of his life. Painted a year after he moved to St. Louis, *The Voyage* (1961; fig. 20) emblematizes, in its title and its form, this transition from the earlier urban views to the growing interest in abstraction that characterizes the later phase of his career. Drawing inspiration from the industrial world, as he had in his paintings from previous decades—indicated by the vestiges of smokestacks, water tanks, and rooftops—Osver reworked the objects into a simplified series of flat shapes painted with luminous browns, oranges, reds, blues, and blacks. Transforming from a cityscape into a graphic interplay of shape, color, light, and texture on the surface of the canvas, the painting embodies the artist's creative journey in the mid-twentieth century from an emphasis on three-dimensional space to two-dimensional forms, from a concern with painting things observed to a subjective exploration of the visual and emotional impact of the formal properties of painting.

The Voyage also indicates, however, how Osver persisted in rooting his abstract works in the observable world, no matter how nonfigurative they might appear. The artist once explained that form and pictorial design were always important factors in his painting, extending to his urban and industrial scenes that are essentially composed of flattened, interlocking geometric shapes inspired by the built environment. In these works, however, the subject matter was of primary importance, whereas in his paintings from the last half of the twentieth century, subject matter gave way to a "grid" or armature on which to experiment with the relationships between shape, color, line, mass, volume, and texture. "I find that the form leans on the story," he stated with reference to his monumental Grand Palais series of the 1970s, "but the form takes over and says: I'm number one, I want full attention to be given me."[1]

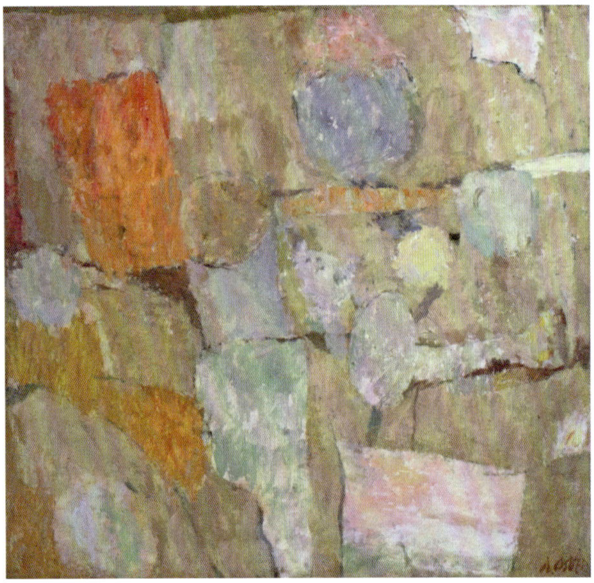

Fig. 21
***Roman Noon*, 1953**
Oil on canvas, 47 x 52"
Collection of Chris and Laura Spence

Osver's turn to abstraction—extending to a variety of sources, styles, and mediums—can be attributed to a number of factors and influences. Reflecting his ambition to constantly experiment in ways that gave shape to his subjective response to the landscapes he encountered during his frequent travels, abstraction can also be seen as an extended struggle to define himself as an artist in relation and in opposition to the art of the time. In the early 1950s Abstract Expressionism and other forms of *informel* painting constituted the most advanced forms of international abstraction. In his writings and lectures Osver often mentioned Willem de Kooning, Philip Guston, Franz Kline, and Jackson Pollock in particular. He remained ambivalent toward their art and ideals, however, admiring their achievements yet wrestling with them, unwilling to jettison his own artistic and philosophical convictions. He engaged in something of an imaginary competition with these figures in the 1950s and even into the 1960s, when Abstract Expressionism had given way to Pop, Minimalism, and other conceptual approaches.

Starting in 1952, when the artist spent two years in Italy on a coveted Rome Prize Fellowship from the American Academy in Rome (known colloquially as the Prix de Rome), Osver led a rather nomadic life. He also spent a year as an artist-in-residence at the University of Florida in 1954, served as a visiting critic at Yale University in 1956–57, spent another year in Italy as a painter-in-residence at the American Academy in Rome starting in 1957, and eventually moved to St. Louis in 1960 to teach at Washington University.[2]

Osver's shift toward abstraction began during his first trip to Rome. Commenting on an exhibition of paintings that the artist executed in Italy, Daniel Catton Rich, director of the Art Institute of Chicago, found that these works moved Osver's art in the direction of "suggestion" rather than description. In paintings such as *Roman Noon* (1953; fig. 21) or *Paestum* (1955; fig. 22), Rich observed, Osver responded to the Italian landscape

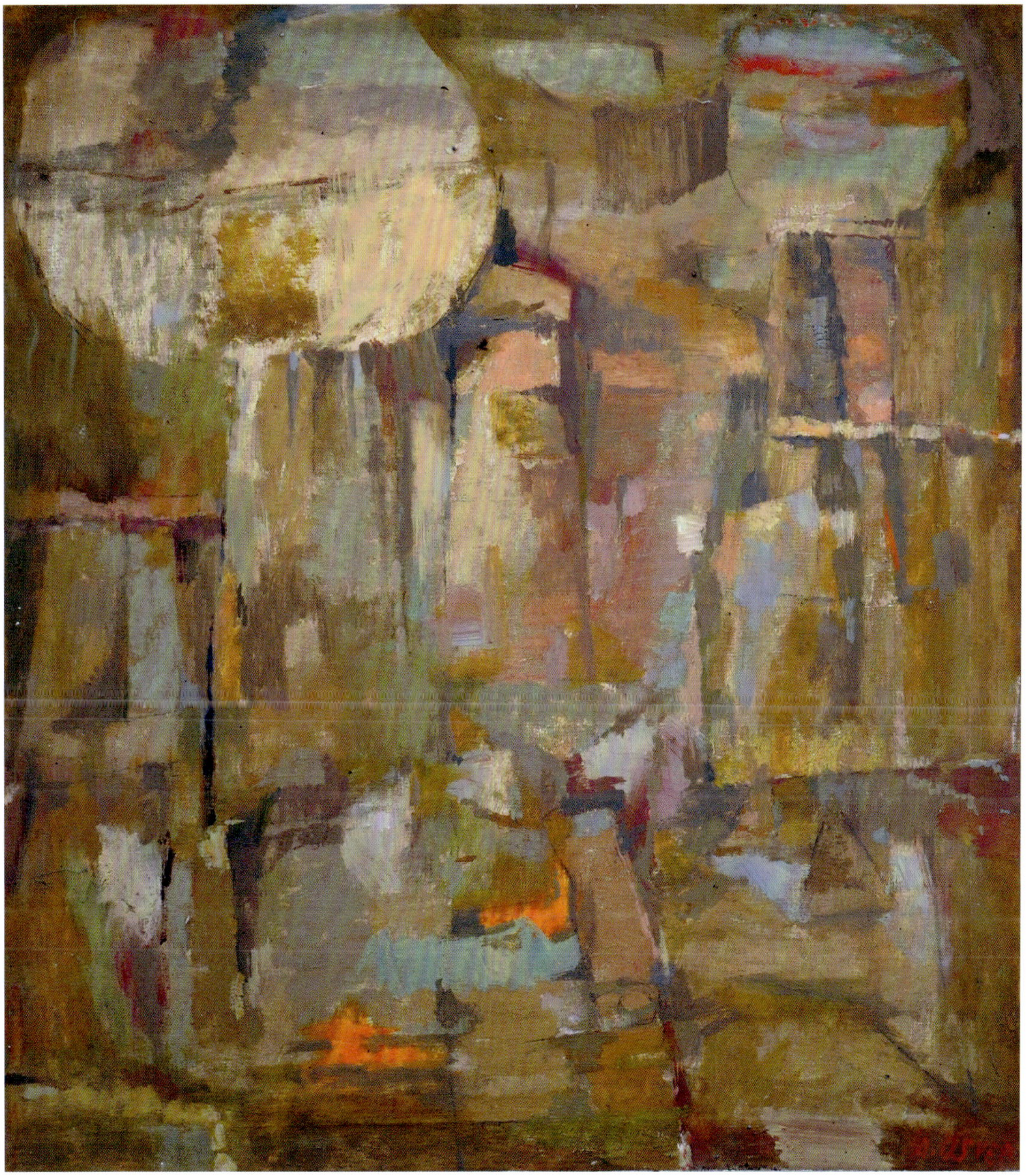

Fig. 22
***Paestum*, 1955**
Oil on canvas, 36 x 32"
Estate of Arthur Osver and Ernestine Betsberg

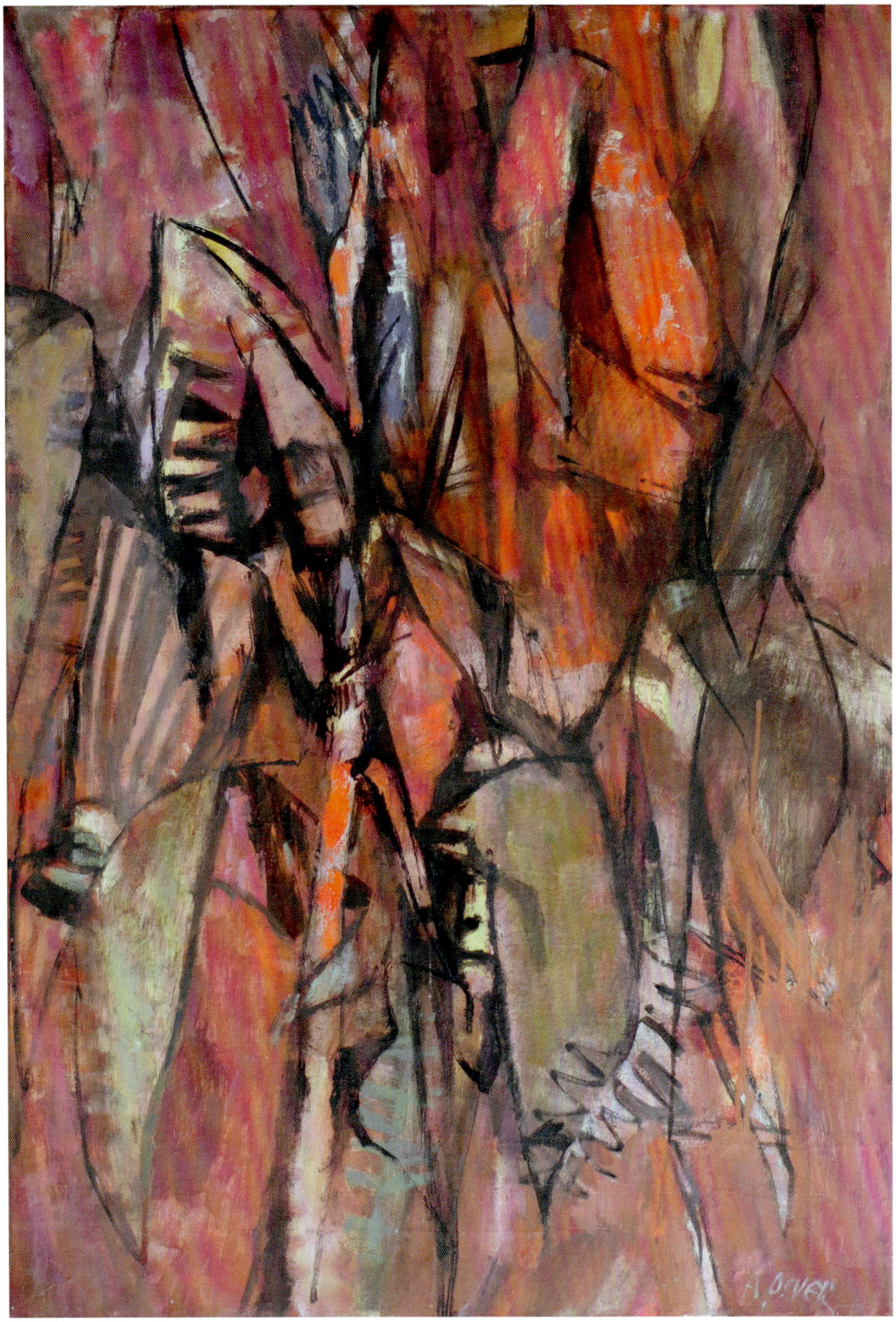

Fig. 23
***Love Garden*, 1956**
Oil on canvas, 29 x 26"
Estate of Arthur Osver and Ernestine Betsberg

and classical architecture with ethereal, dissolving forms and delicate pastel colors that seized the "sun-struck atmosphere of the ancient world."[3] In the same vein the critic Marilyn Robb Trier observed in 1954 that these paintings seem "like poetry opposed to the prose of his earlier work. However the question arises whether this marks a real change of heart or merely reactions to Italian scenery?"[4] Such critical reactions to Osver's early abstractions suggest continuity rather than rupture with the earlier work.

As Osver would later recall, this shift in his artistic style was indeed an aesthetic response to the foreign environment and subjects he encountered in and around Rome. Confronted with Italian structures, spaces, and light so different from the "industrial look" central to his New York work, Osver responded with a more internal examination of the formal, poetic, and expressive languages of art.[5] In his works of this period, the external world is muted. In *Paestum*, for example, the ancient Greek city is reduced to a vivid patchwork of rich, painterly yellows, ochres, browns, blues, and pinks, evoking the golden, suffusing glow of Italian sunlight as well as the architectonic forms of the temples. Osver's botanical studies, such as *Love Garden* (1956; fig. 23), which allowed him to experiment with more amorphous forms than those of the man-made environment, pushed his art even further in the direction of abstraction from nature, as in *Mazzo di Fiori (Rome)* (1953; fig. 24), composed of lyrical, organic washes of vivid high-toned colors bled into the paper. These paintings, he explained, were even more about the decorative properties of form, color, and line than they were about the specificities of the subjects in nature that he took as sources of inspiration.[6] These became catalysts for increasingly abstracted compositions.

Continuing the aesthetic direction he began in Rome, many of Osver's paintings from throughout the 1950s are suggestive of organic forms and were rendered with heightened colors and loose brushwork (pls. 33, 34). As he pushed toward greater degrees of abstraction, Osver also became frustrated with the way his paintings became more and more removed from the external world. During his second trip to Rome especially, Osver vacillated between an inclination to render recognizable objects and a fascination with the sensuous appeal of form, color, and richly textured surfaces. As he came to realize, he needed

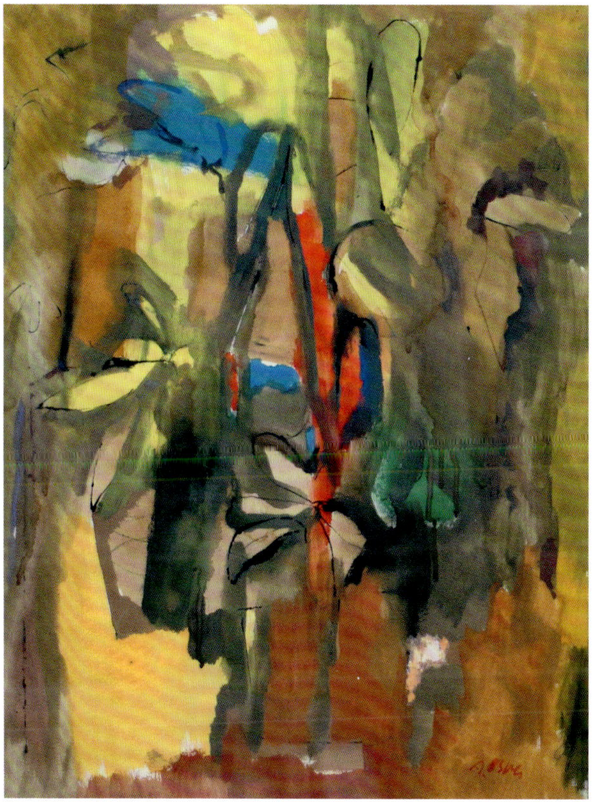

Fig. 24
Mazzo di Fiori (Rome), 1953
Acrylic on paper, 25 x 19"
Estate of Arthur Osver and Ernestine Betsberg

"something to say" in terms of subject. He noted in his diary, "I doubt that I will ever have anything to say in the formal sense like a Kline or a Guston but that my expression must always come from a figurative lead," recognizing that his abstractions from nature differentiated his work from the nonobjectivity of the New York School.[7]

Osver's vision of art as expressing the contact between the self and the world and his notion of abstract painting as the reconfiguration of things observed in nature into the unique language of easel painting reveal another influence on his abstraction: the French modernist Henri Matisse. During the late 1940s and the 1950s Matisse's art and reputation experienced a critical revival, stimulated by a retrospective at the Philadelphia Museum of Art in 1948, an exhibition of important works at Pierre Matisse's New York gallery in 1949, and the purchase of Matisse's celebrated painting *The Red Studio* (1911; fig. 25) in 1949 by the Museum of Modern Art, culminating in the New York museum's Matisse retrospective in 1951. The critic Clement Greenberg, a champion and close associate of the Abstract Expressionists, deemed Matisse the "greatest living painter."[8] Osver's contemporaries in the New York School, however, preferred the more powerfully gripping work of Picasso in their quest for an art of philosophical significance. While they also expressed admiration for Matisse, they were wary of the "aesthetics of pleasure" and the purely material, sensuous appeal they saw in Matisse's work.[9] Osver by contrast seems to have embraced Matisse as a guide in his art and thought, especially after admiring the Museum of Modern Art's retrospective. "The big Matisse show … is something to see! There is such a feeling of rightness to this work," he wrote to his longtime friend Al Leindecker. "Almost a predestined rightness, with every color and form and line building up to an entity you wouldn't imagine taking any other form."[10] Though Osver mentioned in the letter that he was doubtful anyone could achieve the same in painting after Matisse, the French artist's work seems to have been another major impetus for Osver's inroads into abstraction while on fellowship in Rome. The impact of Matisse is revealed in Osver's Italian abstractions, his Grand Palais paintings, and what he referred to as his "pillar and diagonal" series, which accentuate flattened decorative forms, organic lines, and rich, absorptive zones of color in the manner of the French artist. In ways paralleling Matisse's interest in harmony, Osver noted that an artist is someone who "is tirelessly and eagerly searching for the inner harmonies [of] the underlying order to this big blooming confusion we call existence."[11]

Osver's deep sympathy for Matisse suggests a rather different set of loyalties from those motivating many currents of American modernism after 1950. His focus on harmony, beauty, and nature grounded him in a form of conservative modernism that pushed against the agonistic strains of New York School art, with its emphasis on existential choice and a contingent and unfolding engagement with the process and materials of art. Osver also seems to have taken a cue from the older modernist's belief in the use and reworking of external motifs.[12] Osver's abstract paintings from the 1950s on reveal the artist's studio as a site of experimentation in which he transformed and reduced specific motifs into expressive units of form, color, line, and texture, freely altering and reworking paintings and exploring different materials—but always with an eye toward the external world. "The incitement to lay brush to canvas comes from the excitement of the World of Things," he once stated. "Things teach. They point out heretofore unimagined means of disposing my line and color…; my approach has come from the nature of Nature. No rigid prefabricated concepts. Technique has flowed from subject. Manner from Matter."[13] Indeed, as Osver pursued over the many productive decades of his later career an art of discipline, control, order, and harmony rooted in the external world, his work underwent a gradual transition from a dependency on the "*specific* characteristics of the motif" to "more a generalized *evocation* of a motif or a number of motifs."[14]

After Osver's experimentation with a variety of subjects during his years in Italy, he returned to more familiar industrial and urban themes as an armature for his formal investigations of the 1950s and 1960s. Based on drawings, photographs, and memories, these composed abstractions also demonstrate his experimentation with large-scale paintings, his preference for working in series based on particular motifs, and his exploration of the decorative and expressive qualities of color. For instance, using an aerial view of a factory scene, with the suggestion of a

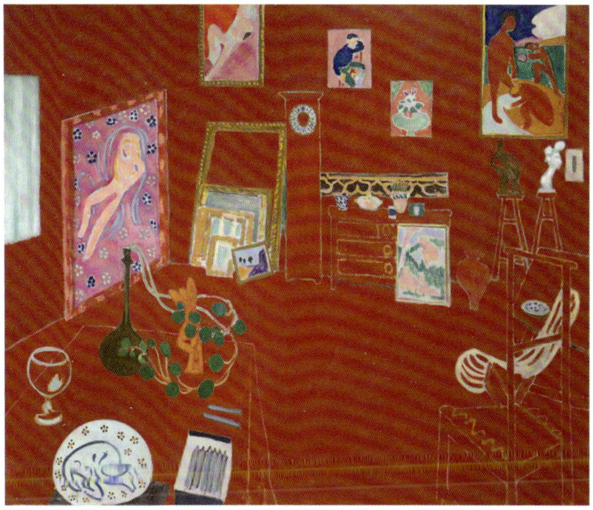

Fig. 25
Henri Matisse (French, 1869–1954)
***The Red Studio*, 1911**
Oil on canvas, 71 1/4 x 86 1/4"
The Museum of Modern Art, New York, Mrs. Simon Guggenheim Fund

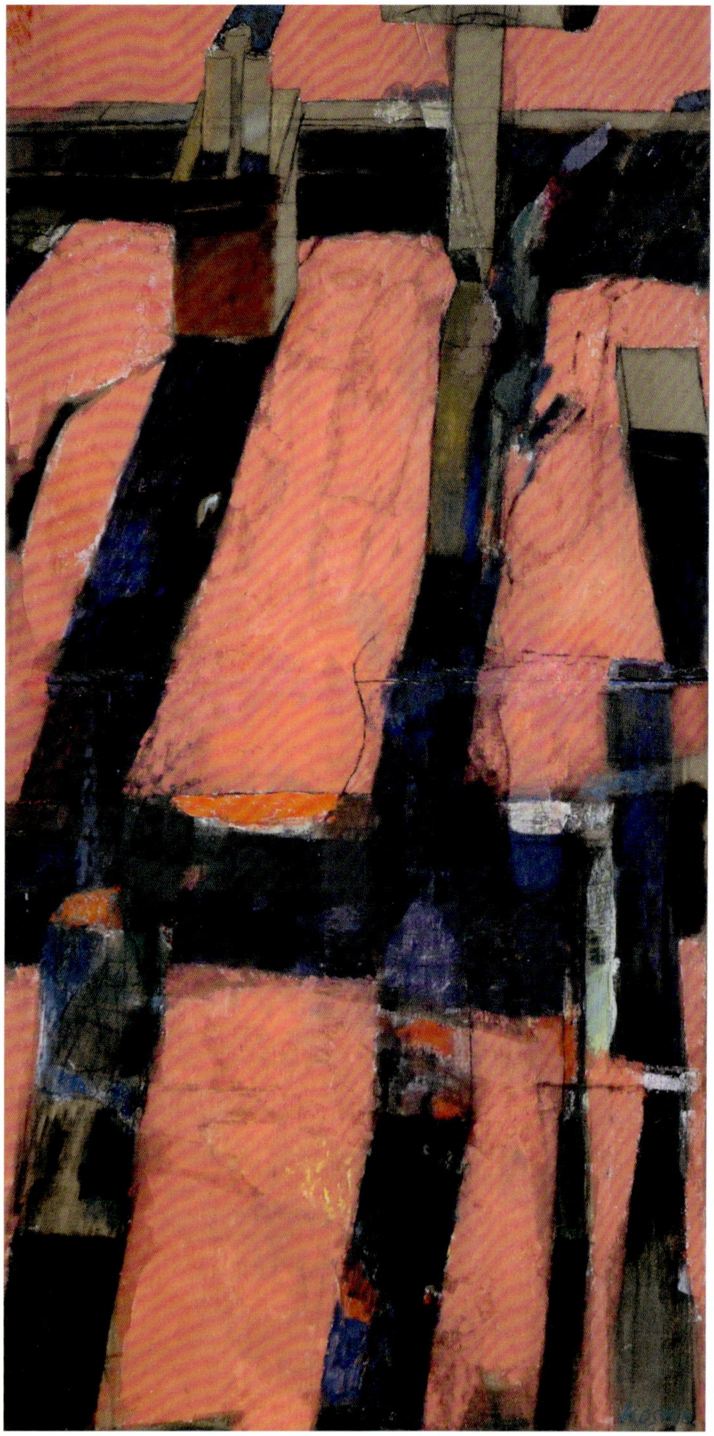

Fig. 26
***The Tall Red,* 1959**
Oil on canvas, 81 x 41"
Courtesy of Winfield Gallery, Carmel, California

series of rooftops and smokestacks receding into space, in the monumental work *The Tall Red* (1959; fig. 26), Osver reduced the positive and negative shapes into a schematic series of flat, interlocking geometric forms, accentuating the purely visual impact of the broad, vibrant reds and painterly blues. Maintaining this path into the next decade, he described many of the resulting works, including *The Voyage* (see fig. 20) and *Duo* (c. 1966; pl. 39), as his "pillar and diagonal" series for the way colors and shapes were yolked to these essential structural elements abstracted from man-made environments. In these works he continued to explore the effects of vivid, dominant hues such as red, blue, and orange while also heightening the sumptuous qualities of his surfaces, building up forms with loose, painterly strokes and scumbles, stains, dashes, and loops of pigment, executed with thick impastos that create a richly textured surface of interlocking organic and geometric forms. In the process the industrial motif became transfigured into fields of color. He also began using a variety of techniques and materials in addition to oils. Experimenting with acrylics and latex paints (even noting the difference in quality between name brands such as Moore's and Lucite house paints), he also tested different amounts and types of shellac and varnish, smeared paint on his surfaces with rags, sanded portions of his works, and scrubbed on pigments with dry brushes and painting knives.[15]

Inspired by the possibilities of these materials and his abstractions of the urban world, Osver was also stimulated by his move to St. Louis to teach at Washington University in 1960. Increasingly absorbed by his studio practice, he again turned away from the kinds of industrial subjects that had characterized his early career (fig. 27). The move to St. Louis helped him focus more on the internal logic of painting and to evaluate his art in a new context. One of the reasons for his decision to leave the East Coast was the dominance of the Abstract Expressionists in the New York art scene and the prevalence of assertively bold, large-scale painting, which had made him feel "a bit alien in my own city."[16] In St. Louis, he wrote, "I discovered a chance to work with a degree of tranquility that let me look inward instead of helplessly trying to ferret out 'the scene.'"[17]

Nevertheless, Osver acknowledged that Abstract Expressionism had changed the way people thought about art

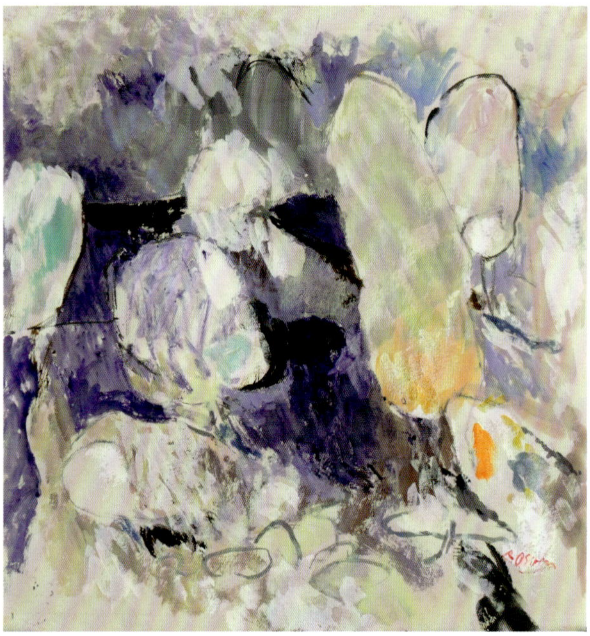

Fig. 27
***Untitled*, 1960s**
Gouache on rice paper, 18 x 18"
Collection of Jeannine and Kent Kalkwarf

and painting. He respected the accomplishments of such artists as de Kooning, Guston, Kline, Robert Motherwell, Pollock, and Mark Rothko, who, he believed, had ushered in the coming of age of American art. "How can one deny the freshness, the spontaneity, the abandon, the force of this new work?" he wrote. Admiring the artists for "seeking new values" and for trying to get at the "inner structure of things" through examination of the principles of painting and its materials, he singled out Pollock for the way he gave "primacy to the painting act itself … the material, its consistency, flow, texture becomes important. We are aware of gesture, of manipulation of materials, of muscle operating material, of gravity & weight (look how the paint *flows*, how it *drips*, *spreads*, *stains*, *blots*)."[18] Osver emulated these techniques, both before and after his move to St. Louis, working on a larger scale and using materials such as latex house paints. He also pushed himself to explore gestural brushstrokes in the manner of de Kooning, and he noted how his diaphanous color fields related to Rothko's.[19]

The New York School, while stimulating Osver creatively in the 1950s and 1960s, also goaded him to shape and define his own distinct art and ideals, especially in contrast to what he saw as the overly fashionable and repetitive work of imitators and art students who thought that all one needed to paint abstractly was "plentiful paint, canvas, muscle and enthusiasm."[20] By the late 1950s the ideal of authentic expression held by painters of the New York School had in fact devolved into a "style," learned and repeated reflexively by art students around the country. In his personal notes Osver also wrote about what he saw as the "perils" of a "destructive" art—art that was driven by "a central principle of the *unformed*, the *irrational*, and the *uncontrolled*" in paintings that were "moldy, broken, corrugated, ragged, dripping" with "brushstrokes executed with the sloppy brutality of cornered men" in their infatuation with the tortured subconscious.[21] His terms of description align closely with the ways in which Abstract Expressionism was discussed both by unsympathetic critics and by those who valued these qualities for other reasons. The artist and critic Cleve Gray, for example, criticized what he—like Osver—saw as the undisciplined formlessness of the work of such artists as Pollock, de Kooning, Motherwell, Clyfford Still, and Kline: "Branded as conservative and reactionary are any suggestions that order is intrinsic to art, that an artist has an obligation of aesthetic responsibility, that individuality should be disciplined."[22] For Gray, these artists' abandonment of the object or the external world in favor of the spontaneous registering of inner sensations was a rejection of discipline and order in art. Their exploration of the psyche and embrace of chance in painting disregarded the responsibility of art to communicate in a meaningful, elevating way through the coherent articulation of form and order inspired by the external world. The result, Gray argued, is that "the unhappy spectator stares at an unintelligible vacuum."[23] Like Gray—himself an abstract painter—Osver clearly differentiated his work from the New York School through assertions of aesthetic will and authorship that would increasingly characterize his form of modernist abstraction. According to Osver, Abstract Expressionism had been an important part of the "revolt against the tyranny of the imitation of the *object*" in art, yet many of the artists had pushed too far in the way they ultimately disregarded the external world altogether in favor of subjective self-examination. As Osver claimed, "one cannot truly escape Nature. It is all we have." A vital art instead should be "a *recreation* of the natural order; a significant transformation of everything which we experience through the eye," which, he was convinced, was "as essential for Art's continued growth and vitality, as is food for the body."[24]

For Osver, being was determined not by actions wrought by the painter in the process of existential reckoning but by the external world of things. "Do not we dream in terms of images—is there such a thing as an abstract dream...? Our world is a world of visual impressions," he wrote in notes titled "The 1960 Art Season." "But the sensory world is the primal world—it is the world we always have with us—outside of perhaps some occult religious states, we cannot escape it. The artist who believes that he is escaping it suffers from a vain delusion—a delusion that cripples his capacity for growth.... The powers of a conscious initiative derive from a conscious exploration of Nature."[25] Here once more, Osver asserted the by then conservative premise of authorship and aesthetic control. But while his painting maintained contact with the world as a source of aesthetic stimulation and guidance, that world remained largely private, disconnected

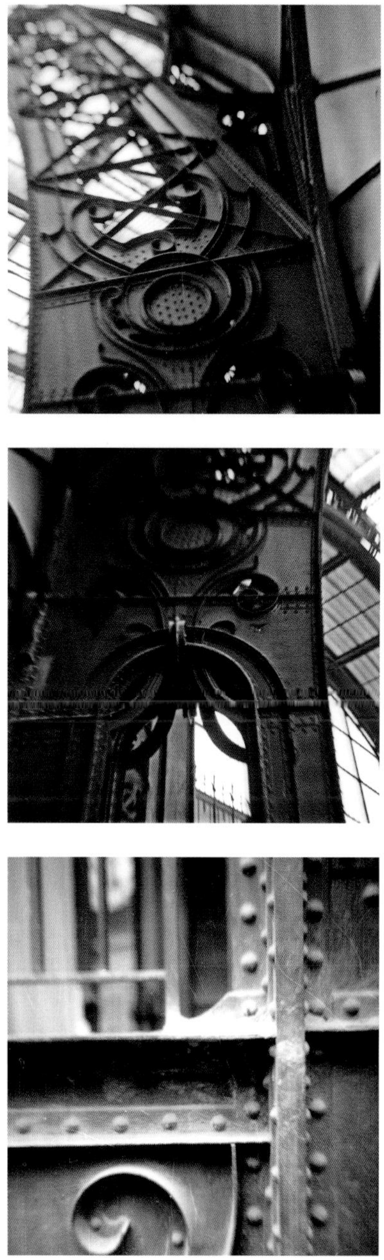

Fig. 28
Undated photographs by Arthur Osver of the Grand Palais, Paris
Arthur Osver Papers, Estate of Arthur Osver and Ernestine Betsberg, St. Louis

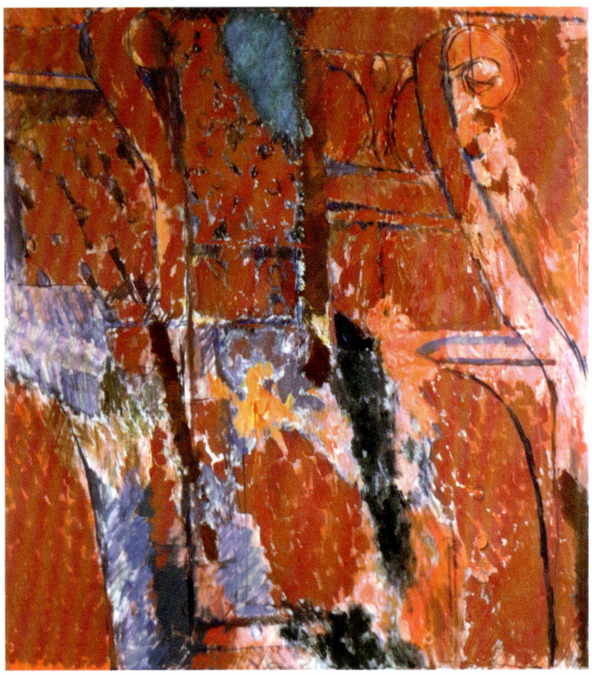

Fig. 29
***Untitled*, 1967**
Oil on canvas, 56 x 52"
Private collection

from the often tumultuous contemporary scenes of modern history as it unfolded over his lifetime.

In the late 1960s Osver found inspiration in the steel, cast iron, and glass configurations of the Grand Palais in Paris. Representing another major turning point in his career, Osver's encounter with the Art Nouveau structure, built for the Exposition Universelle in 1900, while he was en route to the United States after touring Europe on a travel grant from the National Endowment for the Arts, inspired a series of paintings that occupied his attention for more than a decade. Although he had visited the Grand Palais on prior trips, he later recalled that in 1967 he had been struck by the visual impact of the "world of fancifully twisting, curling, steel girders, lacing together vast areas of glass and light," and he took both black-and-white and color photographs (fig. 28) that he used as a basis for his paintings.[26] Looking again to man-made industrial objects for inspiration but departing from more panoramic industrial scenes or cityscapes, he began to employ the intricate patterns created by the interplay of metal and glass as a stimulating motif in his abstractions. As he later explained, the Grand Palais "gave me something that I could *recognize* as being what I had been looking for, and I *knew* it was important for me."[27]

Osver was frustrated with his initial experiments, however, which he executed with the same loose brushwork, vivid colors, and impastoed surfaces employed in his "pillar and diagonal" series (fig. 29). Discouraged, he largely abandoned the Grand Palais idea until three years later, when his students introduced him to water-based latex paints, which dried more quickly than oils and could produce brighter, more luminous areas of color. This helped him expand his palette and his working methods. "With oils," he explained, "I would put down a shape, and then I'd begin to modify that shape, but I couldn't do it with the accuracy and directness and quickness that I could with these [latex paints] because oil takes a long time to dry." As he found, when working in oils, "before I'd get back to it the idea would have somehow evaporated or didn't seem quite as important as it had been in the first place—you might say inspiration had just flown out the window. Using these latex paints I could keep inspiration caged a bit longer." Allowing Osver to work in a more improvisatory manner—painting with the Grand Palais

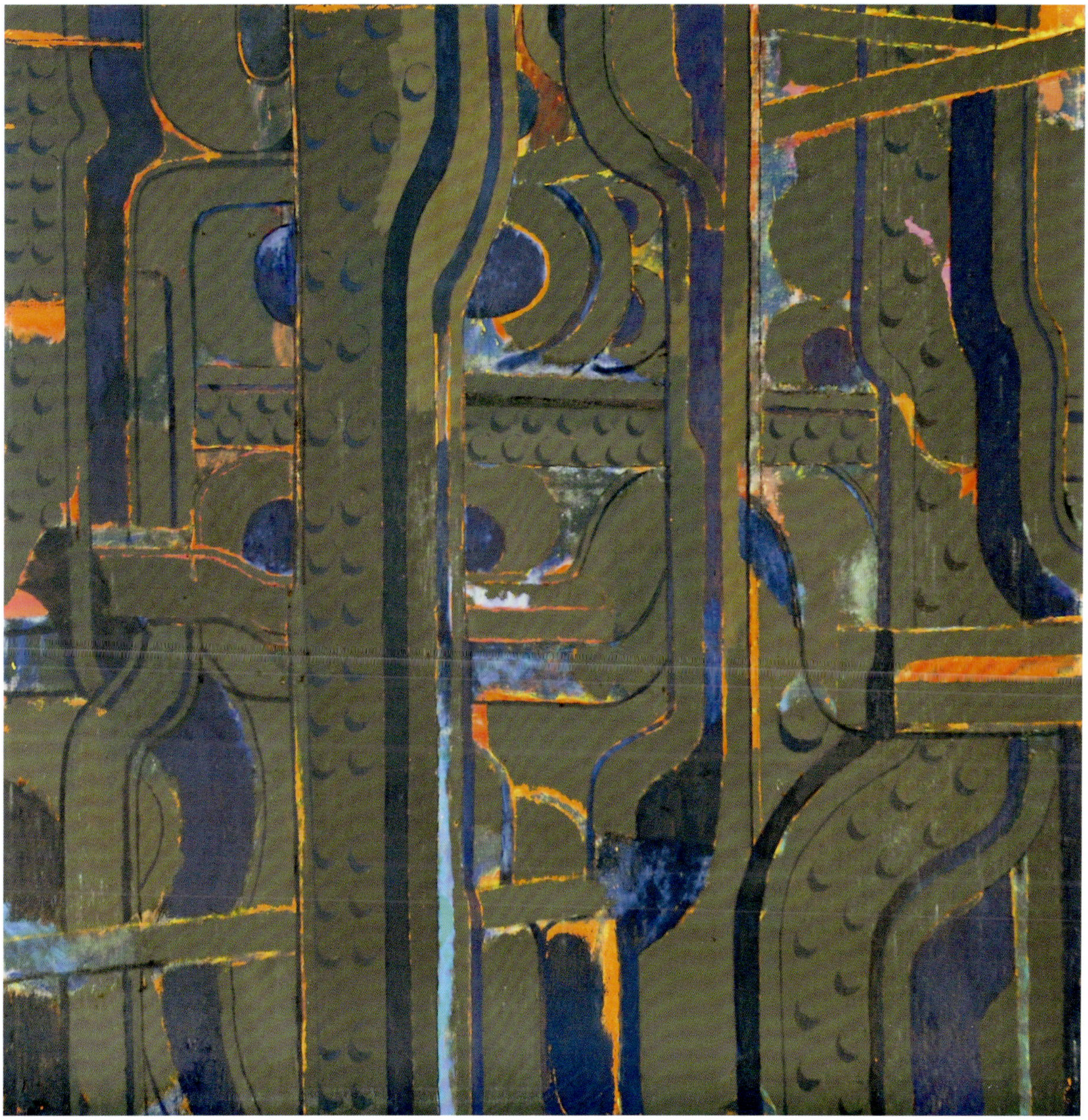

Fig. 30
***G. P. 10-70*, 1970**
Oil on canvas, 61 x 61"
Estate of Arthur Osver and Ernestine Betsberg

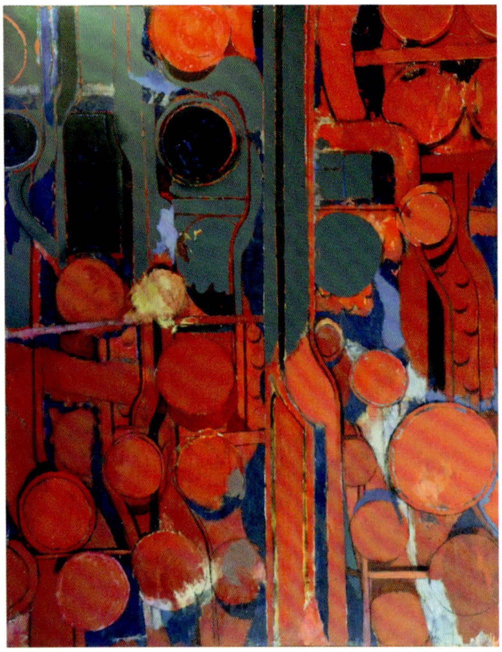

Fig. 31
Grand Palais 10-70 (2), 1970
Oil on canvas, 72 x 58"
Estate of Arthur Osver and Ernestine Betsberg

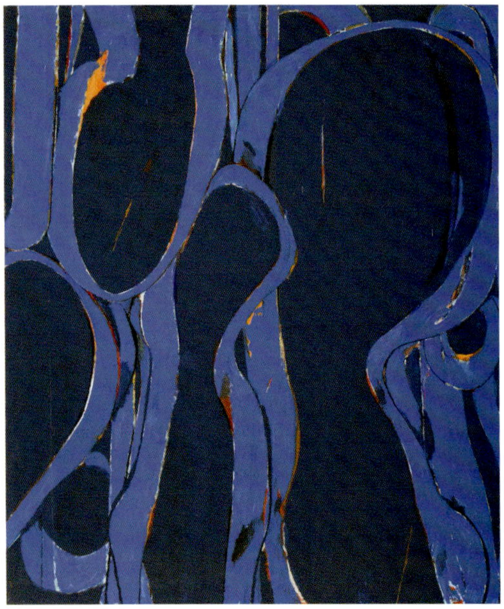

Fig. 32
G. P. 10-72, 1972
Oil on canvas, 96 x 84"
Estate of Arthur Osver and Ernestine Betsberg

in mind yet responding to the formal arrangements that materialized on his canvases—his discovery of latex paints "was a case," he stated, "of the right technique meeting the right idea."[28] Thinking of his paintings as a process of creative discovery, he called his newer, more spontaneous methods "a very disorganized, unplanned, wild plunge into what I hope is going to be a fresh experience, even though that experience has looming in the background the idea of the Grand Palais."[29]

Osver's decision to launch a sustained investigation of the formal components of the Grand Palais at the height of student unrest in Paris and internationally in 1968 points toward his withdrawal from the turmoil of the social realm into an autonomous world of art. This assertion of the gap between art and life was conditioned by his own investment in a visual world of architectural and natural forms. His impulse toward order and harmony was essentially at odds with such movements as Arte Povera and Fluxus, which turned to abject materials and performance to question the autonomy of the aesthetic object. In his working processes both in a single painting and in the Grand Palais series as a whole, Osver generally moved from the more referential to the more abstracted, beginning with an image or memory of the elaborate structures yet becoming involved more and more with the "purity of the painting" in the design and relationships of shape, color, value, and texture on the canvas.[30] Pushing himself to discover new visual and expressive effects, Osver also continually modified his style and technique throughout the series. In addition to switching between different mediums, such as oil and latex paints, he shifted between loose, gestural brushwork and more meticulously painted flat surfaces, as well as between more suggestive organic forms and precise geometric shapes. He also expanded his palette from neutral hues to bright, saturated colors juxtaposed with deep blacks. For instance, in an early example, *G. P. 10-70* (1970; fig. 30), he painted the recognizable forms of the beams and rivets with subdued greens and blues punctuated by brilliant orange contours, imaginatively reconfiguring his memory of the steel girders into a dark, intertwining labyrinth of heavy industrial forms. As he progressed, however, the forms, space, and color of the paintings gradually became even more decorative and arbitrary, as in *Grand Palais 10-70 (2)* (1970; fig. 31), in which

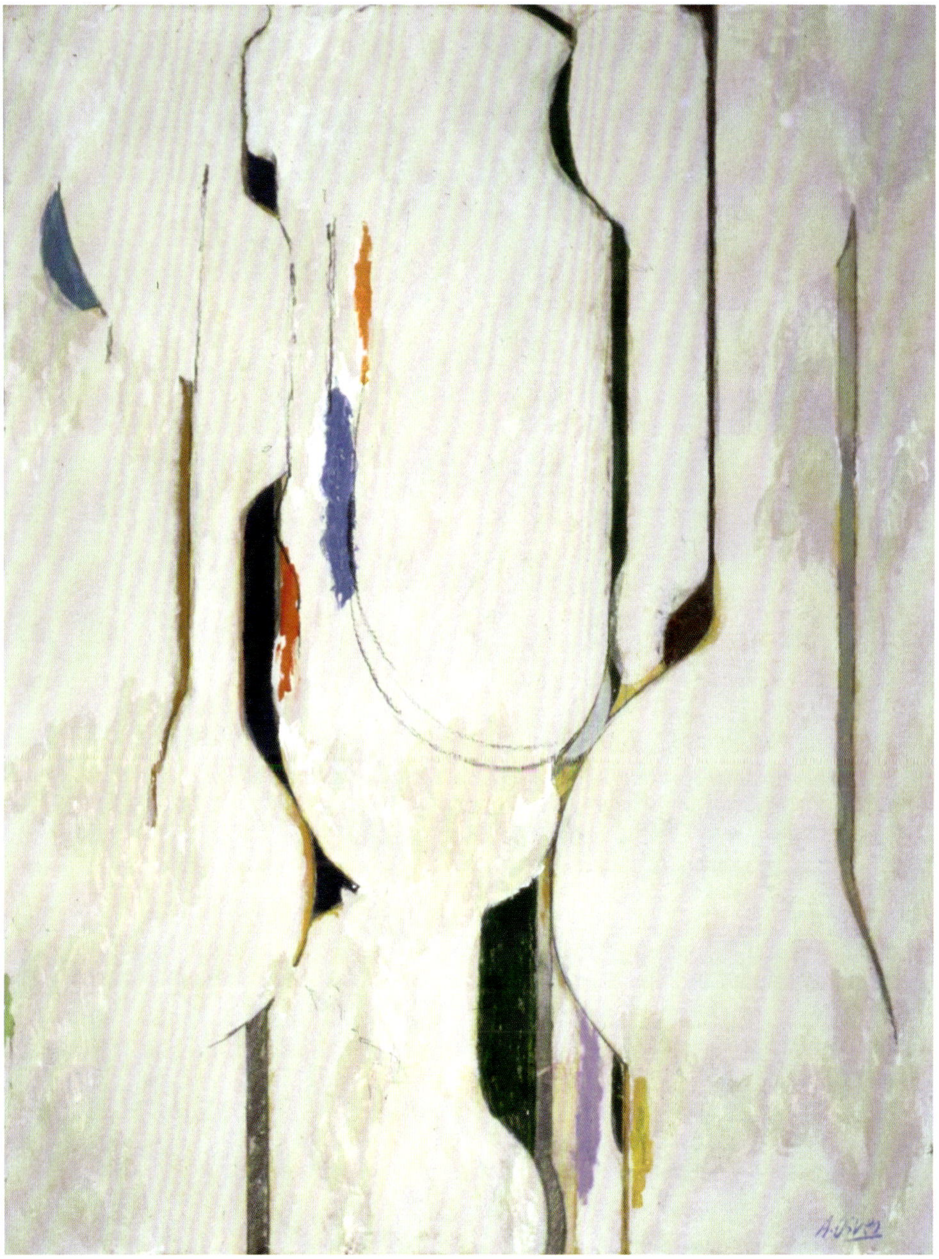

Fig. 33
***GPC: Centennial,* 1980**
Mixed media on paper on canvas, 58 1/2 x 45 1/2"
Location unknown

the motif was transformed into a dense weave of bright red and green circles and tubes. In *G. P. 10-72* (1972; fig. 32), an example of what Osver called his "loopy" paintings, he whimsically mutated the industrial pattern of steel, cast iron, and glass into globular shapes that seem to ooze and expand into one another, fighting for space within the frame.[31] Other works, by contrast, are more austere, with forms and space flattened into a vertical series of subtly modulated red and black curvilinear bands, creating an ornamental pattern of contrasting values that plays with the visual tensions between light and dark as well as flatness and depth (pl. 42, for example). Toward the end of the decade the series became even more decorative, especially with Osver's discovery of the translucent effects of rice paper. Applying the paper over underpainting on canvas, he created broad expanses of lighter, airier forms with the suggestion of mysterious shapes of green, black, yellow, or blue peeking through or around nebulous white curtains (fig. 33).

The manner in which Osver moved between different styles, techniques, and approaches in the Grand Palais series not only points to his resolve to experiment and push his art in new directions but also indicates something of the doubt that continually plagued him. Though he may have looked to Matisse's art as a model of aesthetic balance, serenity, and confident resolution, Osver periodically wrestled with his own ideals and achievements. During these times of uncertainty he often turned to his journal and correspondence with close friends, in particular with Leindecker. In a letter to Leindecker written in 1970, in response to the question of whether Osver had found any "wholeness" or "inner peace" through his art, he explained that his feelings shifted endlessly, "balanced on a razor's edge." If one day he felt fulfillment and accomplishment, the next he "could easily decide that these paintings are really mistakes, blind alleys, just more evidence of myself meeting myself going around in circles." This, the artist found, was the curse of "creativity," which, he wrote, "*is* anxiety."[32]

In 1999, seven years before his death, Osver looked back on his career. Although his art was invariably concerned with form, color, and content, he reflected, it also seemed that just as important was the "unfolding, through painting, of a sense of self, the establishing of an identity." He continued: "Along with this has come the realization that my painting has held a mirror up to life, wherein are reflected images not only as I am today but as I was in the past."[33] Although he pursued different paths throughout his career, alternating between intense creativity and frustration, Osver's constant and eclectic investigation of styles, motifs, and materials throughout the second half of the twentieth century, openly exploring new territories of art, is his most characteristic quality as a painter. Traceable through the many shifts of style—from his urban industrial landscapes to his abstractions from nature, his experiments with mediums, and his turn toward more hard-edged geometric abstraction in the 1970s—is a persistent strain of self-questioning that remained with him throughout his artistic life and that marked his distinct intelligence as an artist.

NOTES

1. Arthur Osver, in transcript of oral history interview conducted by Richard Gaugert, January 13–14, 1976, Archives of American Art, Smithsonian Institution, Washington, DC, 51; hereafter cited as AAA interview.
2. Until his move to St. Louis in 1960, Osver returned to New York in between travel and fellowship periods to live and teach, serving as an instructor at Cooper Union in 1955 and again in 1958–60.
3. Daniel Catton Rich, in *Arthur Osver: New Paintings from Italy* (Evanston, IL: Fairweather-Garnett Gallery, 1954).
4. Marilyn Robb Trier, "Osvers from Italy," *Art News* 53 (May 1954): 46.
5. AAA interview, 43. Indeed, in 1950 Osver described his need to forge an intense bond with his subject matter in a letter to Henry A. (Al) Leindecker, his friend and former student at the School of the Art Institute of Chicago, written while traveling in the Southwest. Although the canyons, mountains, and valleys fascinated him, Osver was itching to return to his studio in New York. "My approach to painting is just too darn subjective," he wrote. "I enjoy those boys who can paint what they see for the first time. I've got to keep working on the stuff like a cow on her cud," as if subject matter had to be thoroughly absorbed and digested if his painting was to have any value. Arthur Osver to Henry A. (Al) Leindecker, May 3, 1950, correspondence between Henry A. (Al) Leindecker and Arthur Osver, 1949–63, microfilm reel 3948, Arthur Osver Papers 1943–1975, Archives of American Art, Smithsonian Institution, Washington, DC; hereafter cited as Osver Papers, AAA. Correspondence between Leindecker and Osver from April 1964 to January 1987 is in Arthur Osver Papers, Estate of Arthur Osver and Ernestine Betsberg, St. Louis; hereafter cited as Osver Papers, St. Louis.
6. AAA interview, 44–45.
7. Osver, Agenda 1958 diary, March 22, 1958, and November 2, 1958, Osver Papers, St. Louis.
8. Clement Greenberg, "Review of an Exhibition of Henri Matisse," *Nation*, March 5, 1949, reprinted in *Clement Greenberg: The Collected Essays and Criticism*, ed. John O'Brian, vol. 2, *Arrogant Purpose, 1945–1949* (Chicago: University of Chicago Press, 1986), 292.
9. See John O'Brian, *Ruthless Hedonism: The American Reception of Matisse* (Chicago: University of Chicago Press, 1999), 169.
10. Osver to Leindecker, November 18, 1951, Osver Papers, AAA.
11. Undated notes, c. early 1960s, Osver Papers, St. Louis.
12. See Henri Matisse, "Notes of a Painter" (1908), in *Matisse on Art*, ed. Jack Flam (Berkeley: University of California Press, 1995), esp. 38, 42.
13. Osver, as quoted in *Mid-America Invitational: Howard Jones and Arthur Osver* (St. Louis: Saint Louis Art Museum, 1973), unpaged.
14. Osver, "Philosophy of Teaching," and "What I Paint," c. 1961, Osver Papers, St. Louis.
15. Osver's notes of December 1962 and January 25, 1963, detail the different techniques and mediums he employed. Osver Papers, St. Louis.
16. Osver to Leindecker, March 14, 1960, Osver Papers, AAA. Part of this feeling of alienation perhaps stemmed from 1950, when the artist's painting *Cranes* (1950; pl. 27) was shown in *American Painting Today* at the Metropolitan Museum of Art, New York. The juried exhibition was intended to celebrate the broad variety of work by artists from across the United States, but many of the Abstract Expressionists refused to submit work for consideration because of what they perceived as the conservative makeup of the jury. Their protest was famously covered by *Life* magazine, which reproduced the now legendary "Irascibles" photograph of the group, their notoriety effectively upstaging the artists included in the exhibition. See "Irascible Group of Advanced Artists Led Fight against Show," *Life*, January 15, 1951, 34.
17. Osver, as quoted in Alexandra Bellos Goldsand, "Arthur Osver: Mondo Mio," in *Arthur Osver: The Saint Louis Years* (St. Louis: Saint Louis Art Museum, 2000), unpaged.
18. Undated notes, Osver Papers, St. Louis.
19. Notes, February 11, 1963, Osver Papers, St. Louis.
20. Undated notes, Osver Papers, St. Louis.
21. Ibid.
22. Cleve Gray, "Narcissus in Chaos: Contemporary American Art," *American Scholar* 28 (Autumn 1959): 433.
23. Ibid., 437.
24. Undated notes, Osver Papers, St. Louis.
25. Undated notes, "The 1960 Art Season," Osver Papers, St. Louis.
26. "Introduction," notes on Grand Palais paintings, July 8, 1978, 5, Osver Papers, St. Louis.
27. Undated notes on Grand Palais paintings, Osver Papers, St. Louis.
28. AAA interview, 54–55.
29. Ibid., 57.
30. Ibid., 59.
31. Notes, December 21, 1973, Osver Papers, St. Louis.
32. Osver to Leindecker, June 30, 1970, Osver Papers, St. Louis.
33. "Artist's Statement," November 30, 1999, in *Saint Louis Years*.

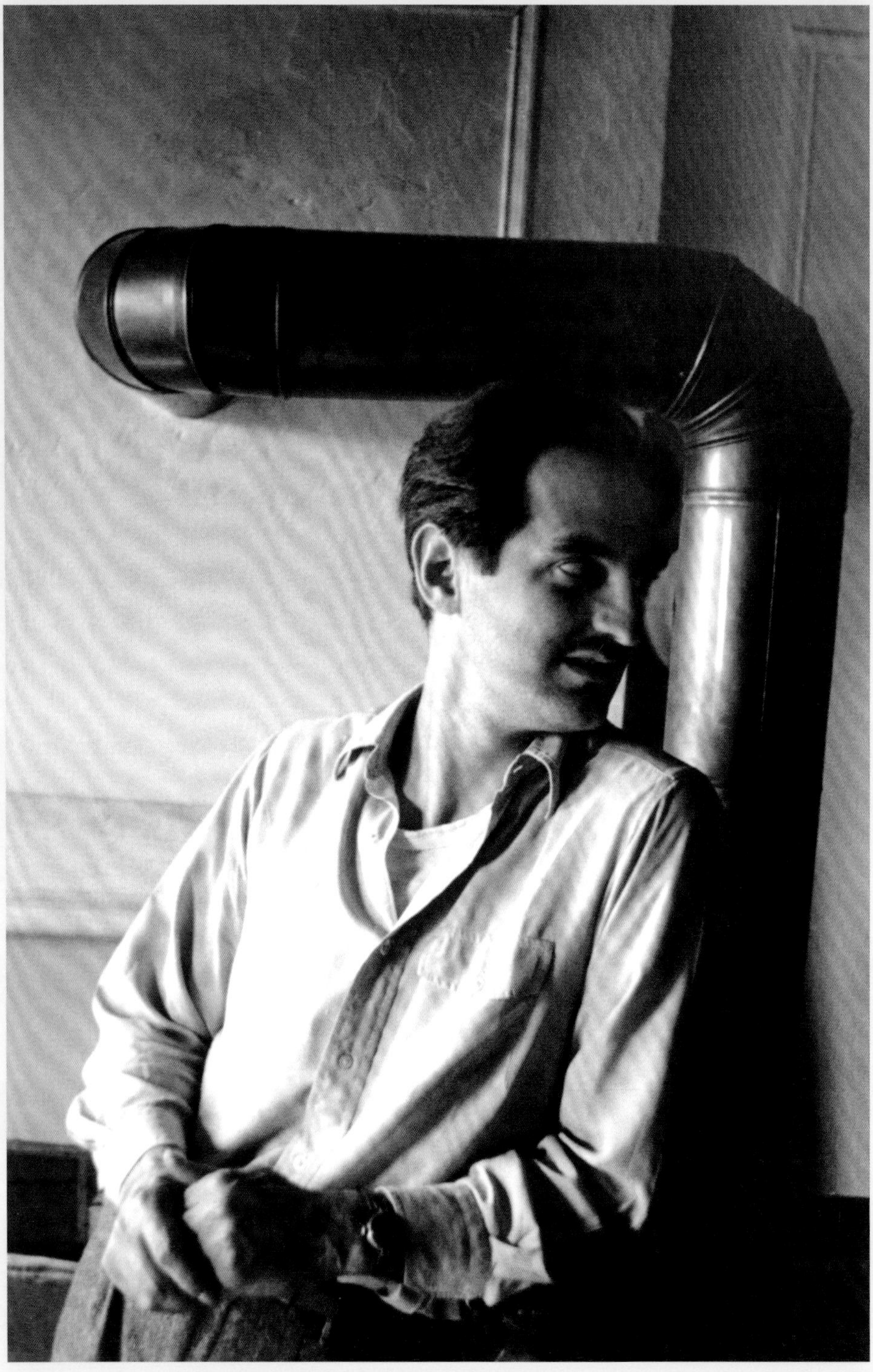

An Interview with Arthur Osver

Conducted by Richard Gaugert

The following is excerpted from a transcription of an oral history interview with Arthur Osver, conducted at Osver's home in St. Louis on January 13 and 14, 1976, for the Oral History Program of the Archives of American Art, Smithsonian Institution.

Experience as a student at the School of the Art Institute of Chicago

RICHARD GAUGERT: You went to the Art Institute of Chicago in 1931 and you studied under Boris Anisfeld. I wonder ... what kind of a study was it?

ARTHUR OSVER: Boris Anisfeld was the senior painting teacher. After you'd gone through your apprenticeship of still life drawing and so on, in your junior or senior year, depending upon your talents, you studied with him. He had a special studio which everyone wanted to get into because he was a very glamorous figure.... He was very much the old-style European professor.... He'd come in one day a week, Thursdays.... Someone would say, "Hey, Boris is coming." We'd all get up to our easels and we'd begin painting. We could hear his footsteps come in. We didn't turn. He'd stand behind someone, perhaps it would be myself.... He'd say, "Osver, this been cheap stuff." And he'd walk away. I'd be standing there. It would be almost like Zen, you know, you've asked a question and you get something that's incomprehensible.... But I found this was very valuable. I began to rely on my own perception of the thing, my own evaluation of it. Why was it cheap stuff, what was wrong about it and so on. Boris ran this very, very tight class. We were all so anxious to get some word of praise from him. Which never came. Sometimes he'd say, "This been not too bad." This was about as much as he would ever give in the way of a compliment.

After I'd gotten my fellowship—which I later discovered was through Boris's help a great deal—and I'd been to France and had come back to Chicago and lived there for a year or so before going on to New York, I looked Boris up. And every time I came to Chicago, I'd look him up because underneath that forbidding exterior was one of the warmest hearts you've ever seen. He was a marvelous, marvelous, human and humane person....

I think one of the most important things in going to school and having contact with older people ... is not so much the ideas they give you, because ideas have a limited life span; what's hot stuff in 1936 is perhaps so dated in 1976 that people don't even know what you're talking about. But the fact that through contact with this person you begin to get some notion of what it meant to be an artist, what made an artist tick—how did he live, how did he think, how did he manage this or that. It's an almost osmosis-like absorption of the artistic essence if you want to call it that.... And I think Boris gave all of us who were in contact with him this sense of what it meant to be an artist....

RG: Do you ever find yourself thinking of him and of what he was saying to you when you are painting or when you are involved in making a statement to your own classes today?

AO: Do I ever! I speak of him a great deal to my students. And also when I'm doing something..., I'll say "Osver" (I'm talking to myself), "this been cheap stuff." It's there; he's at my shoulder.

Urban setting as subject matter

AO: Somewhere along the line I had become interested in the world some stories up.... We had always lived way up, usually on the top floor.... You look out the window and you see a lot of things going on that you don't see at street level. And being up on the top floor, one of the things that interested me tremendously was rooftops. In Chicago I began to do a number of paintings of rooftops. As I recall now, one of these was called *High Wind* [fig. 3], which deals with wind whipping across a rooftop, chimneys, exhaust pipes coming up, the tile ramparts going around the roof and, most dramatically I suppose, clothes on the line with the high wind whipping the clothes. And in that particular painting the clothes have a certain surreal quality by looking as if the person who had worn the clothes was still in them. I did several paintings on that theme.... I was an urban painter, and the urban focus happened to be on this world of wires and chimneys and tar paper and all the rest of it. There was a painting I did in Chicago that had the romantic title of *Melancholy in the Sun* [fig. 13]. It was of a rooftop, the top of a tenement, and sitting in the middle of this rooftop was a man taking a sun bath.... There was something about the context of the whole thing that had this minor key element to it. I sent that painting to the Pennsylvania Academy of the Fine Arts. They had an annual show which was open to anyone.... The painting won a prize. That was the first step that I made, let's say, into professionalism. I felt: well, all right, I've been judged and found to have something not by my peers but by my superiors, I mean these older painters. And I felt that that was a very, very important painting.

First travels abroad

AO: [For my fellowship year through the School of the Art Institute of Chicago in 1936] I wanted to go to France. This is something that now in 1976 I think we tend to forget. At that time Paris was the place. New York was important but—well, not even really important; it was there. But Paris was where Picasso and Braque and all the rest were working. They were the big boys. We had people over here like Grant Wood and [John Steuart] Curry and [Thomas Hart] Benton (who recently died). We admired them and realized they had a certain stature, but their stature was that of pygmies compared to those giants on the other side of the water. And we all had this romantic notion of getting over there and walking the same streets that Braque and Matisse and Picasso walked over. So that had to be the place.

[When I arrived, it] was in November and Paris was getting very, very cold and gloomy, and the days were very short. I hadn't realized how far north Paris is.... I got this tremendous yearning to go to the sun. I got a ticket, got on the train, [my wife, Ernestine, and I] traveled through Switzerland to Italy. That's quite a story in itself. This was in 1936, and of course this was the time of Mussolini.... When we got to Milan, as we walked out of the station, on looking all about us, we noticed that every window that we could see had a rug or a tapestry or a drapery or something bright-colored flung out of the window hanging over the windowsill, and inside the windows were pictures of Il Duce.... We walked around the city all day. Everywhere we went was this color, all these things hanging out, and pictures of Il Duce all over. So that night was an amazing experience. In front of the large railroad station in Milan there was this huge crowd of people. On top of the station they had these big torches.... Il Duce came out. He was very erect, had on this little monkey cap with a tassel hanging on one side.... Il Duce made this big speech, which I understood not a word of. As his voice was bellowing, pounding over this huge throng, every now and then he'd say something and the people would throw up their arms, saying with one voice, "To you, Leader." "You are ours." I had never run into mob hysteria before. It was quite an amazing thing.

Relationship with Ernestine and early career

AO: I met Ernestine Betsberg at the Art Institute of Chicago. She was a year behind me. We went around together, and when I got a fellowship to go to Europe, she said, "You stay there because I'm going to get one too." I thought: well, I don't know about that. But she did get one. So I was in Europe for a year; then she came and she joined me. We got married. We lived for a while in Paris, but most of the time we spent in the South of France.... I had sort of scouted the area out and we lived in a little town called Cagnes-sur-Mer. It was near Nice.... While we were there we did a great deal of painting too.... We were both in the garden, Ernestine at one end and I at the other end. There was this big well there, a sort of big cistern that overflowed and they had a little pond. And I was painting it, and painting it à la Van Gogh, as much as one possibly could. I've told you how much I admired Van Gogh and how much I was influenced by him, and how I had been living his life through these letters he had written to his brother. As I was putting down these big, thick gobs of paint and trying to be as much like Van Gogh as possible, suddenly it struck me how unfair things were. I thought to myself almost in tears: if Van Gogh hadn't come upon this way of painting, I would have because it's so natural and so right, and I would have been the famous one, you see. And I believed it, I honestly believed it....

Then we returned to Chicago. I was looking about for something to do. There was the Federal Art Project waiting. It was possible for only one of us to get on the project. Somehow we decided that I should be the one to try to get on. Which I did. I was on it for eighteen months. Then you had to get off and stay off for a certain period. This was in 1938. People have asked me about the Federal Art Project, what it meant to me as an artist, was it important and all. I thought it was tremendously important. It meant that here I was out of school, I had spent two years in Europe painting, I came back to America, and I could still continue painting. Otherwise, if it hadn't been in existence, I might have had to do something I had done earlier, like selling shoes.

Life in New York

AO: Ernestine and I had been talking about my difficulties of being an artist. The thought: let's go to New York; that's where the action is; there's much more action there than in Chicago. She said: let me go; I can work up some designs and see if I can't get some luck in textile houses or wallpaper houses and so on. So she worked very hard and got this portfolio together, and she took off. A very brave girl. I would have been scared to death to do it myself.... She ended up working for a wallpaper firm. When she had this under control, I followed her to New York. We lived at first in a place on West Twelfth Street ... in the Village. It was a railroad flat. The light was very poor for us really. The rent was cheap. We were able to get things done. We lived there for a number of years. I ended up working for an outfit ... located in Queens, so I had to travel to Queens. And by virtue of being in Queens and looking about, I liked the neighborhood. Somehow it sort of materialized, began to be like Chicago—commercial buildings, bridges, strange structures that turned me on as an artist. It was visually wonderful material for me. So we decided to move to Queens....

As I rode around Queens, of course I began to soak up this visual material more and more and get more and more excited about it.... Now the interesting thing is that I didn't necessarily paint any specific thing that I saw, but this mix of impressions that I picked up resulted in my doing a great many city paintings, which were, in a sense, composites. There was nothing that was specifically this bridge or that building or that rooftop; but they were a composite of all of the bridges and rooftops and buildings that I had seen.... What I did during those years in Long Island City was to take a lot of 35 mm shots of the elevated structure, railroad yards, junkyards, barges along the river. I'd look at these, project them, and try to arrive at some sort of distillation of this material....

We lived in Long Island City for eight years. They were the most productive years of my life. I've never done as much work. And things began to happen. I won a number of prizes. I got a Guggenheim fellowship that was renewed. I eventually ended up with a Prix de Rome [from the American Academy in Rome].... I left Long Island City, and my life has never been the same since. But it was a wonderful, wonderful experience there.

Travel and work in Italy

AO: When I first came to Rome, I wanted to pick up in Rome what I had left in New York. I couldn't do it. I couldn't find these old warehouses or bridges. I couldn't find the sense that America has in terms of its industrial look. There's something about the fences we put around places, just the whole makeup of it. In Rome I found this layer upon layer of civilization—ruins of Roman times, of Renaissance times, of medieval times, and so on. So I began to do what you might expect: I painted buildings. I painted some churches there, churches that I'd seen not only in Rome but outside of Rome. Perhaps one of the most successful paintings was one I did—again a distillation of various cathedrals—but based on these black-and-white-striped stone cathedrals; there's one in Orvieto, and there's one in Florence.... I did paintings of the Roman Forum, the ruins of the Colosseum. I did a number of paintings of Venice because we traveled around Italy a good deal. But looking back at that experience, I begin to see some things a little more clearly now than I saw it then. I didn't have quite the involvement in that subject matter that I had with the American city. I couldn't get into it as much. It was a little for me like being on top of it instead of under it and within it. When I look back at the paintings I did just before leaving America and the paintings that I did in Rome, I feel that ... the American paintings had more intensity. And I think that ... was due to the fact that, as I said before, they meant more to me. I wasn't seeing them with a tourist's eye but with the eye of an actual denizen of this lair of strange creatures that we call habitations and factories and bridges and everything else that goes to make up the American industrial scene. And I think as a result of not feeling as deeply into my material—that is, the Roman material—as I had before with the American material, I began unconsciously to move into a more formal awareness of what was taking place. In other words, if I wasn't that concerned with capturing the essence of a particular structure, I then would ask myself what was I concerned with. And I began to see more clearly that I was concerned—as I always had been, but I hadn't seen it as clearly—with the language of form, with color, shape, mass, line, everything that goes to make up the abstract elements of a painting. The later Roman paintings moved away from buildings and eventually got into botanical things [figs. 23, 24]. You know, the Romans have this wonderful habit of trimming their trees and making all sorts of strange and beautiful shapes out of them. I think it's called topiary art. And they've been doing it for generations. I remember going to places like Ostia, where they have beautiful ... pine forests, which have been sculpted. Just marvelous. But the result of working on this organic material instead of this man-made material, this botanical stuff, I began to see the tree shape, the trunk shape move into pillars, cloud-like forms. They began to be forms almost in terms of forms for themselves. So the identity of the object began to move out ... and the other thing, that is, the formal element, began to move in. I think that was the beginning of something in the Rome experience that hadn't happened there before.

Return to New York and new opportunity in St. Louis

RG: Were you happy to get back to New York after the Prix de Rome experience?

AO: Yes and no. It was very curious. When we were in New York, we lived in terrible places in terms of space, in terms of heat and everything else.... But we didn't mind. We believed in ourselves. This was a new experience. We felt it was high adventure. We got to Rome, and we were seduced, we were spoiled. When we got back to New York, it was never the same truly. In Rome at the American Academy we had these splendid studios. Ernestine was given a good space to work in. I had a studio which was enormous.... A marvelous view over all of Rome. We had servants doing things for us.... We got back to New York. We had very little money. We began looking around for a place to live. Rents had gone up enormously, incredibly. We couldn't find much. Finally we did manage to find a place. They had something called professional apartments where there was no rent ceiling so they could gouge you without running into the law. We ended up getting a ... very poor apartment, very high rent, in one of the most rundown parts of New York—Sixth Street and Avenue D. It was like living in a state of siege, warfare and so on down there. We worked there for a while. Even there the light was poor, the space was poor.

For years Ken Hudson had been after me to come to St. Louis. After a while we thought: well, let's try something out of New York just to see what it's like. So on one occasion when Ken Hudson said, "Why don't you come to St. Louis and try it out for a year?" we thought all right.... We found it nice. We were able to work. We had gone through roughly twenty years of the New York experience, so we felt we had that and we had a certain idea of who we were as artists, we weren't in the process of inventing ourselves as actively as we were earlier on.... New York was a terrible scramble economically.... At this particular time of my life it was good to come here and sort of pull my resources together instead of ... having them dissipated in New York. And this has been reinforced by the experiences of friends of mine who have stayed on in New York, people of my generation who sometimes live in New York in a way that's more provincial than my living in St. Louis.... These artists will live in a neighborhood and not venture beyond it.... So I find that perhaps they see less, or are less exposed to what's going on than I am here. I have this feeling of ease and of being away from the scene and of being more objective and less caught up in the middle of it than they are.

Teaching

AO: While I find teaching stimulating, sometimes I think that if I ... were in a city like New York maybe I could get by without teaching. But in St. Louis I think it's important that I am teaching because the students present the challenge, sometimes the irritation, sometimes the stimulation that I'm not getting from the city itself, the art life of the city. And also without their knowing it, the students have the faculty of being my scouts, my outriders, my avant-garde. They're out there poking through *Artforum*, *Art in America*, *Art Digest*, and they come up with ideas, which then eventually end up in their canvases. I'll come across something, and I'll say "Gee, where did you get that? What's that about?" And I'll find out that they were excited by this article or that article. Unfortunately, so often they don't see the real thing. And by virtue of this challenge that they pose to me, I am kept on my toes in a way that without them I wouldn't be. So in that sense I think teaching has been very valuable....

When I went to school, the idea of the artist as teacher was just not there. There were no teaching jobs. There were a few artists who were artists-in-residence.... But the idea of so many art schools contained within a university—you know, now every university has an art school, and of course having an art school they have people teaching. So you have hundreds and hundreds of teachers. In those days there wasn't that possibility. When we were going to school, we were very humble about our opportunities, about what we could do in the future. We hadn't this idea of a long, patient servitude to some mystical idea of art, you know. We'd just plod along. This was the way I really felt.

The Grand Palais series

AO: I get down around the riverfront in South St. Louis, and there's a lot of industrial material there that reminds me very much of New York, of those earlier experiences in New York. Sometimes I get a certain twinge, I wonder: gee, why didn't I stay with it? I still get the charge from that that I did then, but somehow, although I've made a few efforts to get back into that sort of material, I find that I can't do it.... I can't quite get into it in the same way. Let's say I'm more aware of what form for form's sake is doing.... Perhaps I know more—and I hate to say this—but feel less.... I still have this emotional involvement, but I have this other involvement now in the more formal aspects of art. So that in recent paintings, for example in this Grand Palais series [fig. 32, pls. 40–42], which has now occupied me for at least the last five years, I find that the Grand Palais idea, which would have been foremost and in the forefront in the old days, is secondary. It becomes a grid into which to throw the ideas of form, color, shape, mass, volume, and all the rest of it. So there has been a reversal of this old split thing about the story and the form. You see, before, the story was very, very important, and the form came along and tried to perform its function so it just didn't become an illustration. But now it's been reversed. I find that the form leans on the story but the form takes over and says: I'm number one....

When I began with the Grand Palais, there were these dark, somber colors, which satisfied something in me. In recent years ... it's gotten very contrasty, and I'm less aware of this industrial look in the paintings, and I'm much more aware of the formal contrast, ... the pattern of dark and light, almost black against white. What can I begin doing with various shapes? And the various shapes, while they may originally have come from the Grand Palais, begin to take on an authentic life of their own, and they begin to exist as shapes. Yet without the Grand Palais I wouldn't know where my shapes were to come from. So I need the Grand Palais, but I need it in a less direct manner.

I think the building was built ... for the [1900] Paris Exposition. It's Art Nouveau, you know, where they take these heavy beams of steel and twist them around in floral, wavelike, tendril-like shapes and all. I thought: I can do something with this.... So what I did was to rush back to the hotel—I had a 35 mm camera and I had a Rolleiflex. I came back with the two cameras, and I went around and took all sorts of pictures of it [fig. 28]. When I got back I had them developed and had some blow-ups made. I began painting, basing the paintings on my memory and what these photographs were telling me. The paintings were terrible, actually impossible. I put the whole idea aside and got onto something else. Then a number of years later, working with my students—again this is where I feel my students often give me so much more than I give them—they were working with latex colors because they were cheaper. One of my students had discovered that Central Hardware here in St. Louis had what they called Accent colors; they were strong reds, yellows, greens, blues, and all; they cost only $2.49 a can. When that student left, he asked me, "Do you want any of these?" So I took it home. I had a lot of this paint, and I began fooling around with it.... I began to play with these latex colors and I began to expand my palette.... I discovered that they did something for me that I liked. They enabled me to develop an idea and keep with it because they dried so quickly. The reason I couldn't do anything with the Grand Palais idea earlier was because I was working with oil paints. With oils I would put down a shape, and then I'd begin to modify that shape, but I couldn't do it with the accuracy and directness and quickness that I could with these others because oil takes a long time to dry, and before I'd get back to it the idea would have somehow evaporated or didn't seem quite as important as it had been in the first place—you might say inspiration had just flown out the window. Using these latex paints I could keep inspiration caged a little bit longer.... It was just as if it were waiting to have the door open for it to come in. And it came in. I then began to work on the Grand Palais paintings. I did a lot of them very quickly. I was very excited about the idea. I did drawings, I did paintings. But the determining factor was the change in technique.... I've never gone back to oil since; though, let me tell you, that is a love affair that I remember with a great deal of longing because oil paint can do things that acrylics or latex can't do. Oil paint to me is the king of mediums. But it didn't serve the idea at all. This was a case of the right technique meeting the right idea. And so this meant everything to me. As a result I've been working with acrylics and latex now at least these past five years.

Artistic process

RG: Tell me a little bit about your technique. You've told me about the Grand Palais, you saw this building, you had this idea, you took these 35 mm photographs and all that sort of thing, but what happened from there to the point where we see what we see with the canvases, which of course are all terribly different even though there is a unifying theme.

AO: It would be very nice if I could present some picture of a very rational, organized person who says: all right, I have my idea and now I'm going to take step one, two, three, four, five, and eventually when I've reached step ten I'd have the thing done. But it's the other way around. It's sort of a mad throwing together of a lot of material that I think will provide a future yield. I throw in bits of colors and shapes and all. I have, of course, the Grand Palais idea as the ultimate. It's going to be conditioned by that. But when I begin each painting or drawing, I'm hoping that that conditioning will present some little aspect that I hadn't seen before. So instead of going into it with a prefabricated idea of what it's going to be, I just put down anything that comes to mind.... This could be just a blob of color, which it very often is. I put various bits of color down, then I begin putting in verticals, some diagonals, perhaps a horizontal or two—that interloper, the horizontal. And as this begins to function ... I can begin to see correspondences. Something over here is beginning to set up a little conversation with something here. I try to make that conversation a little more eloquent and one responds a little more beautifully with the other, and so on. And this is the way everything I do works. I think this is true for every artist. You put a lot of things down. Then they begin to suggest things. They begin to point ways that you hadn't imagined. And this is what you hope for.... So to get back to your initial question, it's a very disorganized, unplanned, wild plunge into what I hope is going to be a fresh experience, even though that experience has looming in the background the idea of the Grand Palais.

RG: How do you know when a painting is finished?

AO: You never know. May I quote Monsieur Paul Valéry? He said, "A work of art is never really finished, only abandoned." And this is so true. Very often, or almost always when I get something back, or pull something out of the racks, I see something that I could do on it. And the only thing that keeps me from doing something with all of these things I pull out or get back is that sometimes I tell myself: it's not going to make that much difference. But sometimes when I feel it will make a significant difference, I will take out an old painting.... I did this just a week or two ago. I pulled out one of the early Grand Palais paintings. I saw something that I thought could be simplified and strengthened. I worked on it, and I think it helped a great deal. I remember Ernestine coming up and saying, "Oh, that's much better." I felt so good about it.

Life with Ernestine

RG: I assume your wife always went with you when you went to Rome and wherever you were traveling. Was she also painting with you in a sense? Or had she given up her painting career by this time?

AO: Ernestine never stopped painting. Once she left the job that she had in New York she continued painting, has continued to the present time. She hasn't exhibited as much as I have. But I think that's not been her fault but the blindness of the public, if you like. She has had shows, and she's planning to have a show this coming season. But she's always been there to give me support, and I hope that in some way I've been able to give her support too. It's been very interesting to me in recent years with women becoming more conscious of the fact that they … have certain rights, et cetera.... My girl students ask me: how have you gotten along over the years where you have two artists in the same family? Are there jealousies? Does one have to stand back and let the other one push ahead? Or do they both go ahead at the same time? Just what manner of life do you lead together?

And I've gone into that a bit because it's obviously meaningful to them. It's been very important to me…; it's not always easy. Sometimes you find that if you're doing well the other person isn't. You have to share your joy with another person's frustrations, if you like.... Sometimes there's a certain feeling of guilt as to why am I chosen for this sort of recognition and that other person is not. So the usual ups and downs that an artist always will have … are doubled. Sometimes I point this out. I say, look, be careful, because an artist's life is a life that has to do very much with the abrasiveness of ego, of the spirit, and all things happen which will ruffle you and which sometimes are very disturbing.... But to counteract that, I think the fact that people can mature and become adults and realize that you have to take what comes along with as [much] good grace as you possibly can.... I think Ernestine and I have been able to do that over the years. And also we've been able to do it because we've accommodated our lives to making it possible for each of us to fulfill or express himself or herself as fully as we possibly can as artists.

Gallery representation and interaction with collectors

AO: I've been affiliated with the Fairweather-Hardin Gallery [in Chicago] … it must be over twenty years. I had a gallery in New York … for a number of years, Grand Central Moderns. When the gallery closed, I made some attempts to pick up a New York gallery. This has been a great disappointment to me not to have an outlet in New York....

RG: Do you work directly with collectors much? Or are you uncomfortable with them? Would you rather have someone else do the negotiating with the people who own your work?

AO: Very much the latter, yes. I hate the idea of having people come to the studio to look at work.... Somehow I feel almost, I suppose, like a woman who is disrobing and wondering if this john is going to say, "All right, Baby…" It's very uncomfortable for me.... So I'm delighted when there's this intermediary, the dealer, or someone who, removed from the studio, is showing my work also. If good things are said about it, fine; if bad things are said about it, fine. I'm not aware of it.... I realize more and more that the important thing is to keep a certain sense of self-possession, of self-esteem, equilibrium and all that, which you need for your work. If you begin to worry too much about its value or its reception or how it's going to do or how it's not going to do, you're immobilized. You have to believe basically in the importance of what you're doing and as much as possible keep the world outside the door. Let someone else be your intermediary, your agent, the person speaking for you.

Working habits

AO: There's something I've formulated for the benefit of my students called Osver's law, which is: if you stay away from your work for a day, it takes a day to get back; if you stay away for two days, it takes four days; if you stay away three days, it takes nine days. It's a geometric rather than an arithmetical progression. So if you stay away too long, it's going to take you a long, long time to get back.

RG: Besides Osver's law, what other special advice do you have for your students?

AO: Well, generally it stems from the application of Osver's law.... This is what I do myself: you hit a dry run, things don't go well. I tell them: go into the studio and go through the motions. The motions may be just sweeping up the studio, or rearranging the paintings you have there, or sharpening a pencil, seeing if any brushes need washing; anything that might through some little indirect door lead you back into where you want to go. I tell them that the worst thing they can do is get away from it or give in to it. Maybe because I'm an ex-Boy Scout at heart ... I tell them that if you shirk something it just makes it that much harder to get back to it the next time. In other words, habits are reinforcing: good habits reinforce good habits, and bad habits reinforce bad habits.

PLATES

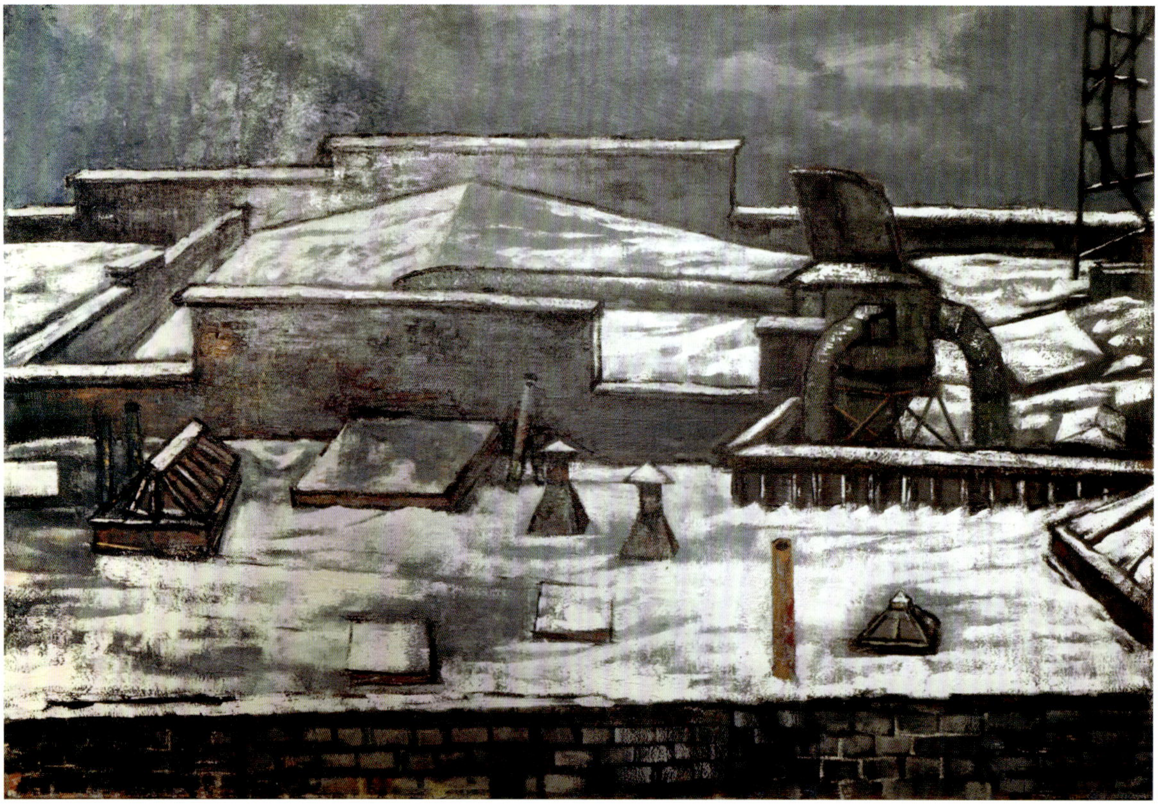

1
***Garage Roof,* 1940s**
Oil on canvas, 30 x 42"
Location unknown

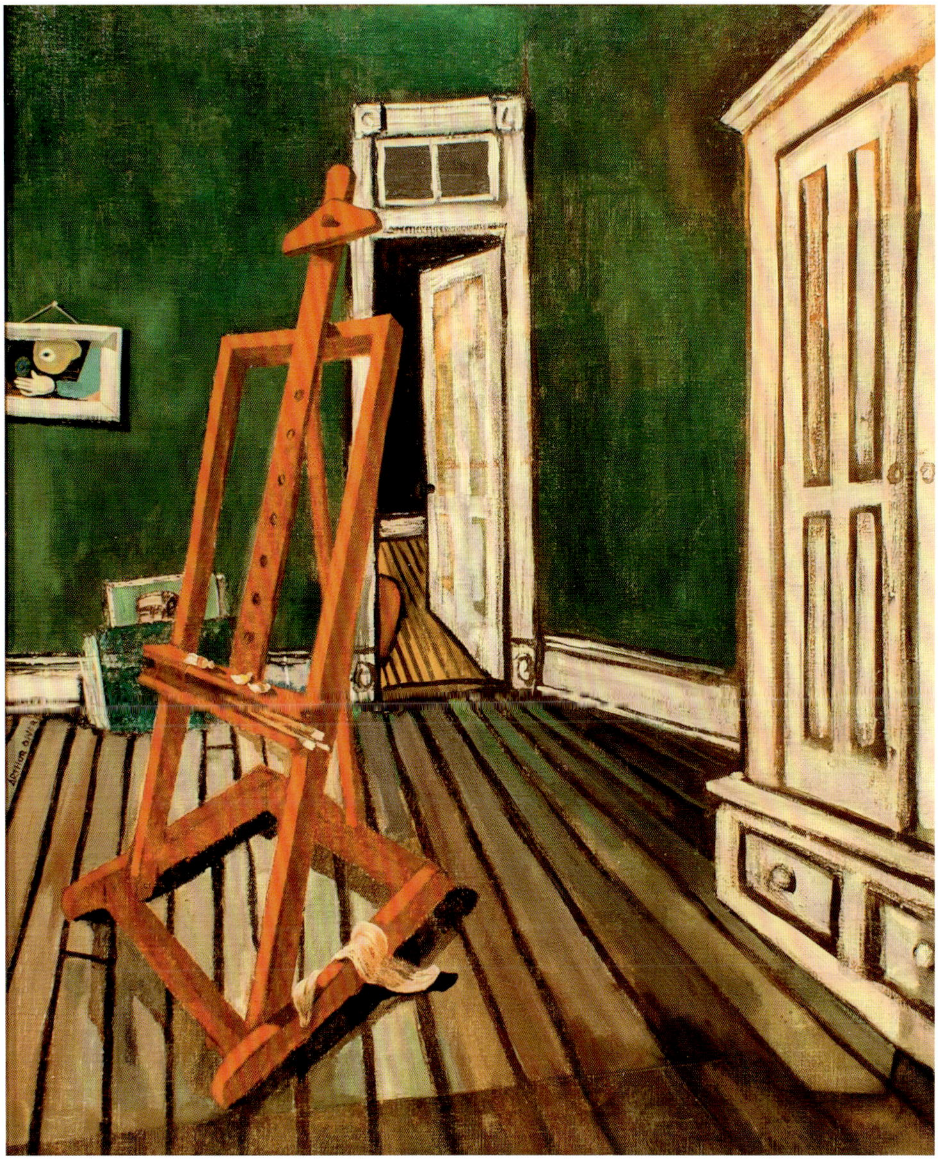

2
***The Studio,* 1941–42**
Oil on canvas, 37 x 30"
Courtesy of Tyler Fine Art, St. Louis

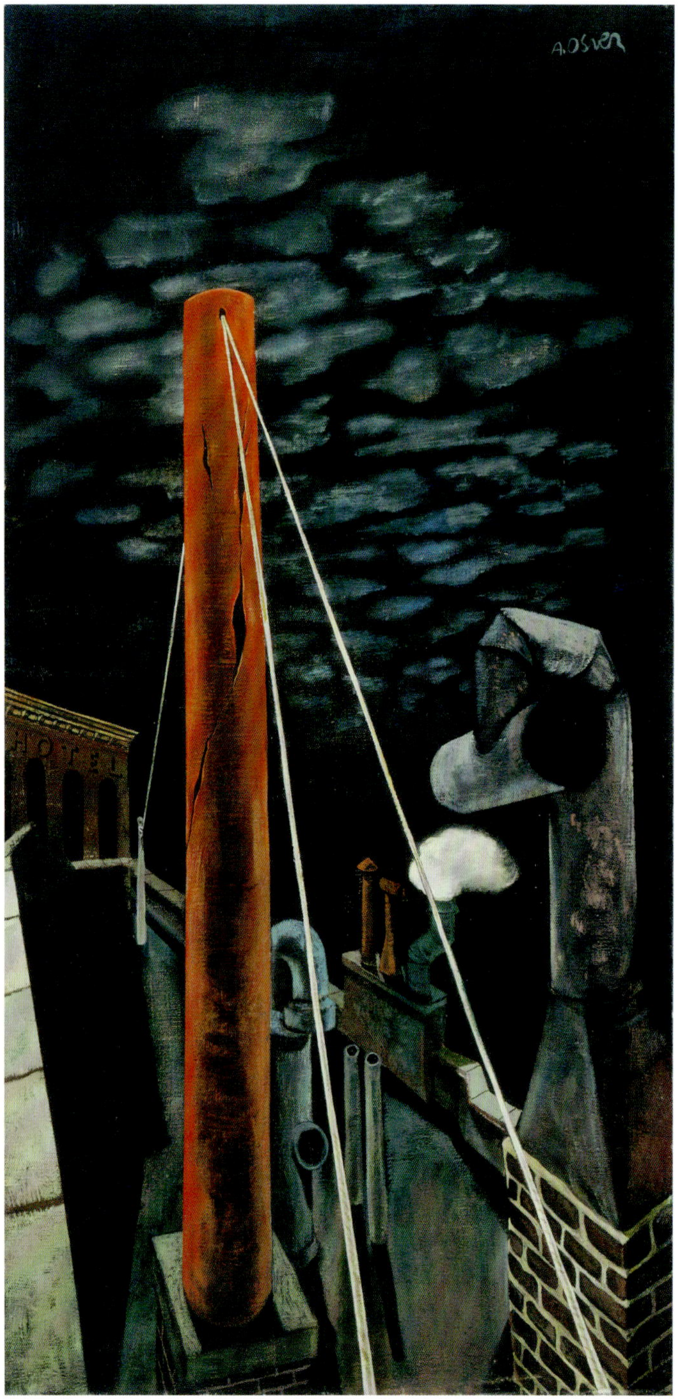

3
***Melancholy of a Rooftop*, 1942**
Oil on canvas, 48 x 24"
The Museum of Modern Art, New York, Purchase

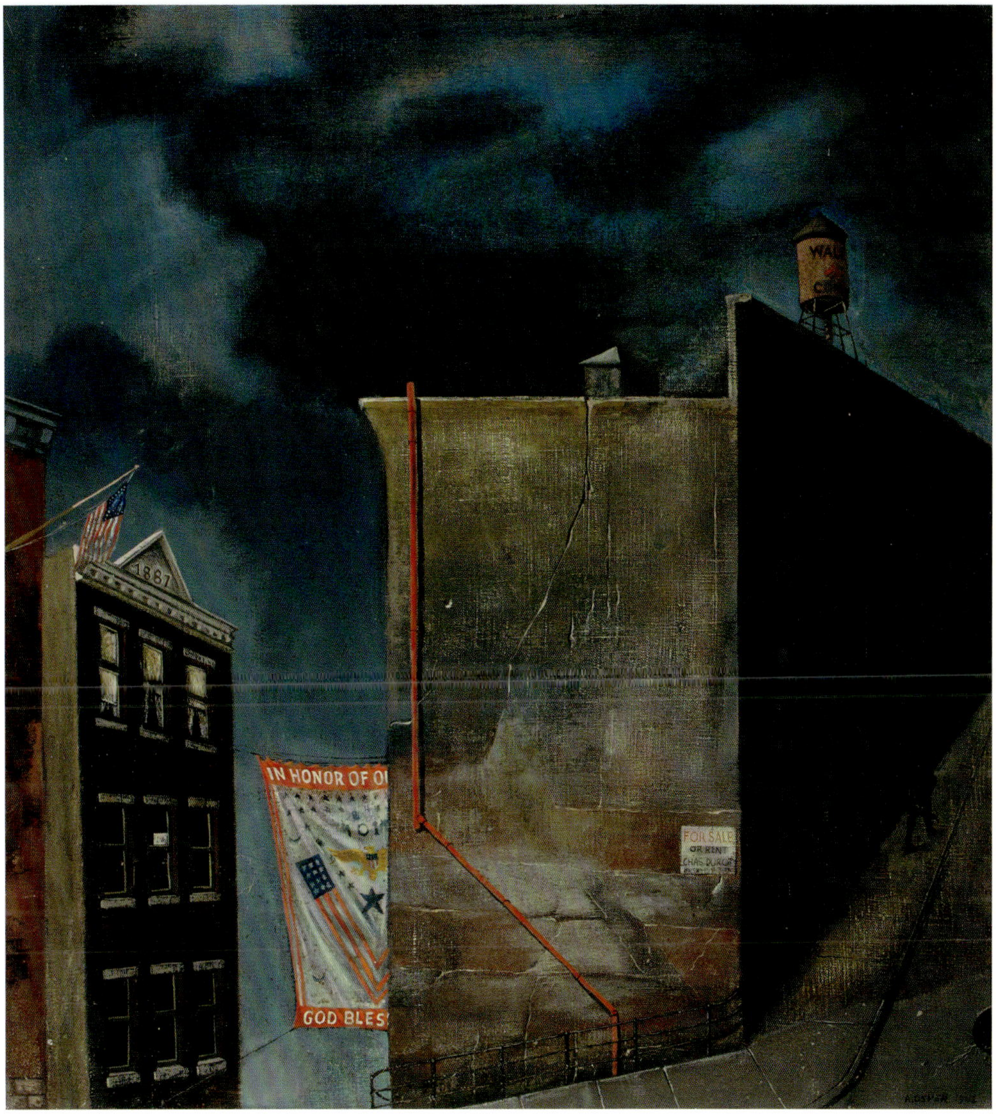

4

***Sunday Morning*, 1942**

Oil on canvas, 30 1/8 x 27 7/8"

Mildred Lane Kemper Art Museum, Washington University in St. Louis, Gift of Peter Lehner, 1994

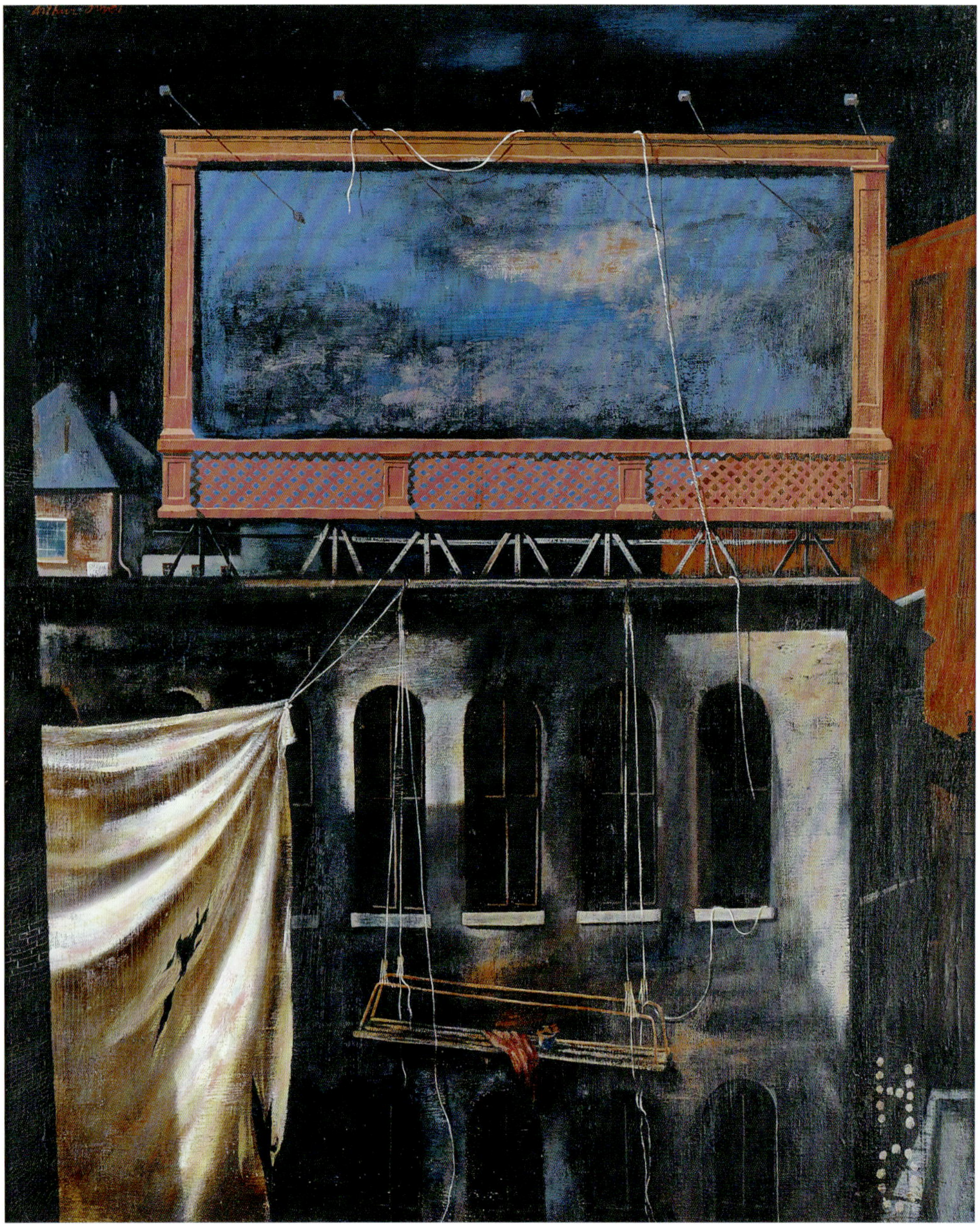

5
***The Big Billboard*, 1944**
Oil on Masonite, 36 x 30"
Georgia Museum of Art, University of Georgia,
Extended loan from the Jason Schoen Collection, Miami

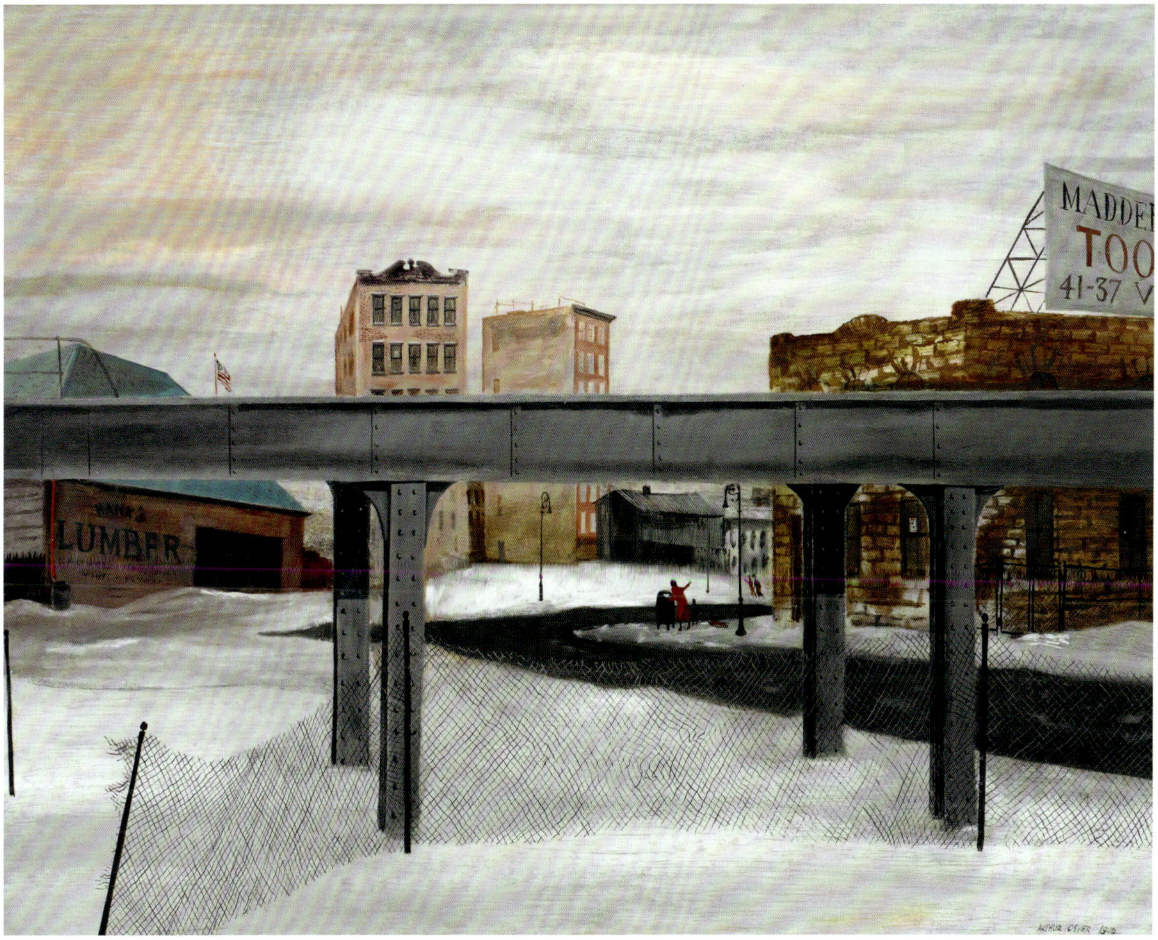

6

***West Side*, 1944**

Oil on board, 22 x 28"

Collection of Jeannine and Kent Kalkwarf

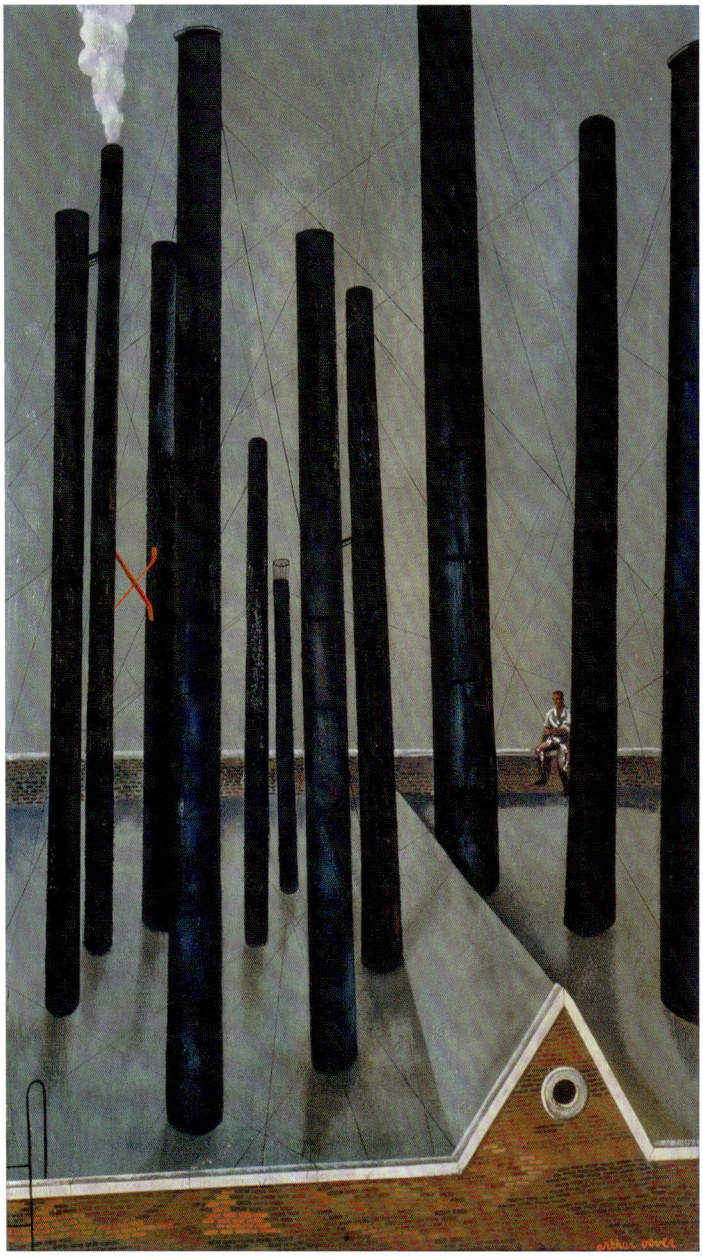

7

***Forest of Chimneys*, 1945**

Oil on canvas, 36 1/4 x 20 15/16"

Museu de Arte Contemporânea da Universidade de São Paulo

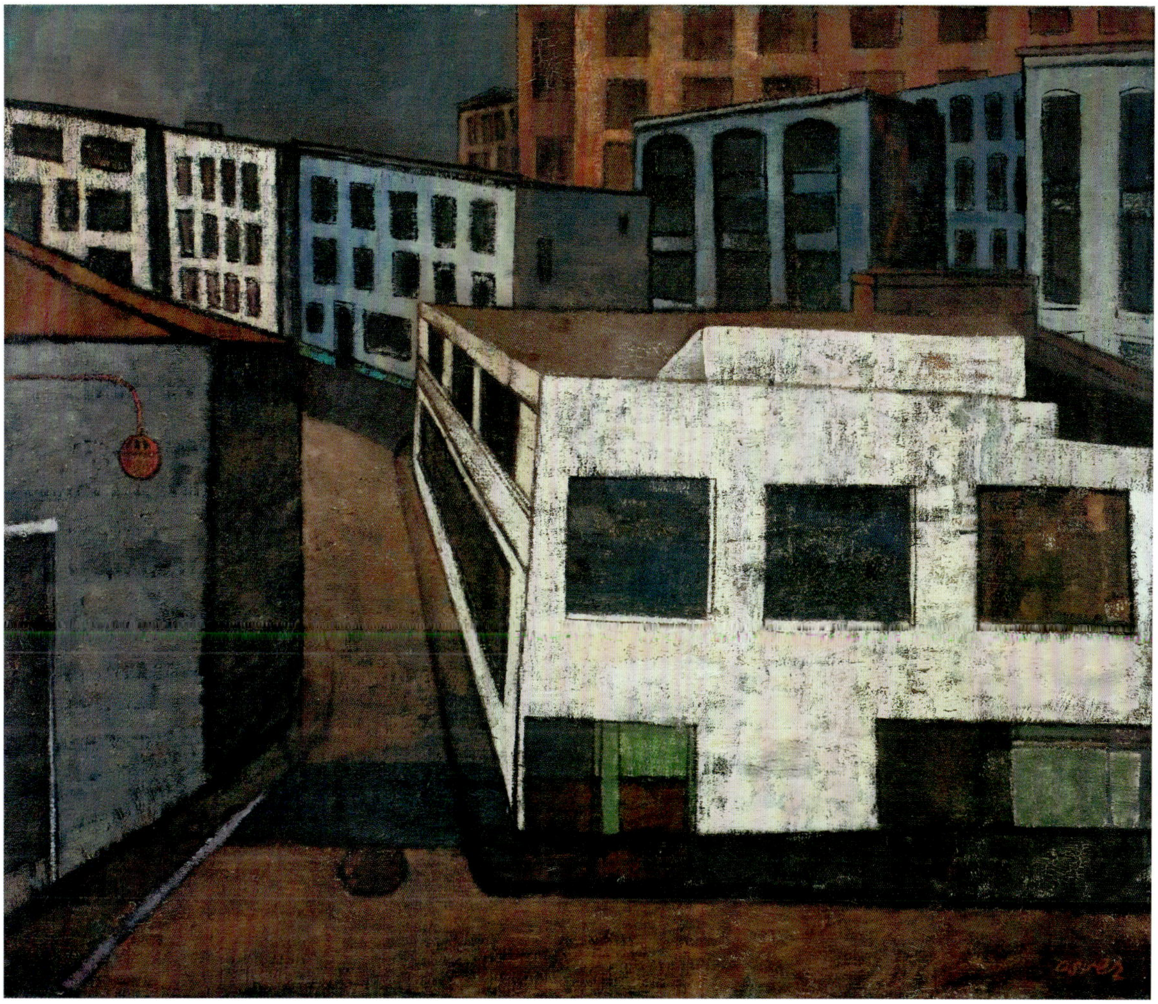

8
***Greenpoint Windows*, 1945**
Oil on canvas, 30 x 36"
Collection of Peter Shank

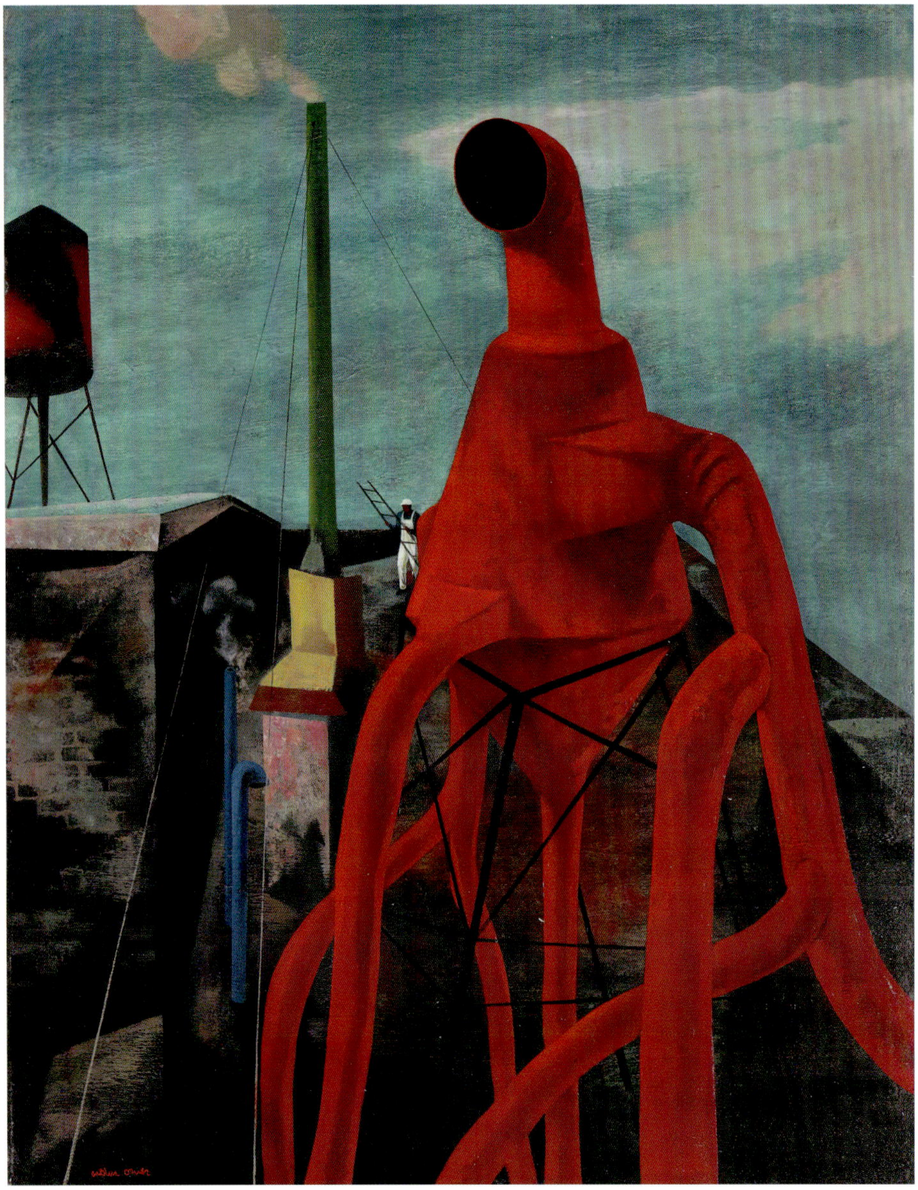

9
***Red Ventilator*, 1945**
Oil on Masonite, 30 x 23"
The John and Susan Horseman Collection, St. Louis

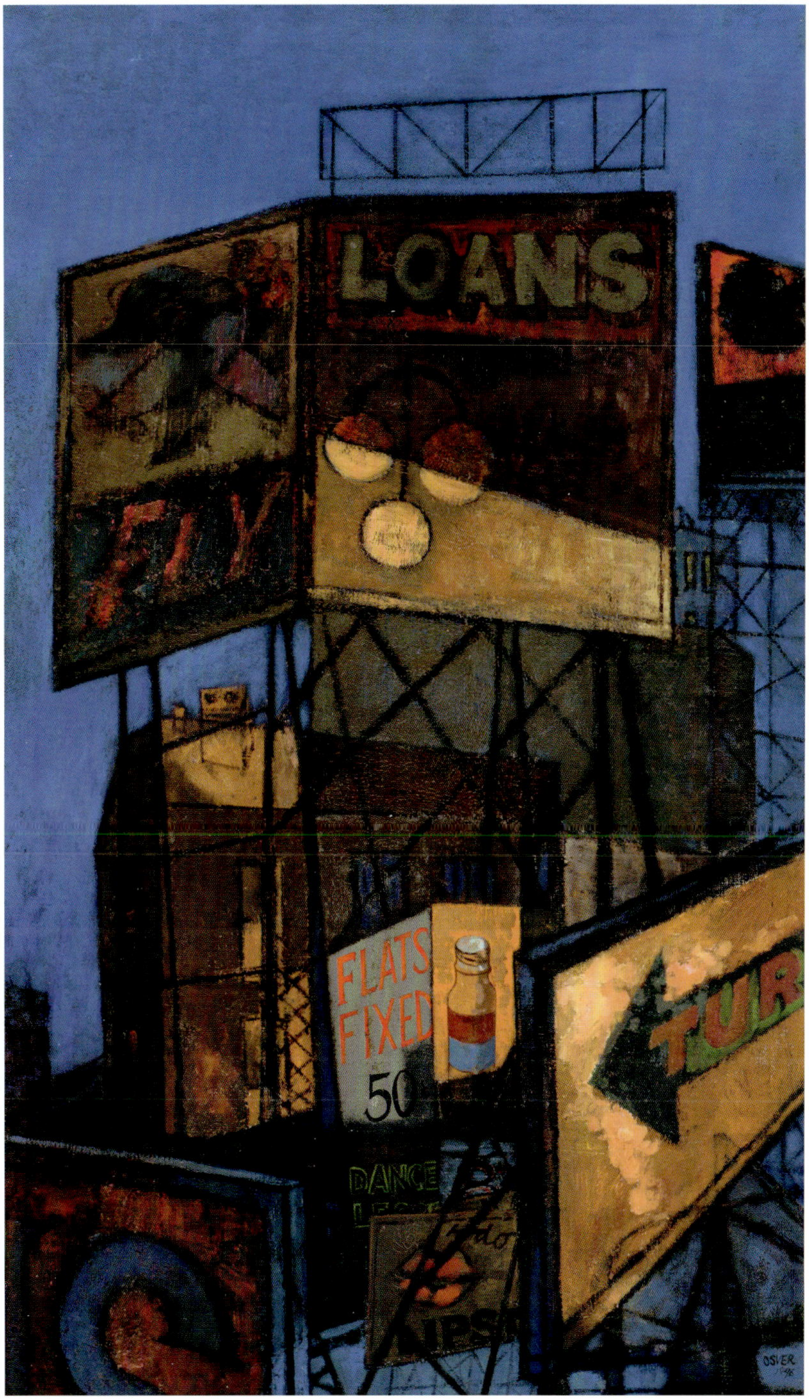

10

***Billboards*, 1946**

Oil on canvas, 45 x 27"

Private collection, courtesy of Keny Galleries, Columbus, Ohio

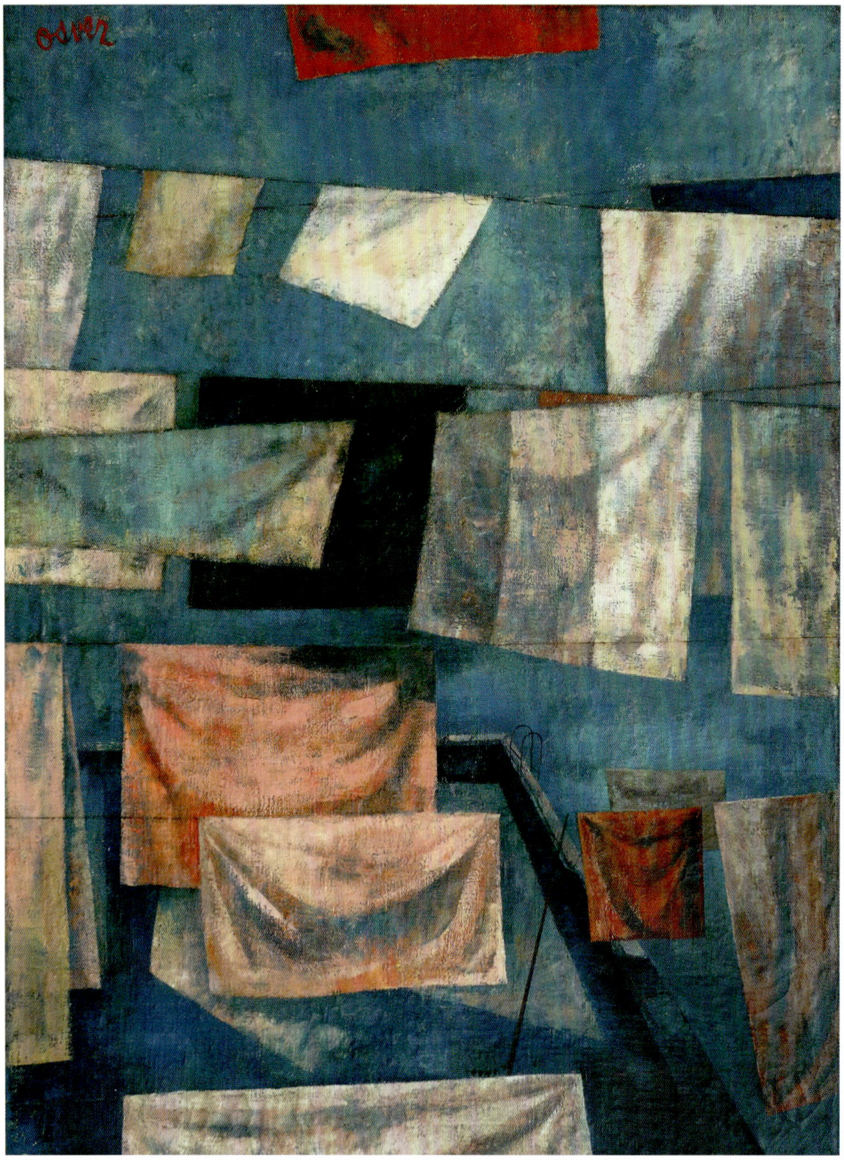

11
***Monday Morning*, 1946**
Oil on canvas, 40 x 30"
Collection of Paul Shank

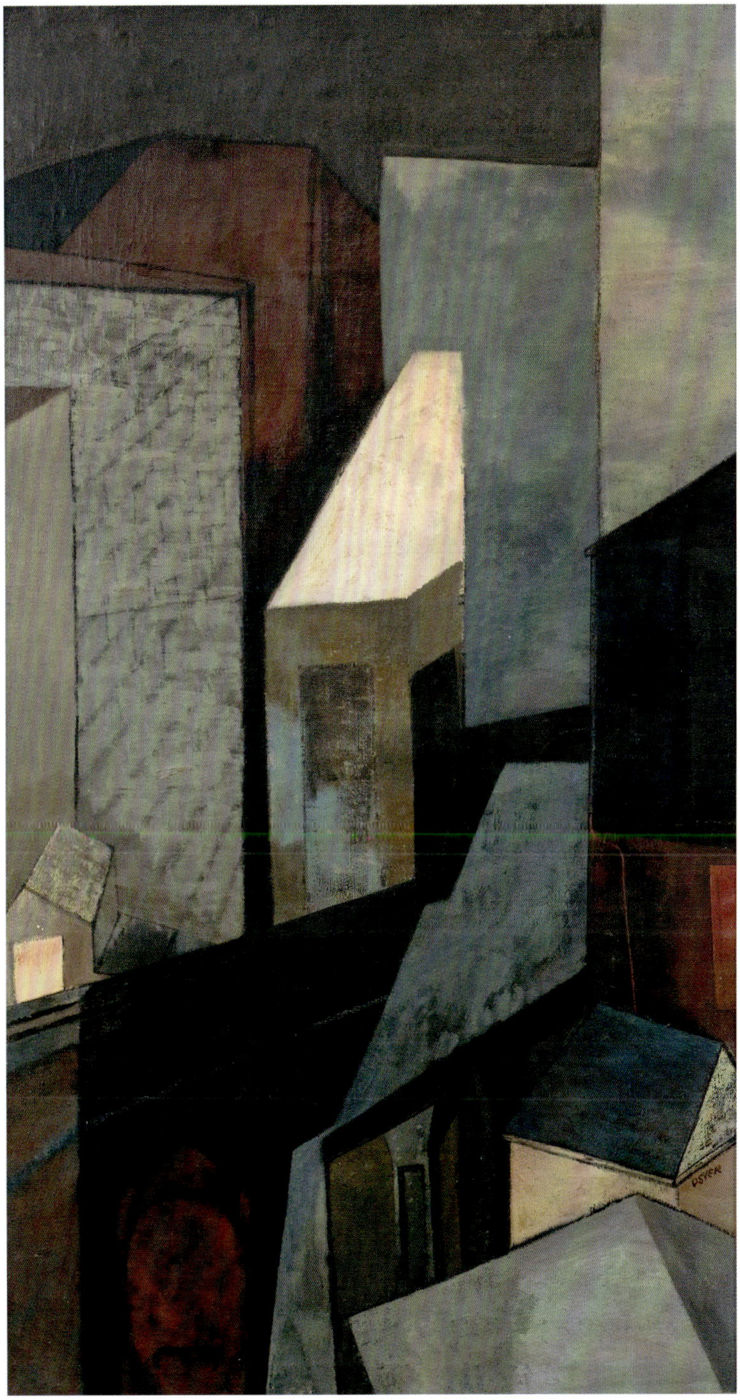

12

***Queens Elevated Highway,* 1946**

Oil on canvas, 55 x 30"

Collection of Paul Shank

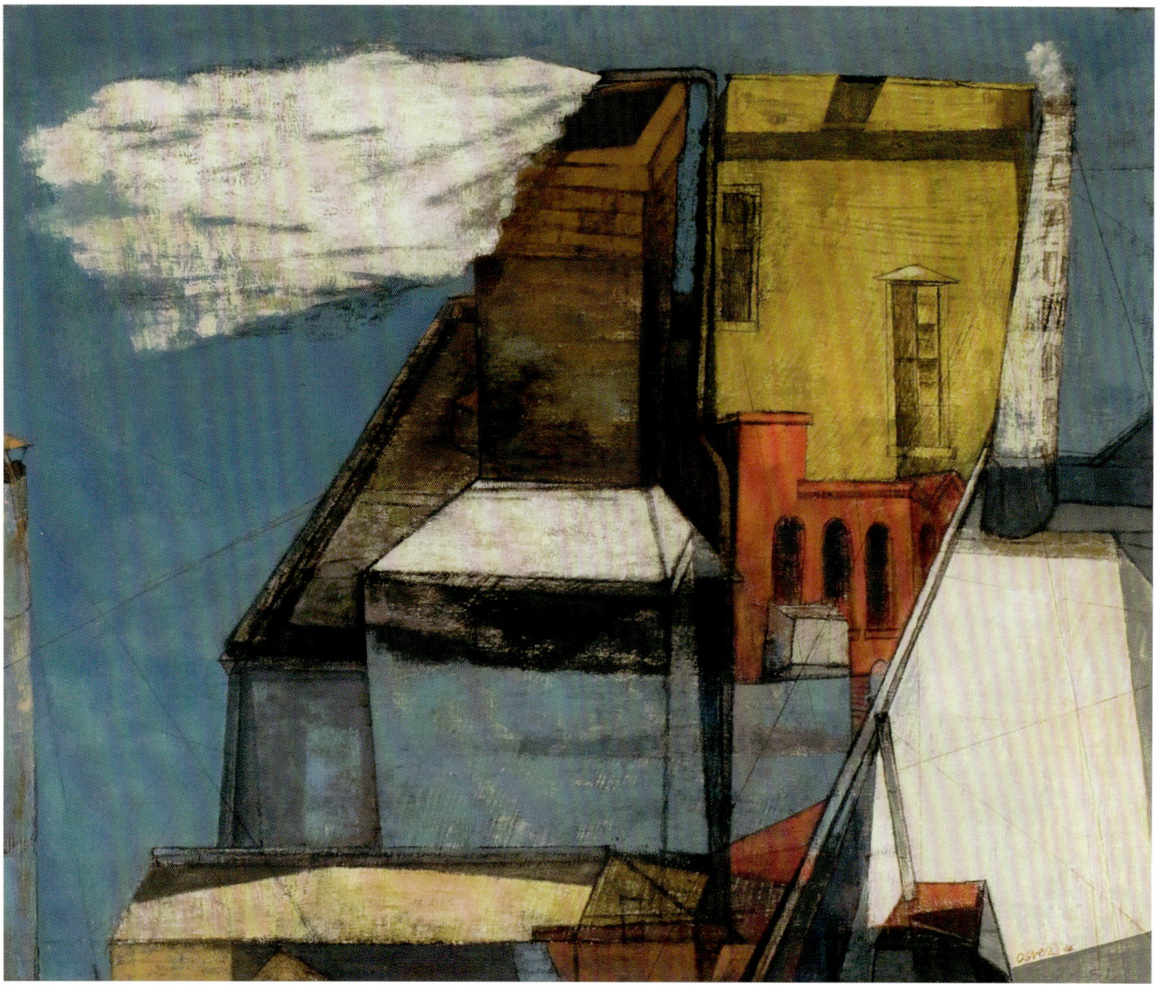

13
***Steam Jet,* 1946**
Oil on canvas, 36 x 44"
Private collection

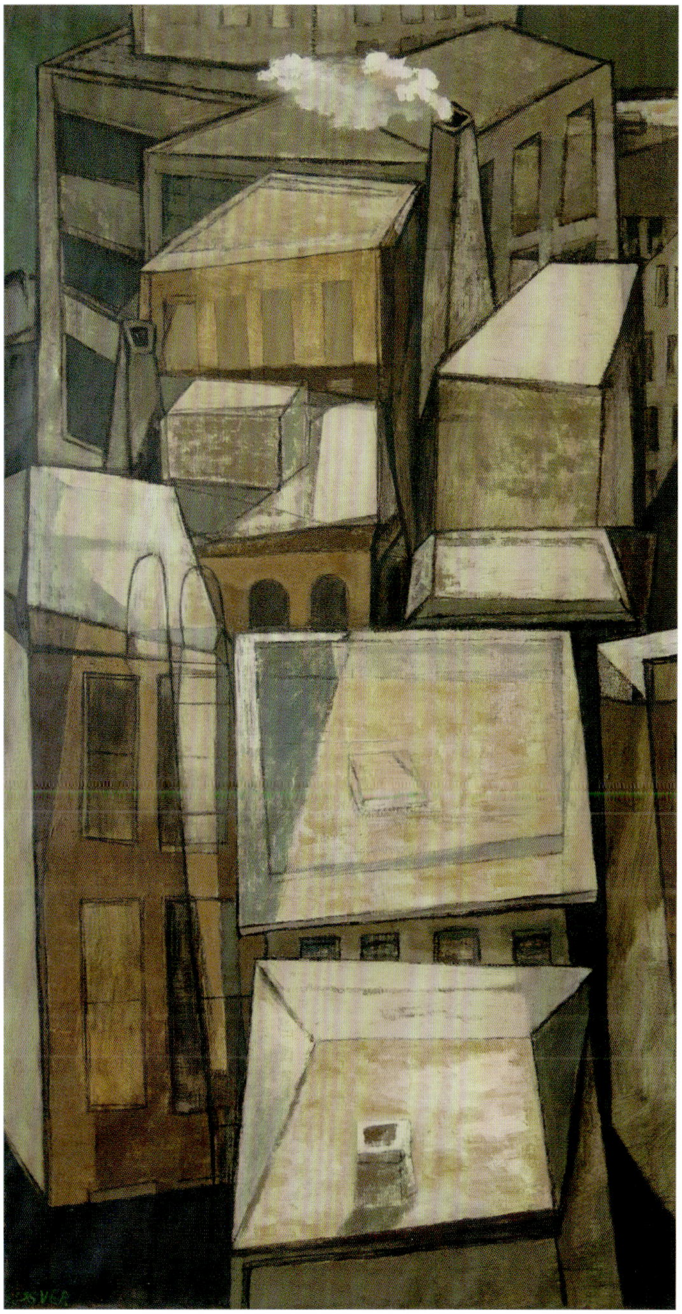

14
***Winter Landscape*, 1947**
Oil on canvas, 48 x 26"
Private collection

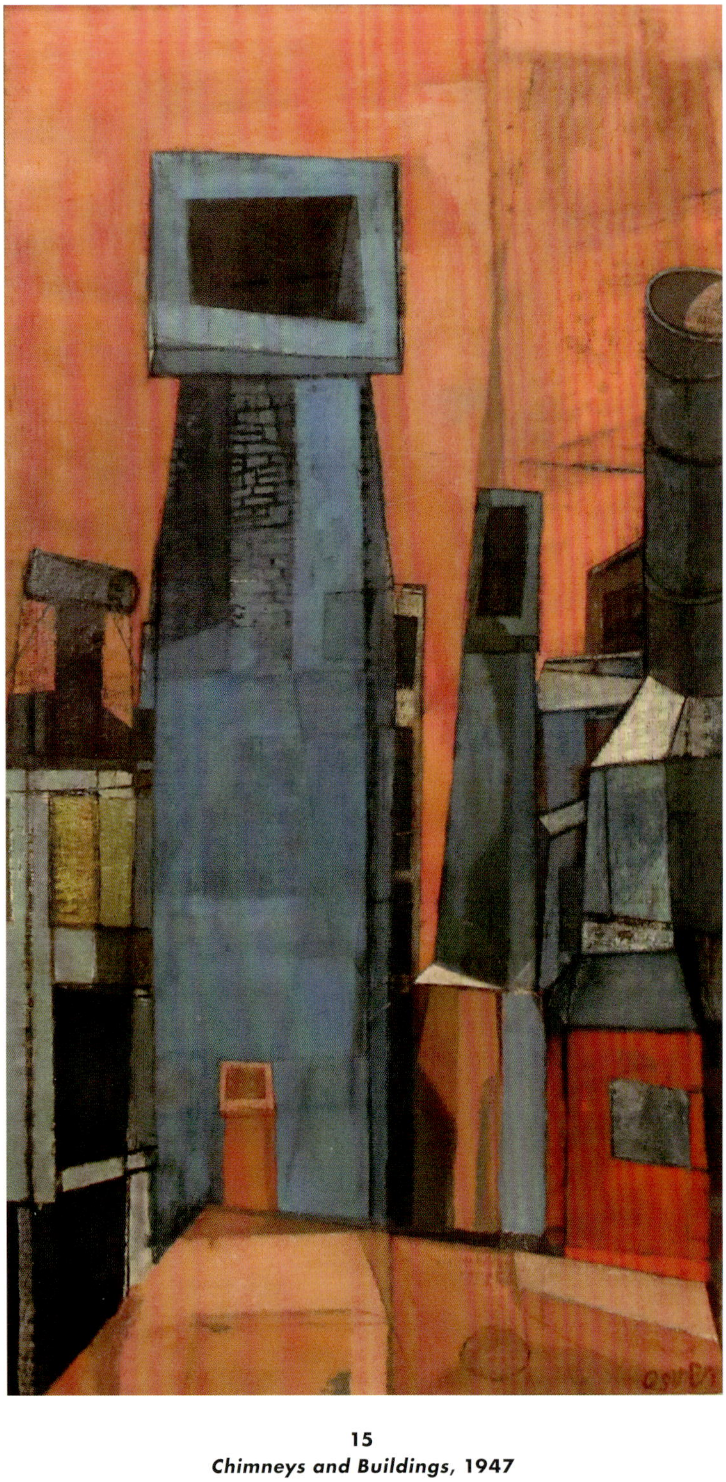

15

***Chimneys and Buildings*, 1947**

Oil on canvas, 55 x 30"

Board of Trustees of the University of Illinois on behalf of its Krannert Art Museum, Festival of Arts Purchase Fund

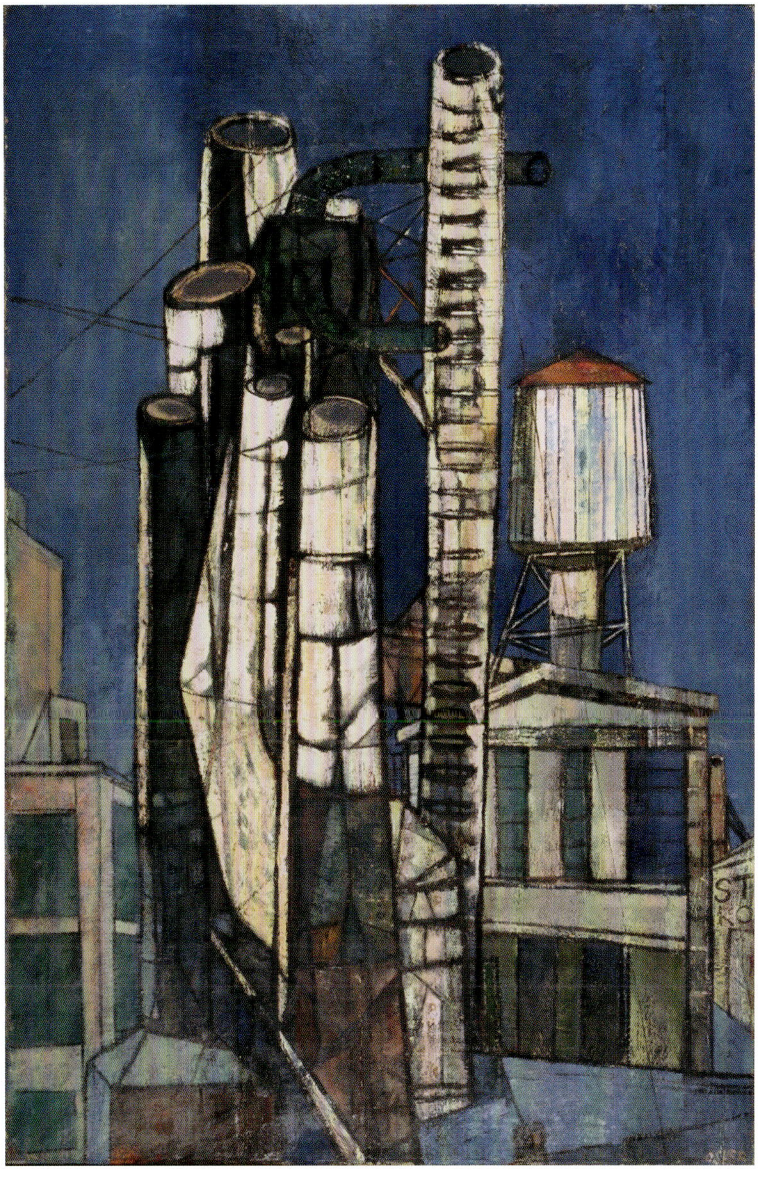

16

***The Cluster*, 1947**

Oil on canvas, 42 x 28"

University of Michigan Museum of Art, Museum Purchase

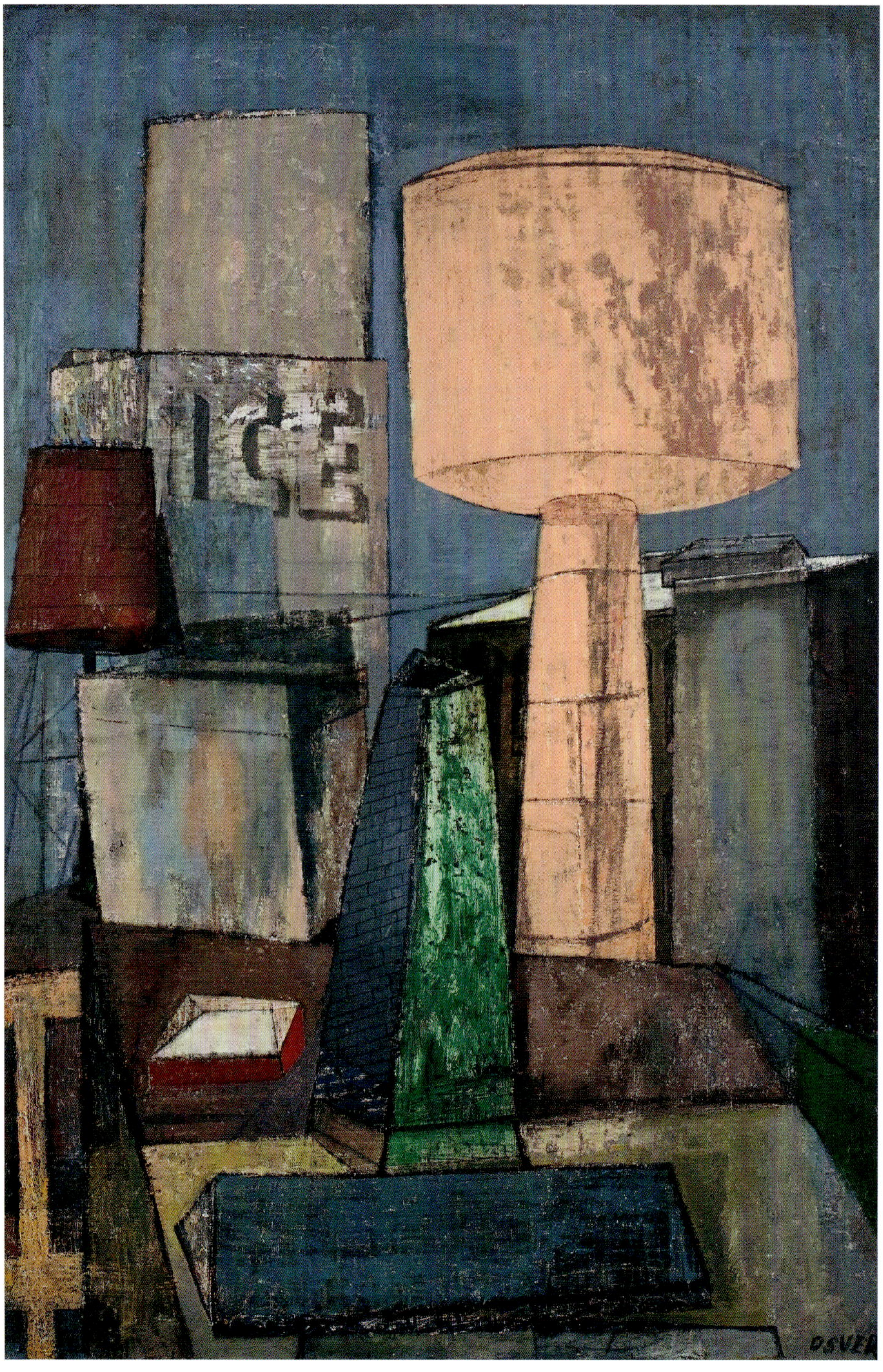

17

***Ice House*, 1947**

Oil on canvas, 40 x 27"

Collection of Paul Shank

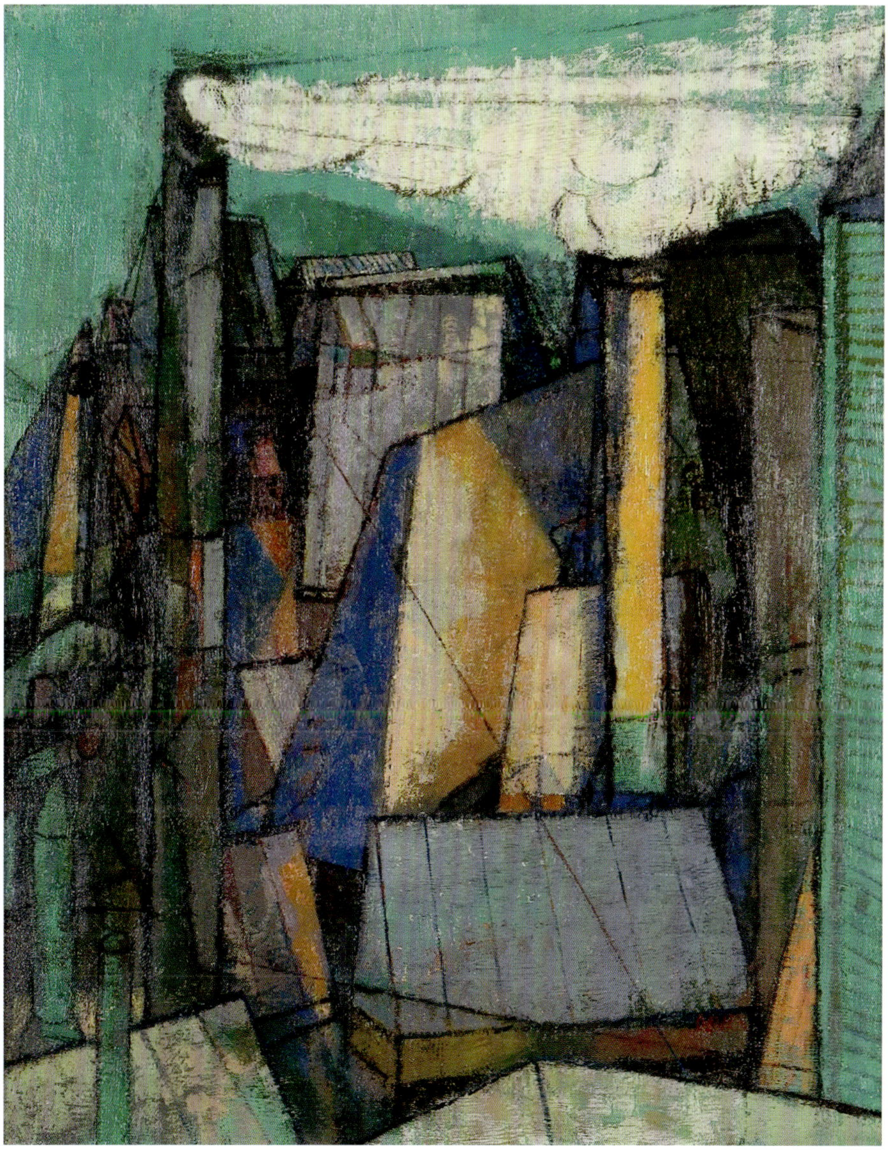

18

***Skylights*, 1947**

Oil on canvas, 19 1/2 x 15 3/4"

Des Moines Art Center Permanent Collections, Purchased with funds from the Edmundson Art Foundation Inc.

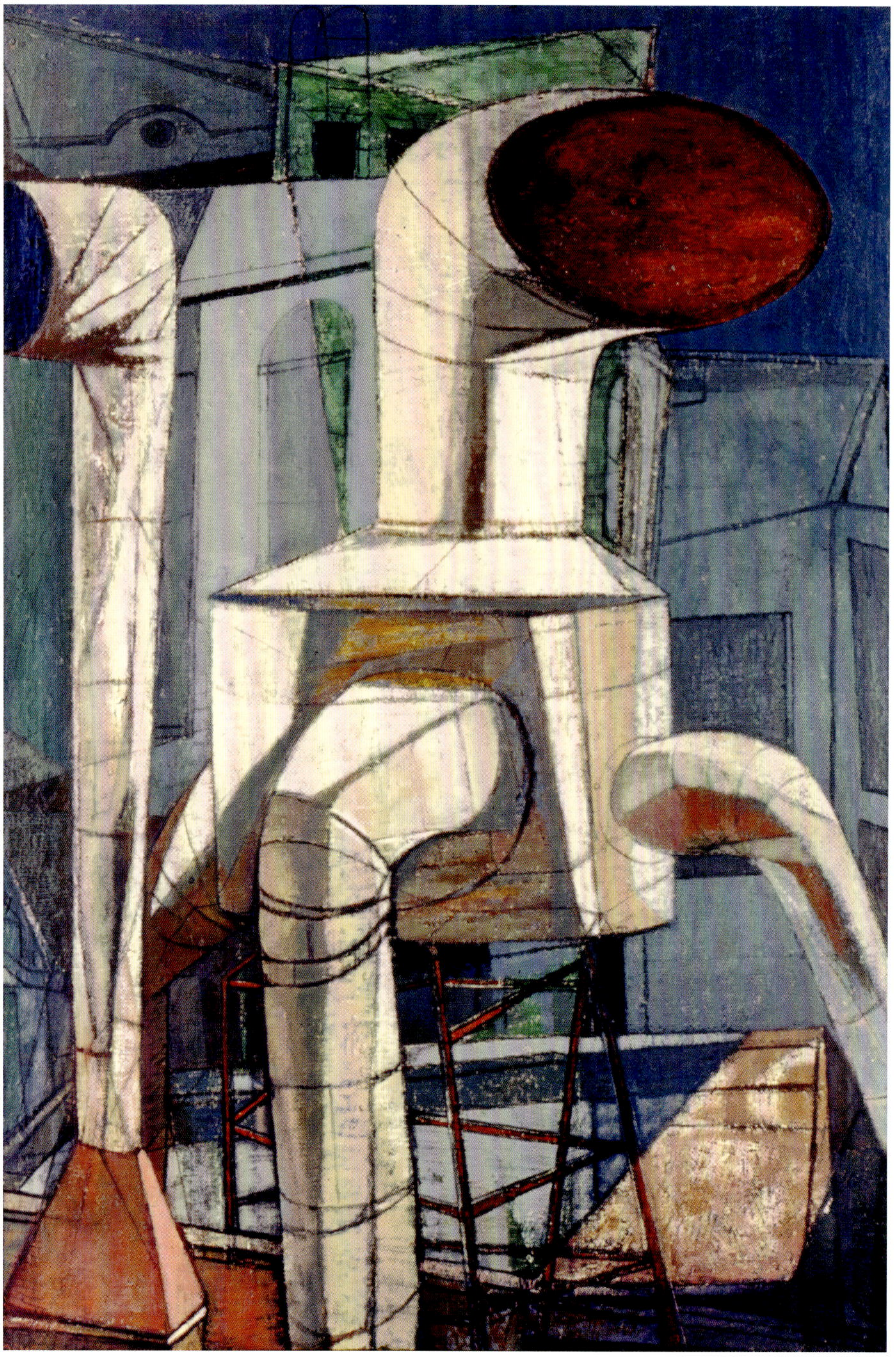

19

Two Ventilators, 1947

Oil on canvas, 39 3/4 x 27 7/8"

The Metropolitan Museum of Art, New York,

Arthur Hoppock Hearn Fund, 1950

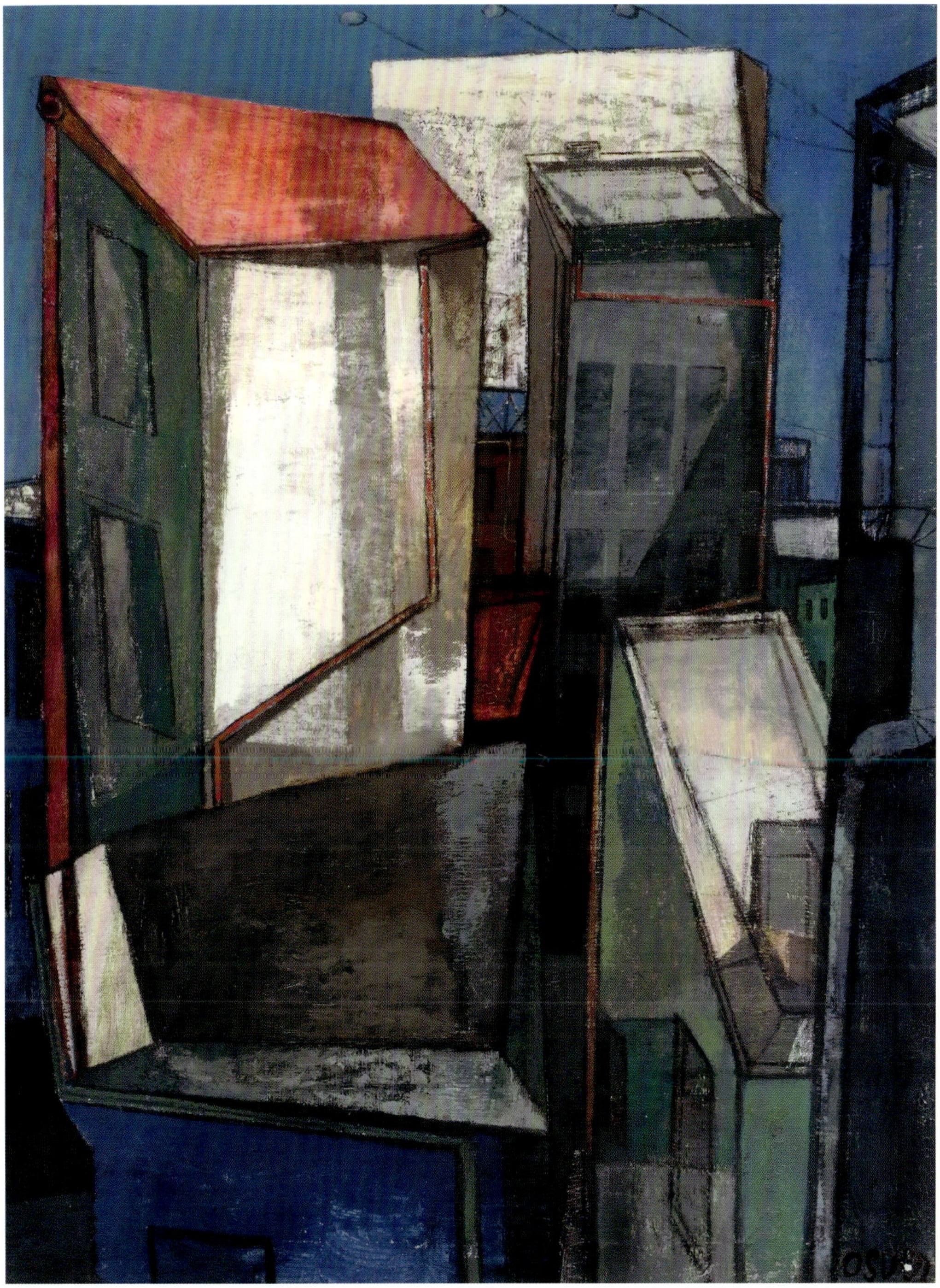

20

***The Rainpipes*, c. 1948**

Oil on canvas, 41 1/2 x 31 1/2"

Delaware Art Museum, Bequest of John L. Sexton, 1955

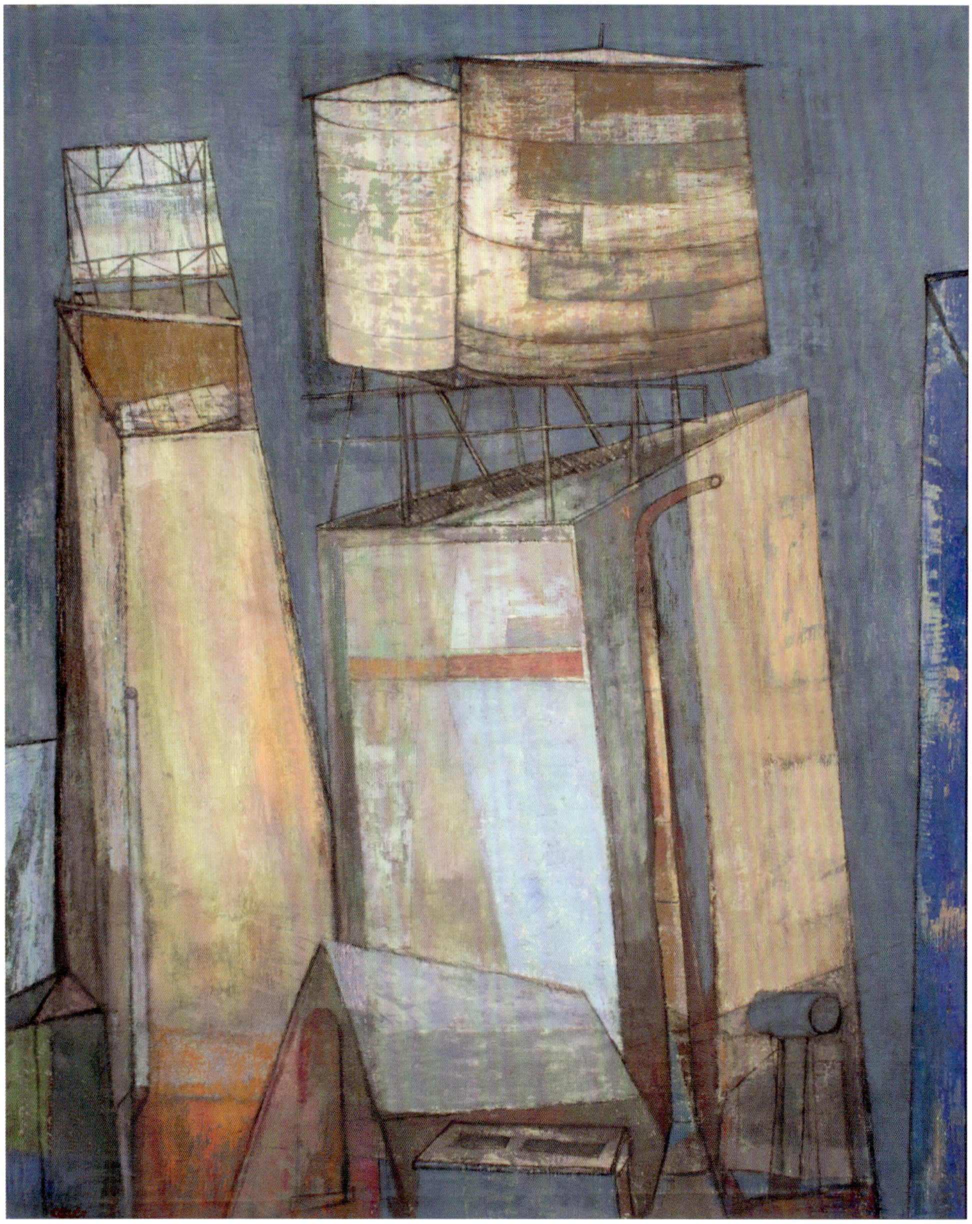

21
***Billboards and Tanks*, 1948**
Oil on canvas, 55 1/2 x 47" (framed)
Colorado Springs Fine Arts Center, Friends of the Fine Arts Center Purchase Fund

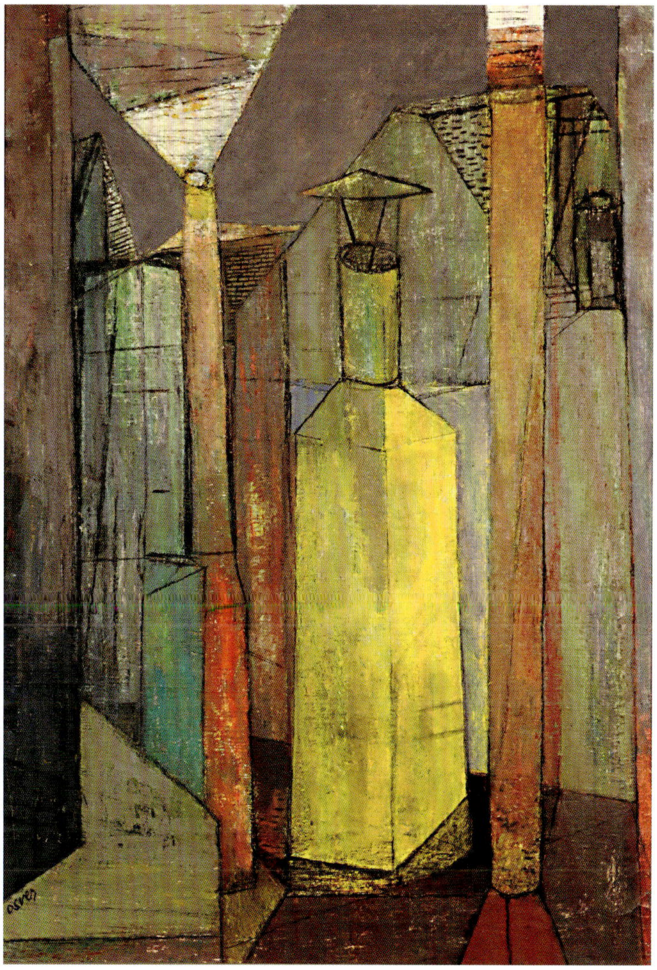

22

***The Enclosure*, 1948**

Oil on canvas, 33 1/2 x 23 3/8"

Figge Art Museum, Davenport, Iowa

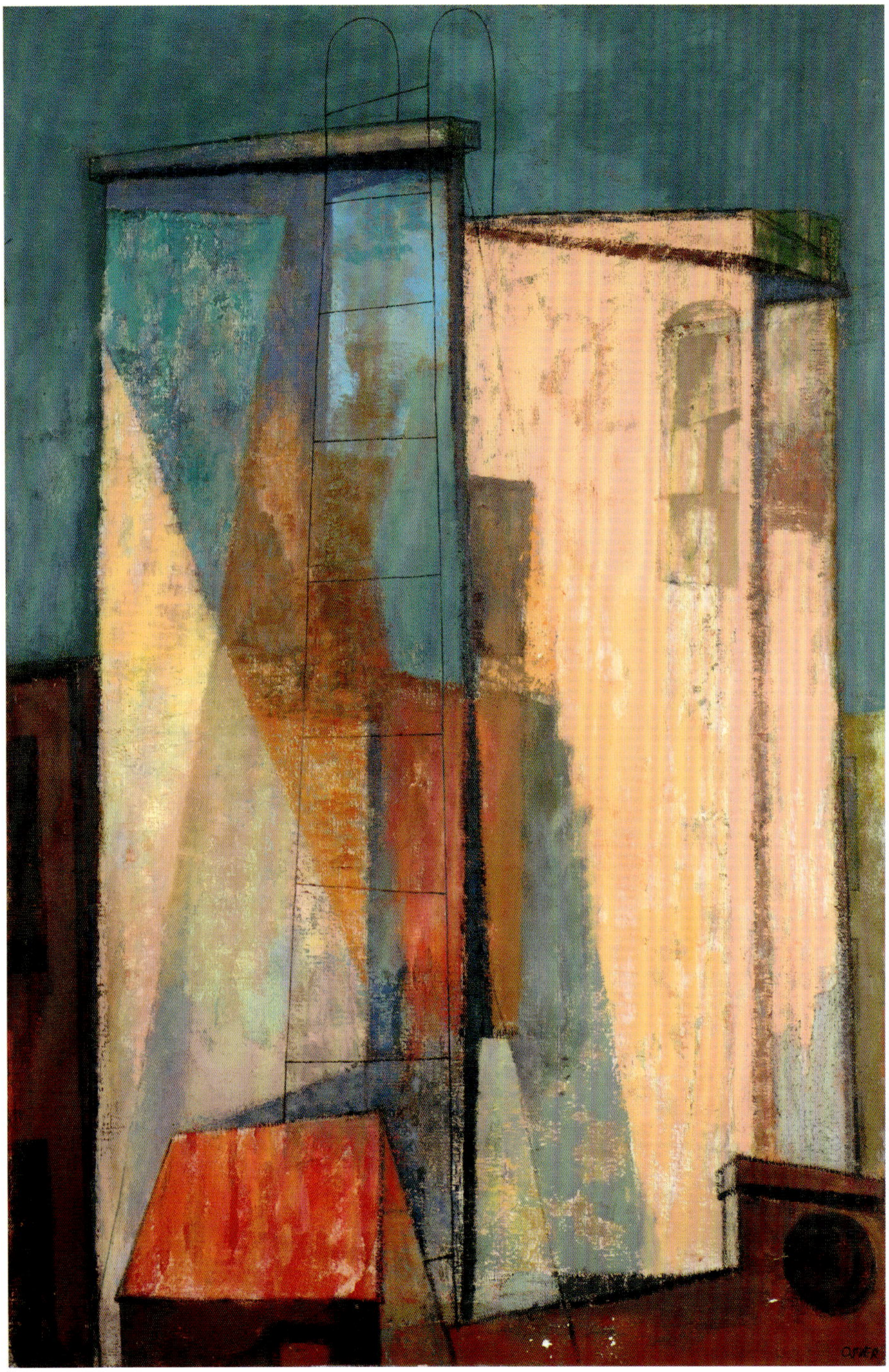

23
***Fire Escape and Facade*, 1948**
Oil on canvas, 47 3/4 x 32"
Sheldon Museum of Art, University of Nebraska–Lincoln, Anna R. and Frank M. Hall Charitable Trust

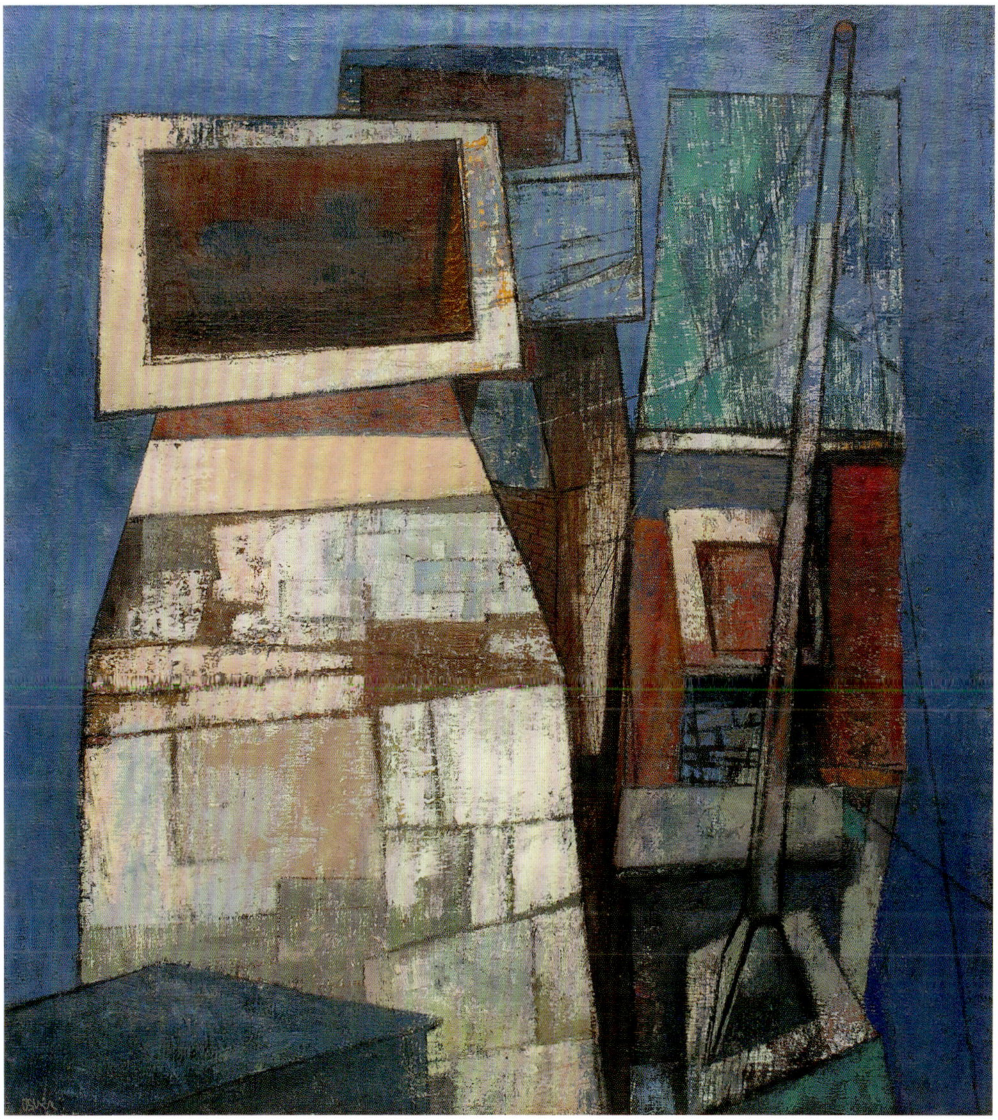

24

***Greenpoint Chimneys*, 1948**

Oil on canvas, 32 x 29 1/2"

Walker Art Center, Minneapolis, Gift of the T. B. Walker Foundation, Gilbert M. Walker Fund, 1948

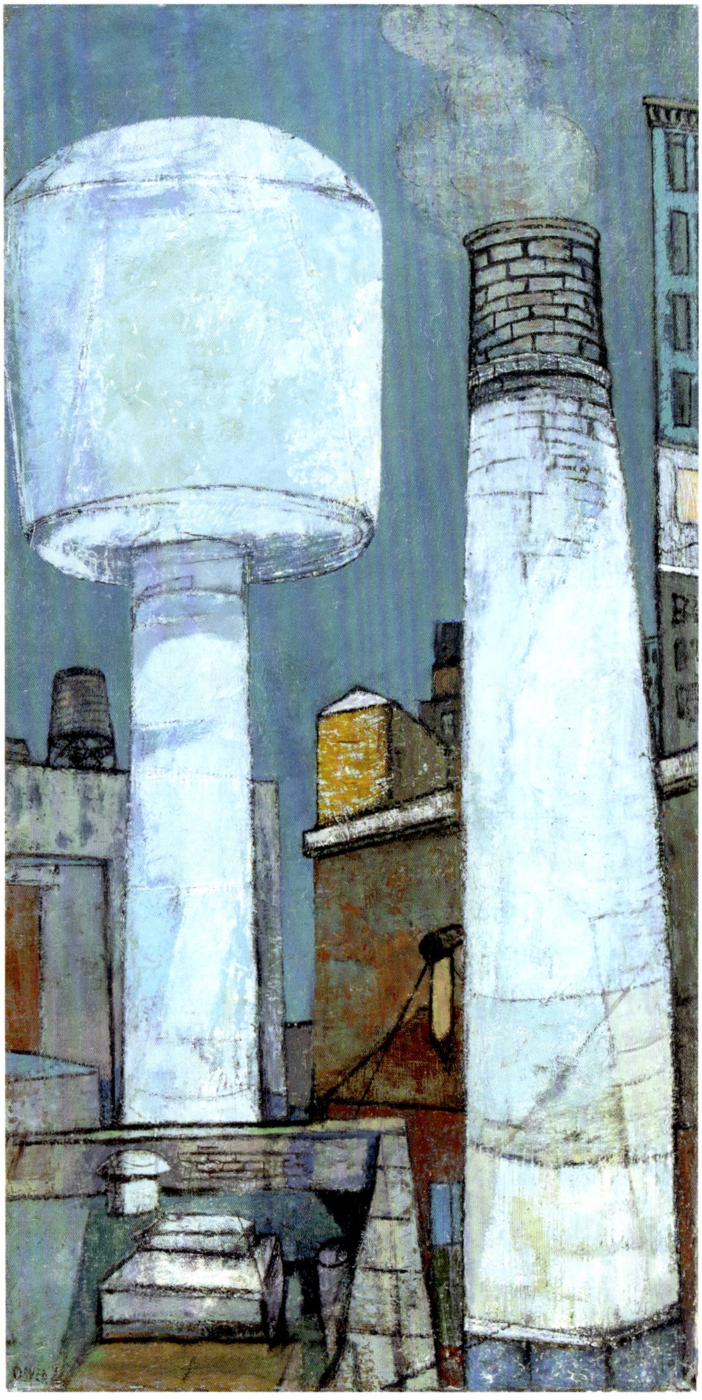

25

***Smokestack and Tank*, 1948**

Oil on canvas, 44 3/4 x 25 3/4" (framed)

New Orleans Museum of Art, Museum purchase

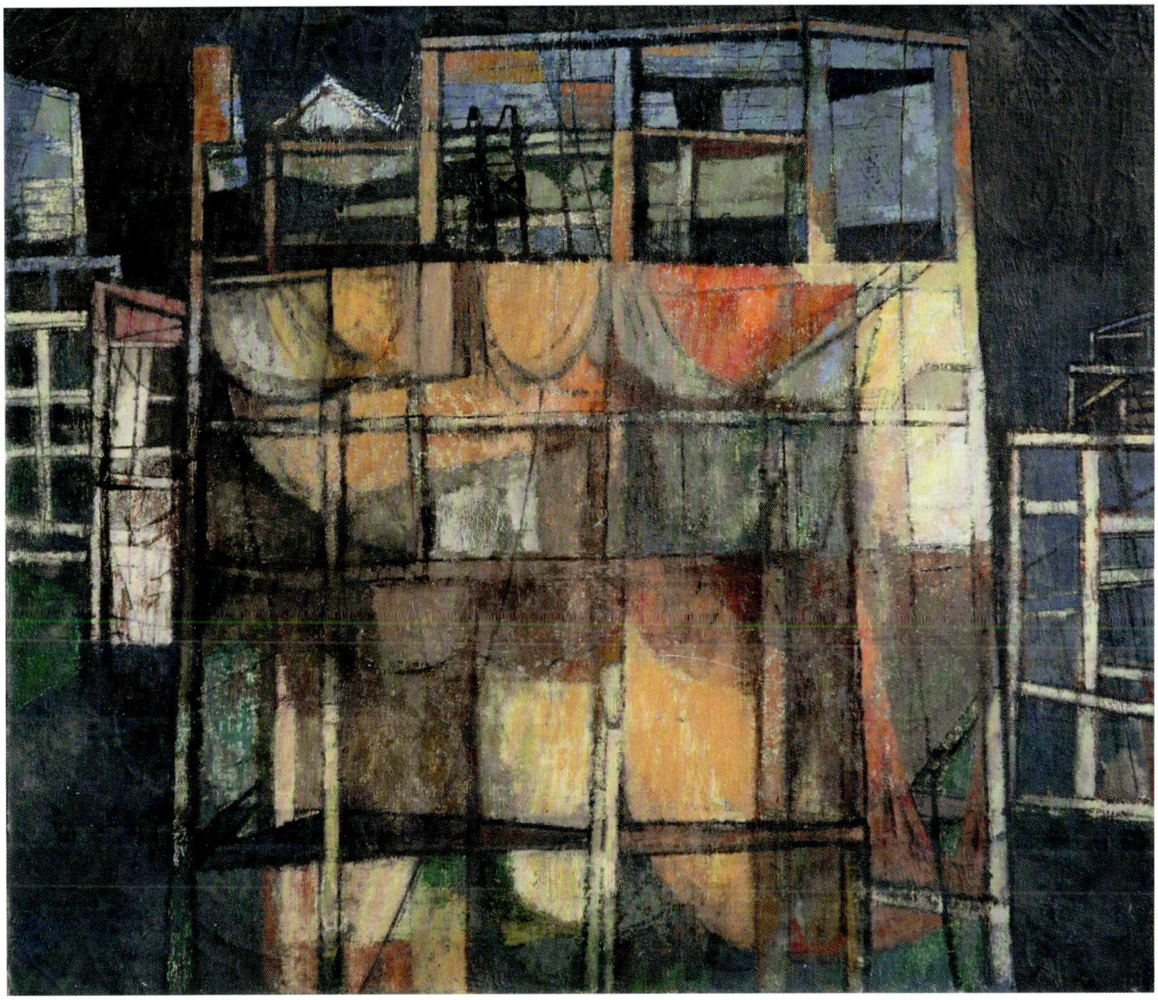

26

***Construction: Spring*, 1950**

Oil on canvas, 31 x 37"

Collection of Jeannine and Kent Kalkwarf

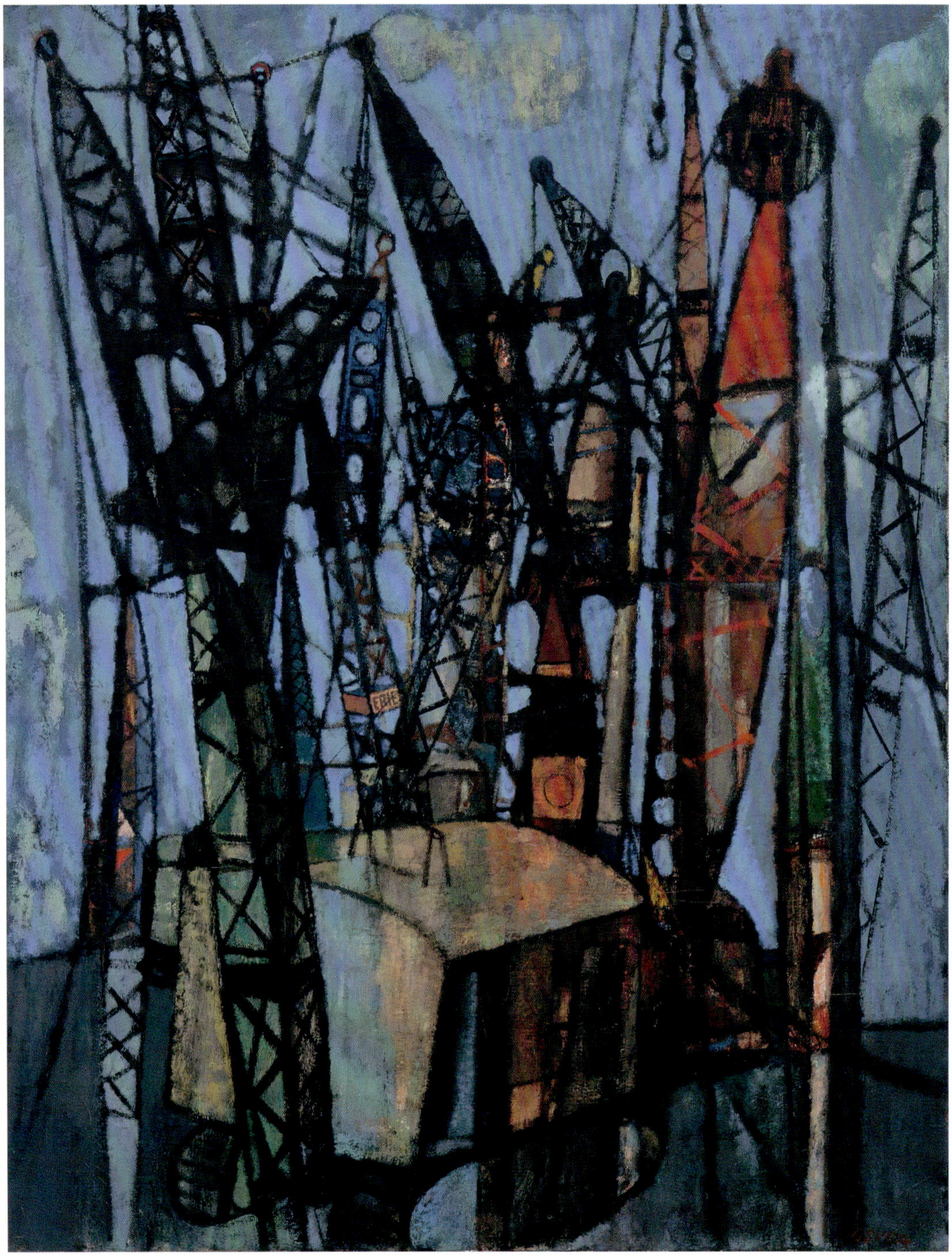

27
***Cranes*, 1950**
Oil on canvas, 60 x 45"
ArcelorMittal Collection, Chicago

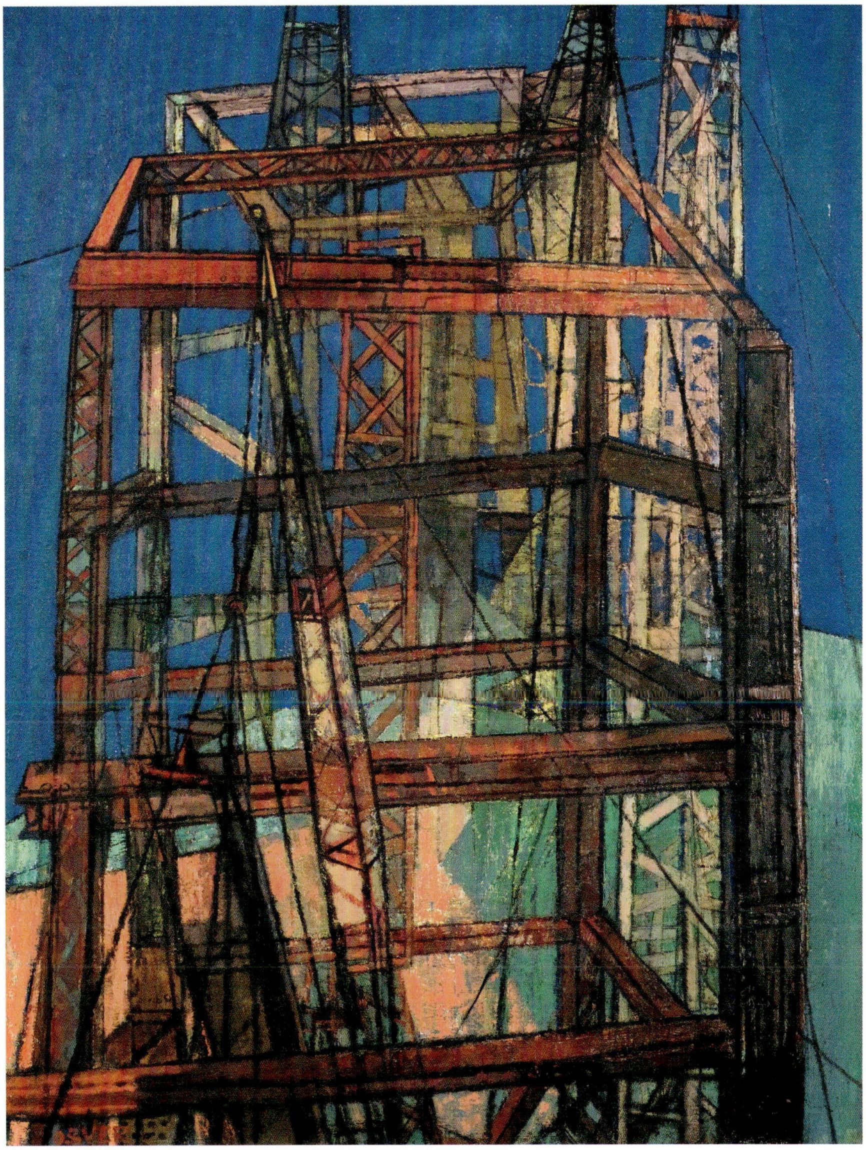

28

***The Framework*, 1950**

Oil on canvas, 42 x 33"

Estate of Arthur Osver and Ernestine Betsberg

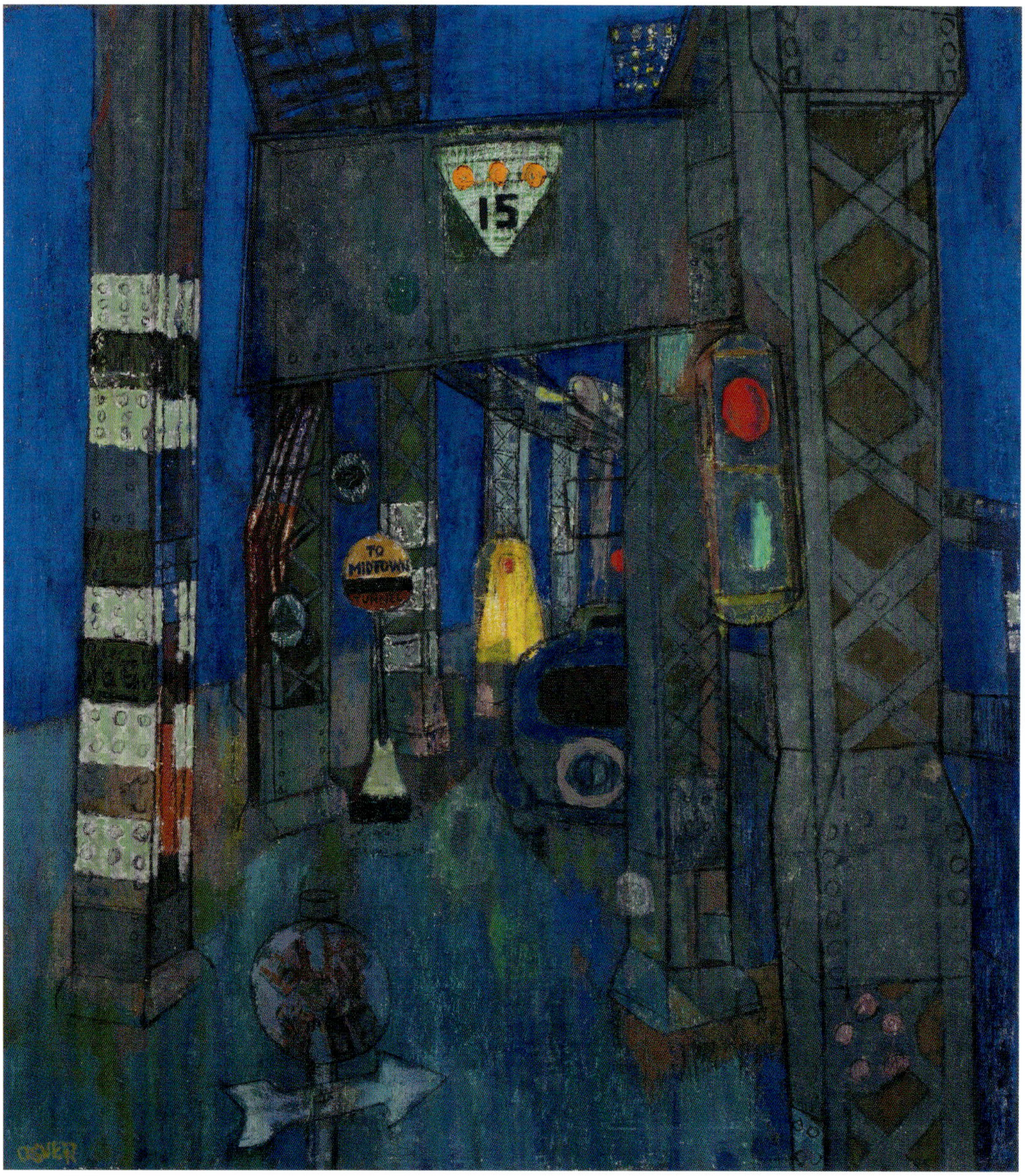

29

***Under the Tracks,* 1951**

Oil on canvas, 40 x 36"

Saint Louis Art Museum, Eliza McMillan Trust

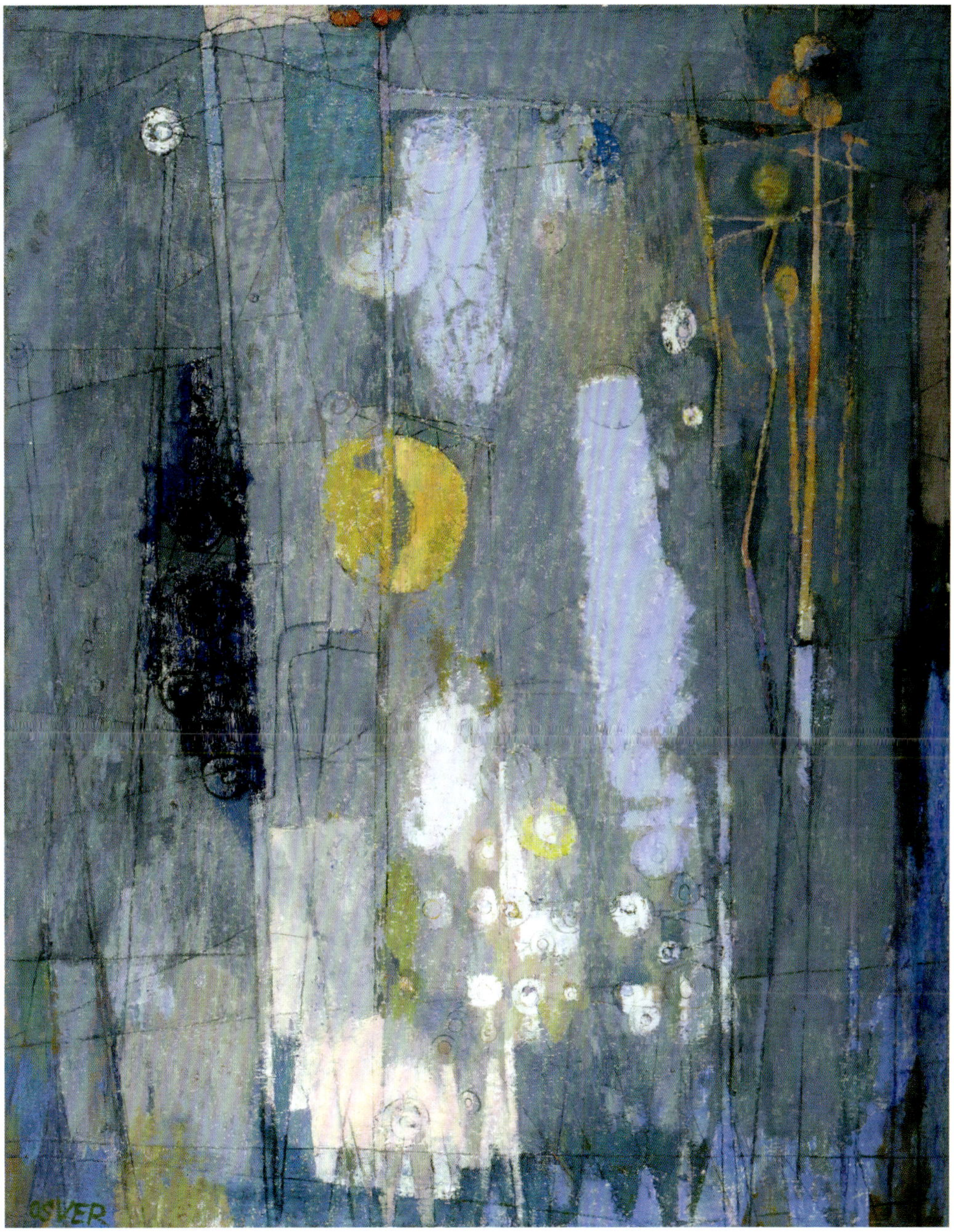

30
***Gray Night*, 1952**
Oil on canvas, 43 x 33"
Acquired 1954, The Phillips Collection, Washington, DC

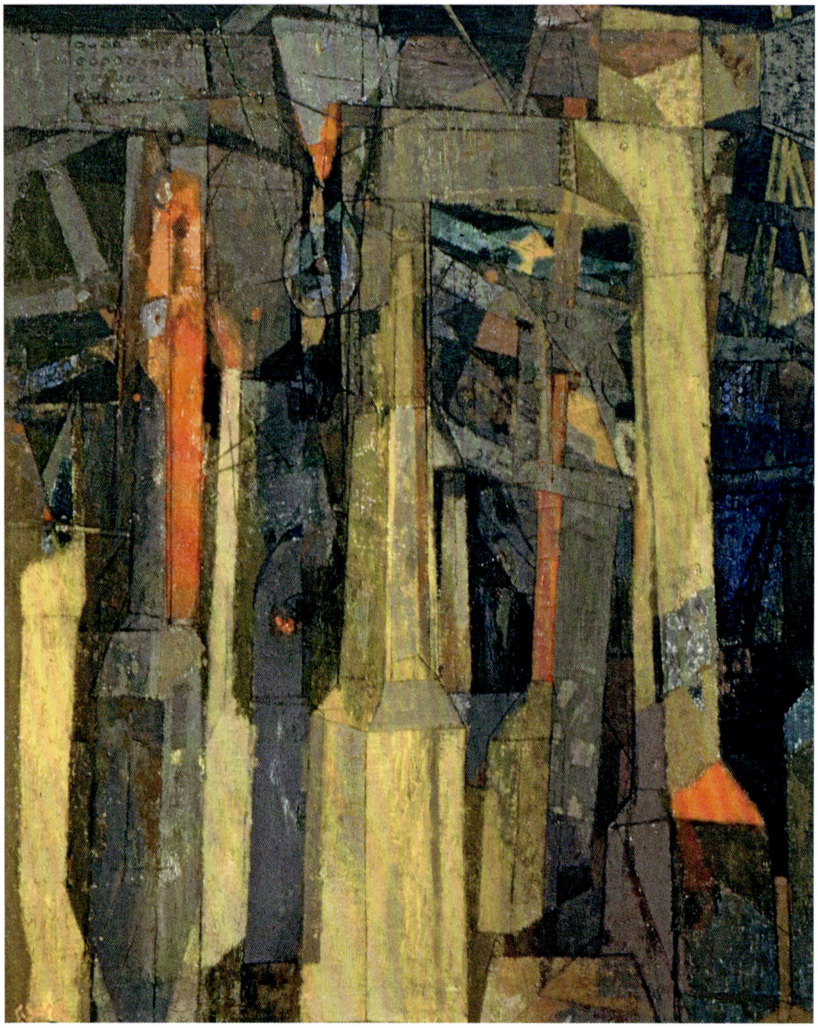

31
***Pylon*, c. 1953**
Oil on canvas, dimensions unknown
Location unknown

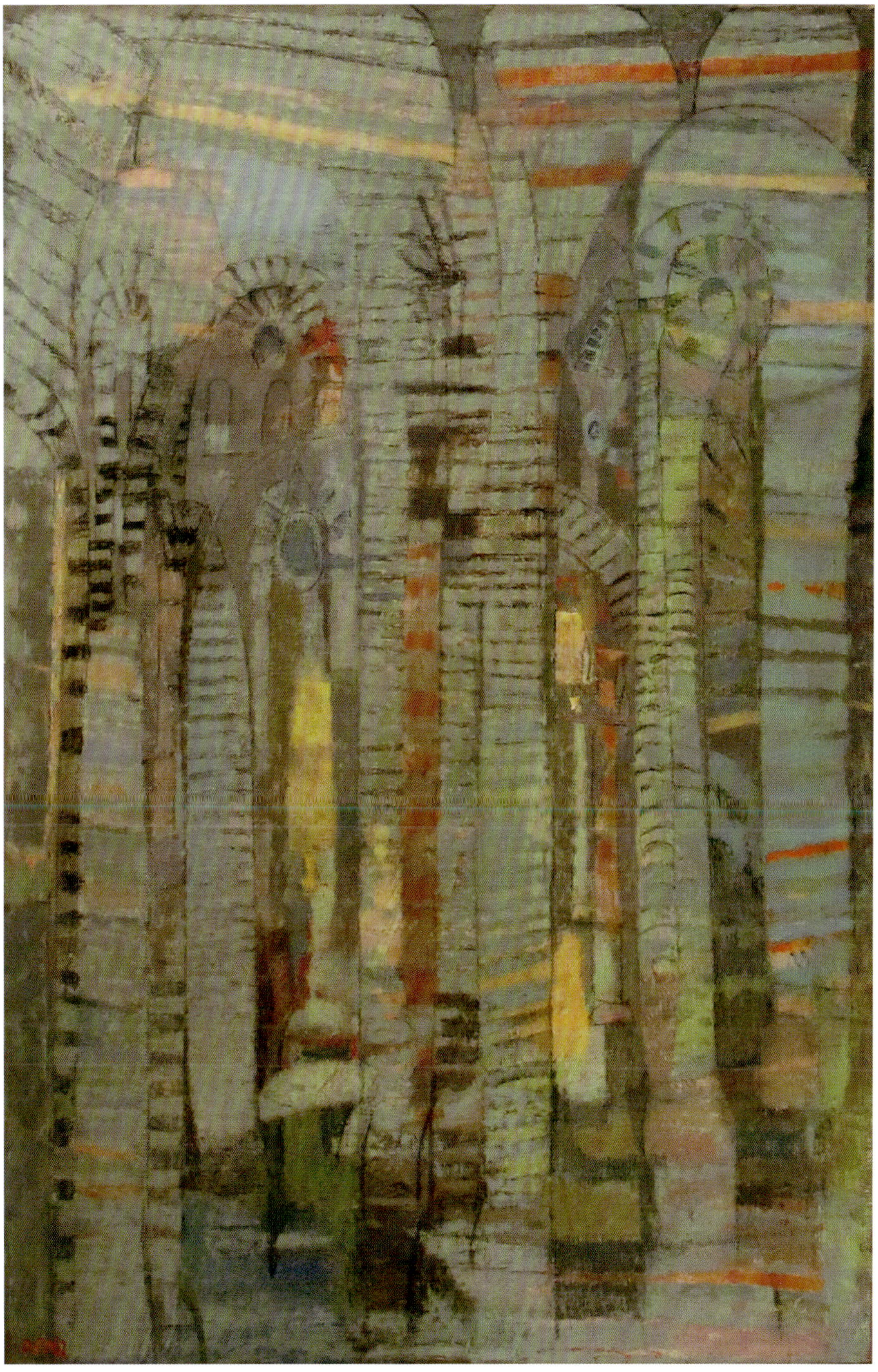

32
***Siena Interior*, 1953**
Oil on canvas, 50 1/2 x 33 7/8"
Board of Trustees of the University of Illinois on behalf of its Krannert Art Museum,
Gift of Mr. and Mrs. Morton G. Schamberg

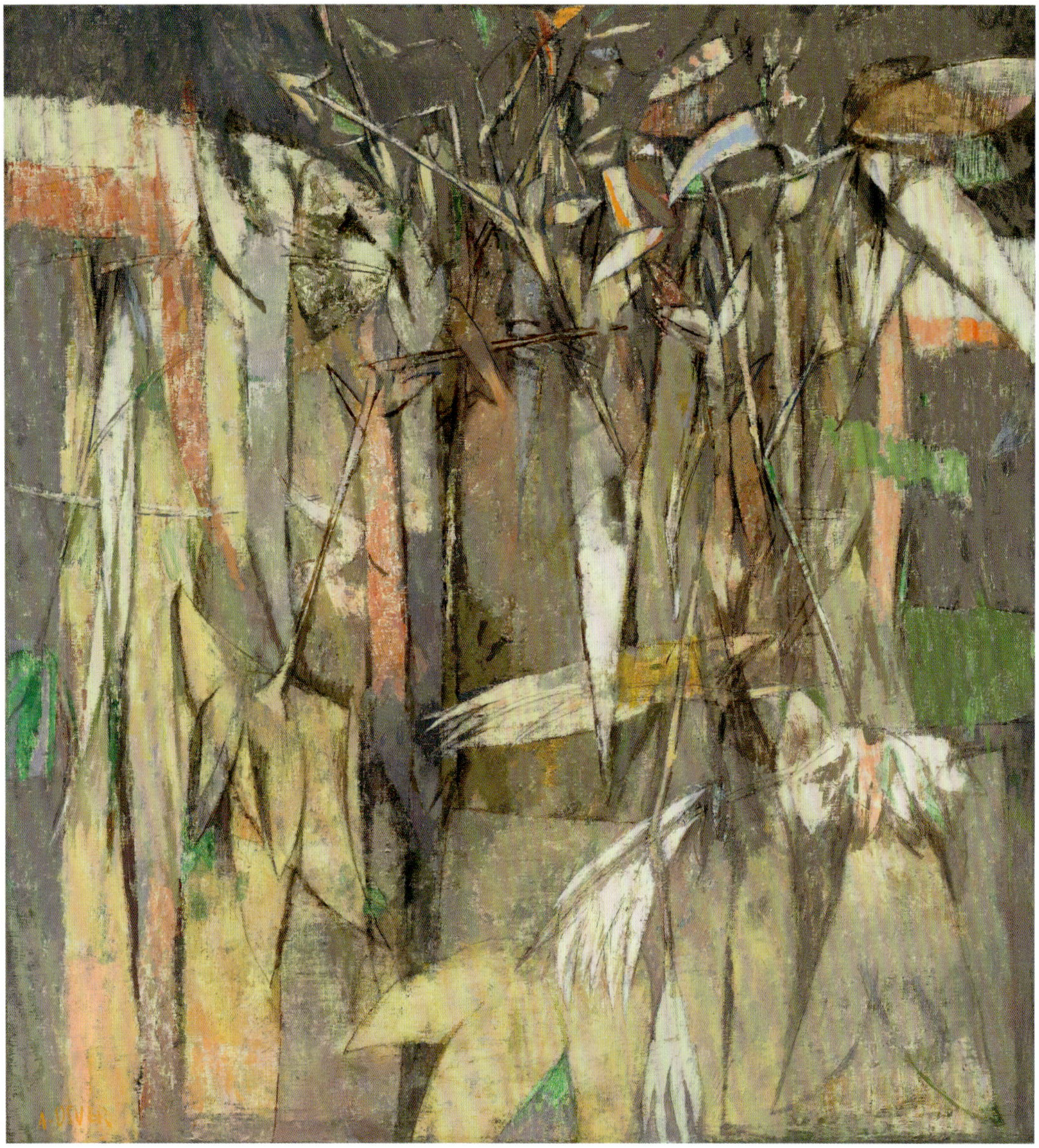

33

***Big Withalacoochee,* 1953–55**

Oil and lithographic crayon on canvas, 54 3/4 x 51"
Whitney Museum of American Art, New York, Purchase, with funds from the Living Arts Foundation Fund

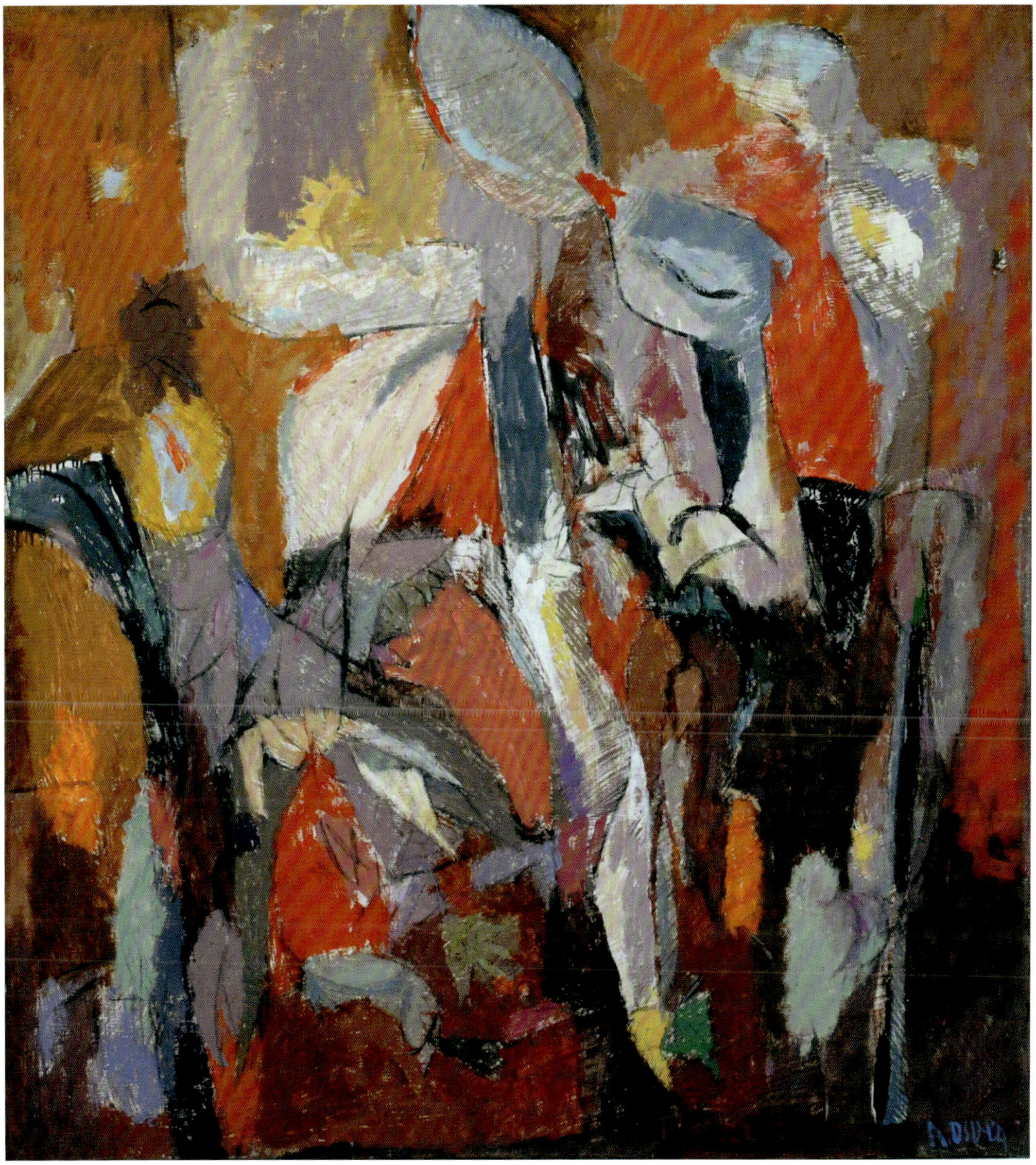

34

***Growth*, 1955**

Oil on canvas, 56 x 51"

Collection of Jeffrey and Leslie Lewis

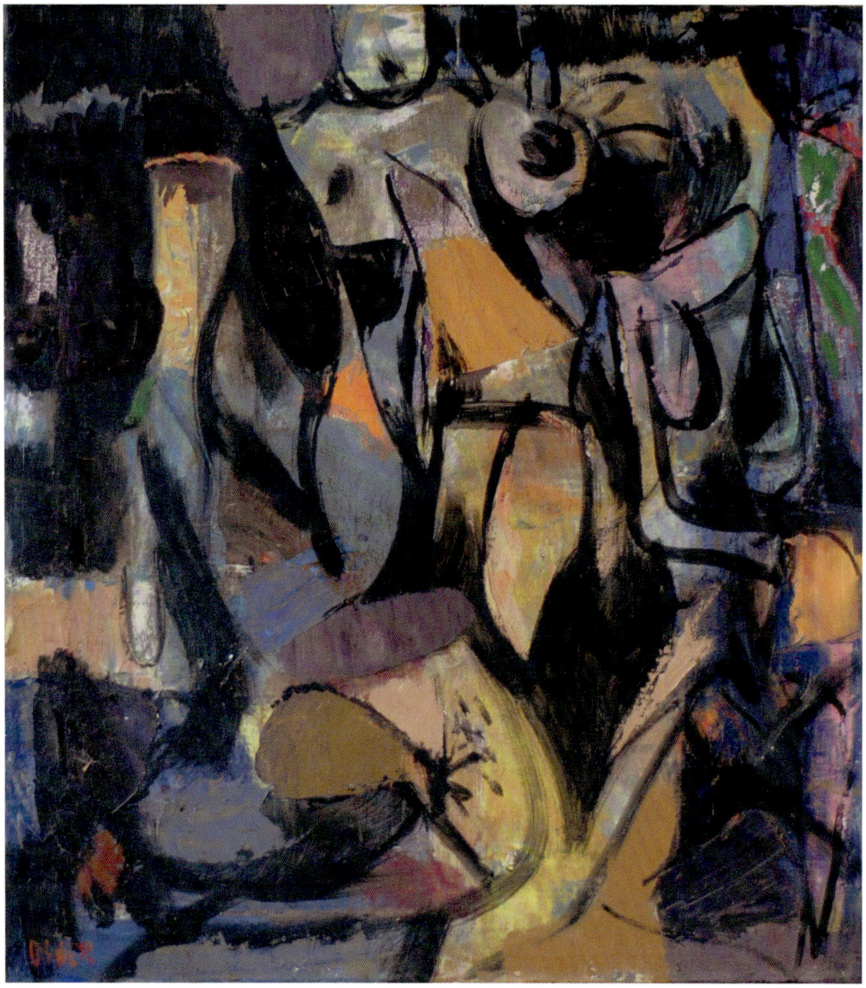

35

***Swamp Fire,* 1956**

Oil on canvas, 23 x 21"

Estate of Arthur Osver and Ernestine Betsberg

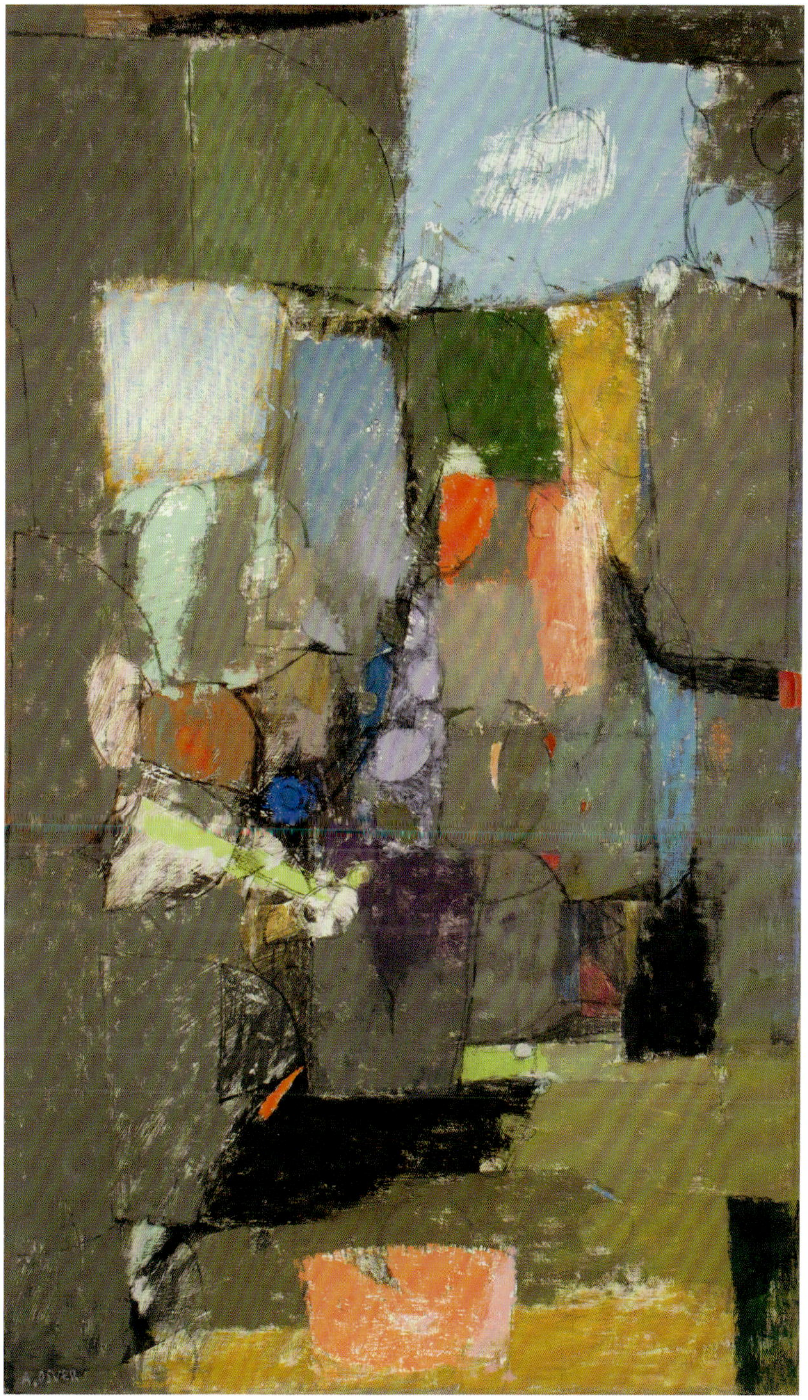

36

***The Tall Green*, 1956**

Oil on canvas, 63 x 37 3/16"

Mildred Lane Kemper Art Museum, Washington University in St. Louis, University purchase, Bixby Fund, 1957

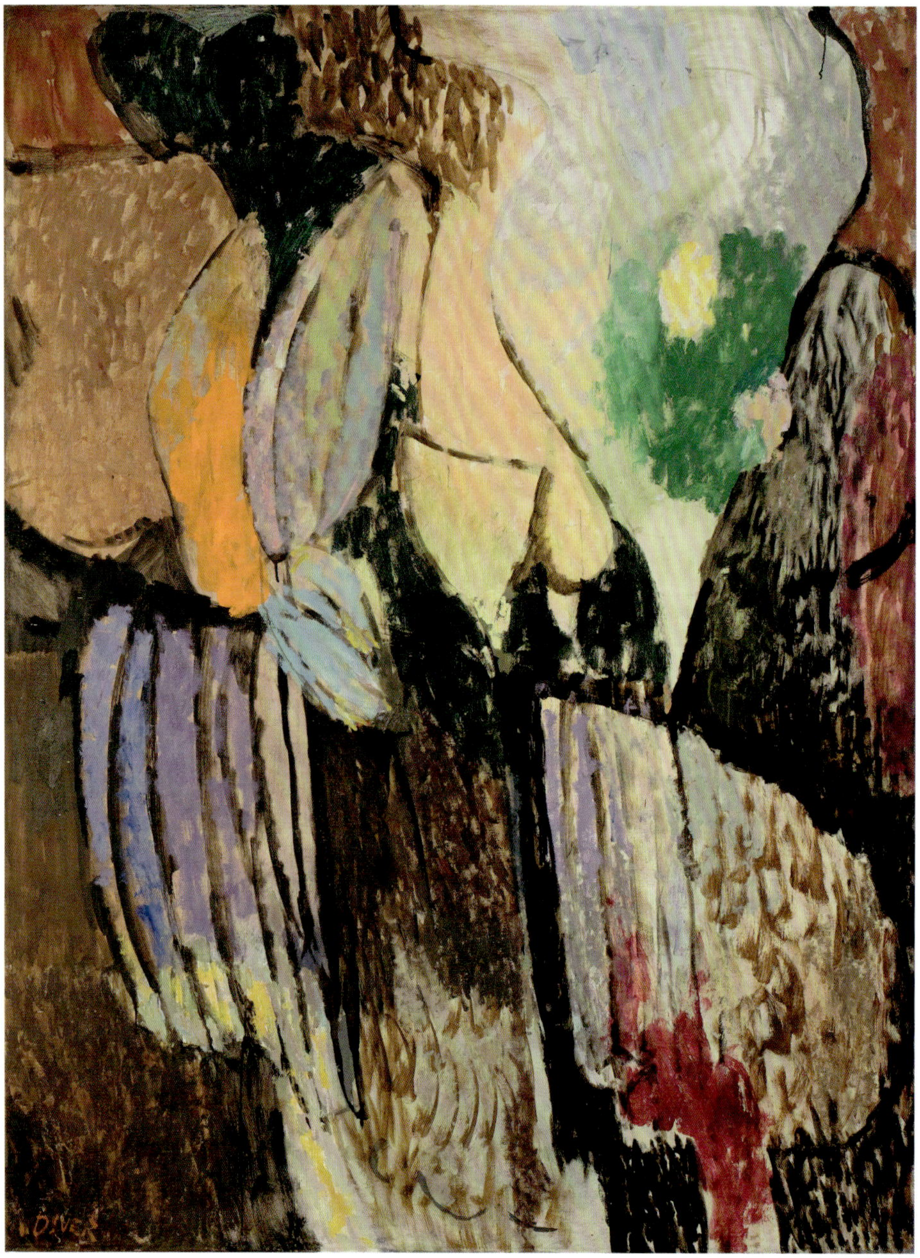

37
***Resurgence*, 1958**
Oil on canvas, 68 x 52"
Courtesy of Philip Slein Gallery, St. Louis

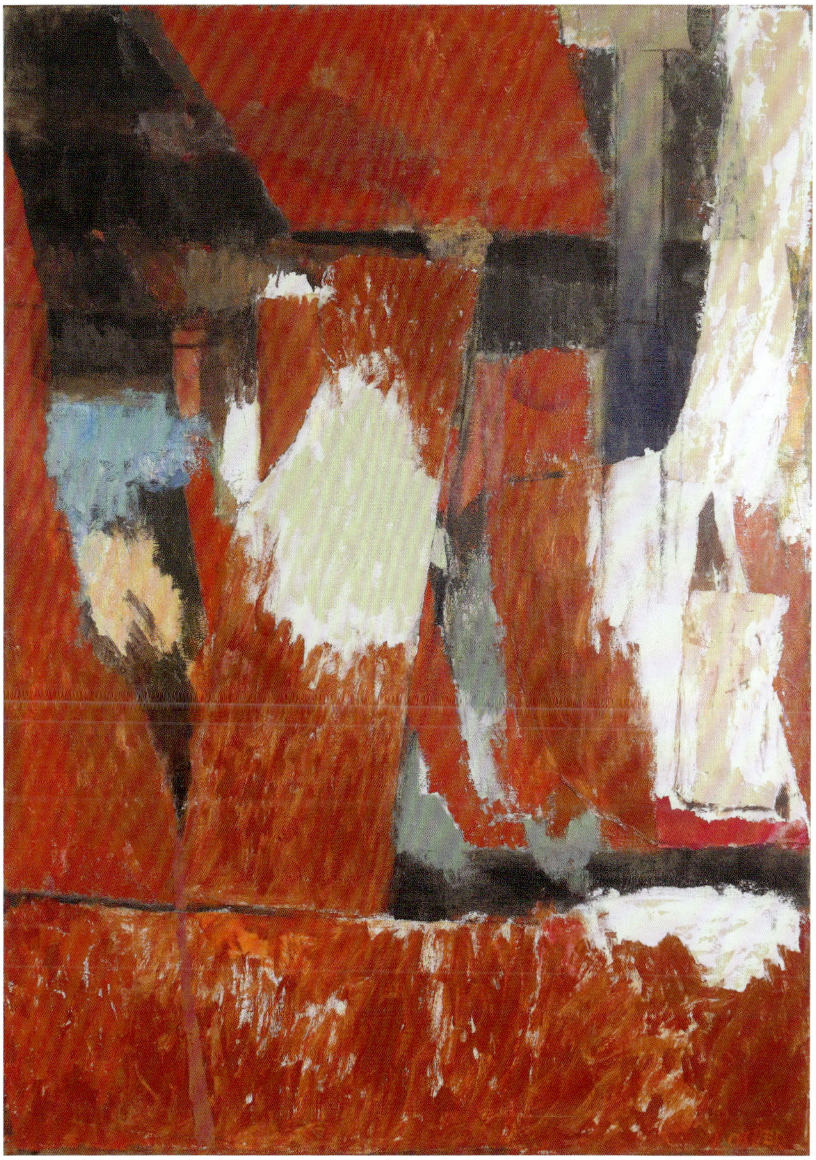

38

***St. Louis Red*, 1961**

Oil and rice paper on hemp, 62 x 34"

Collection of Yvette and John Dubinsky

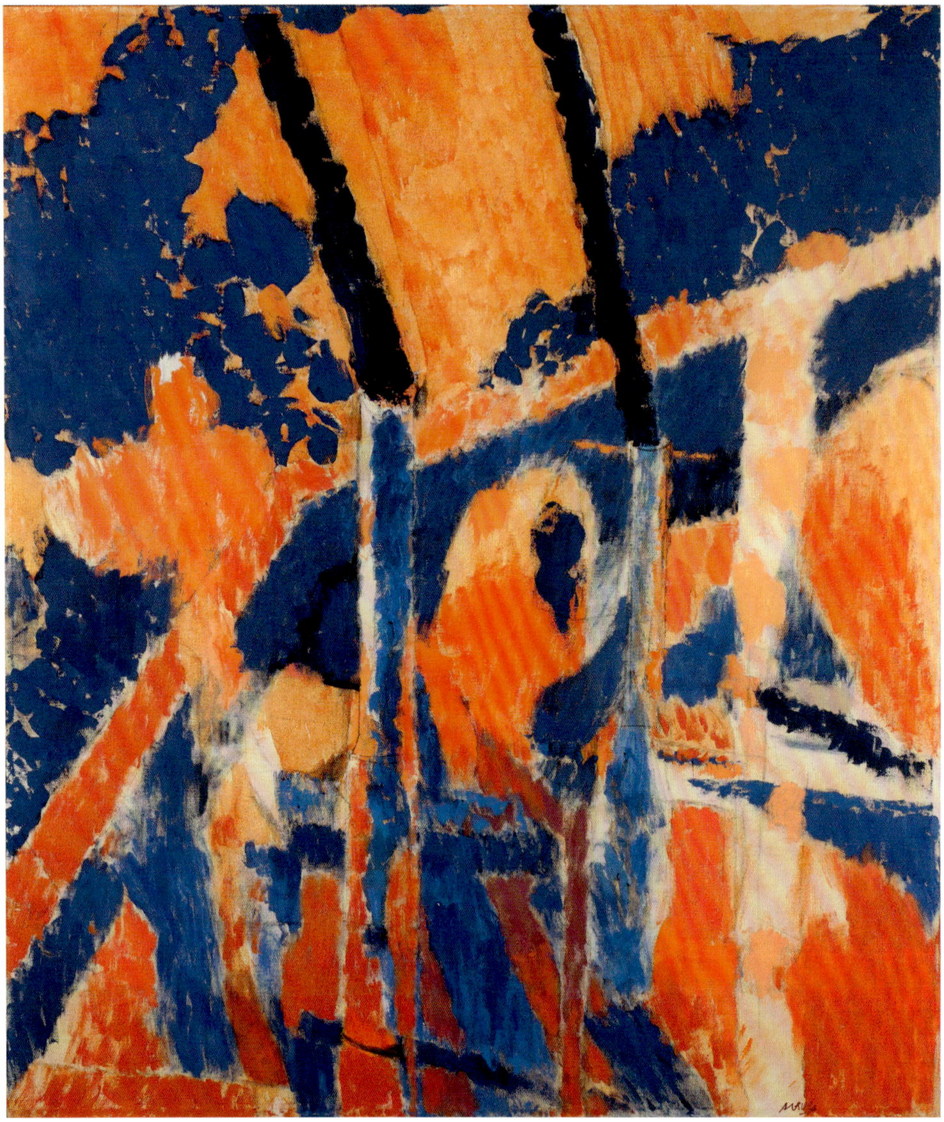

39

***Duo*, c. 1966**

Oil on canvas, 62 7/16 x 54 5/8"

Saint Louis Art Museum, Gift of Morris Moscowitz

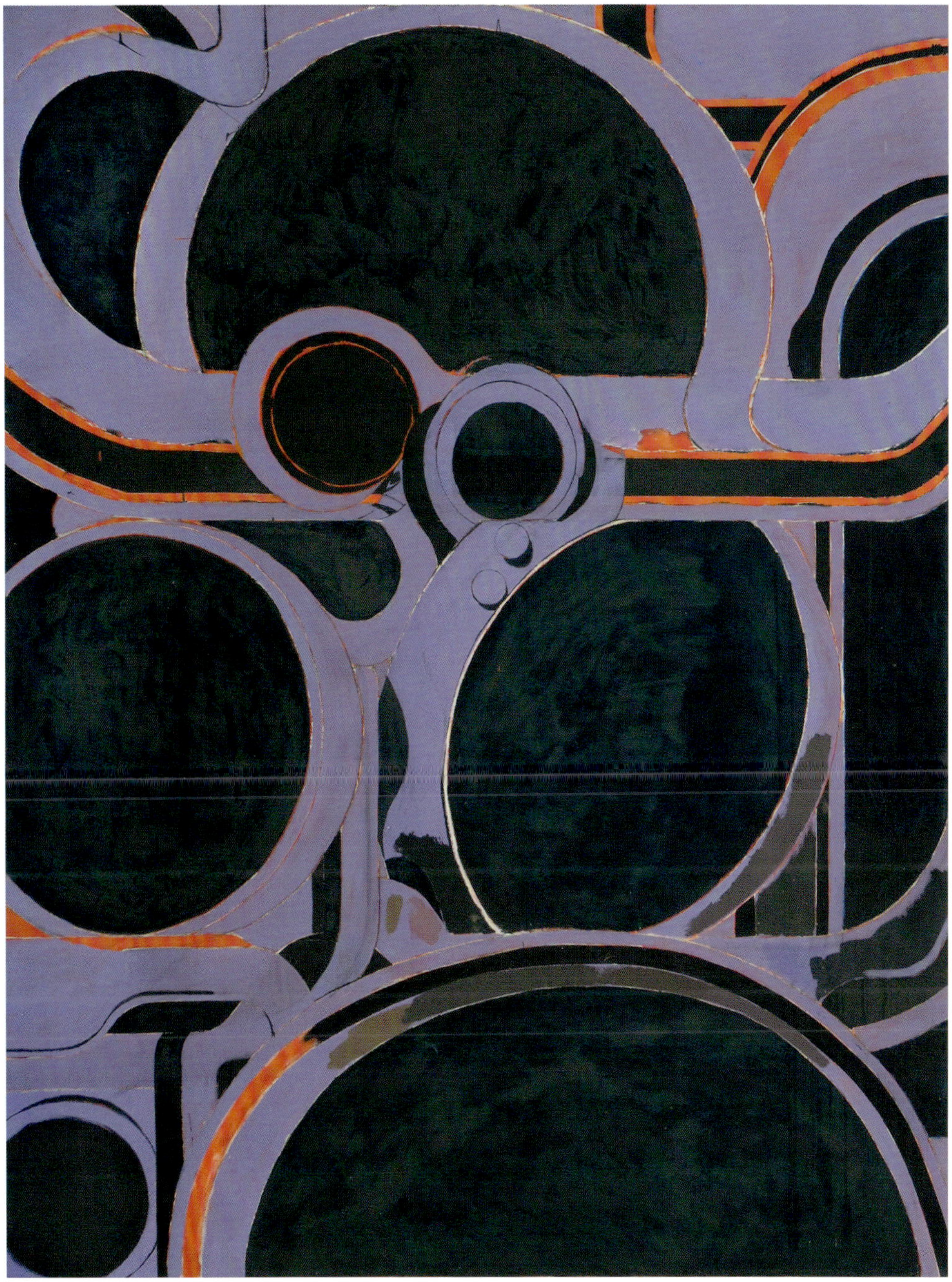

40

***G. P. 2-71*, 1971**

Oil on canvas, 80 x 60"

Estate of Arthur Osver and Ernestine Betsberg

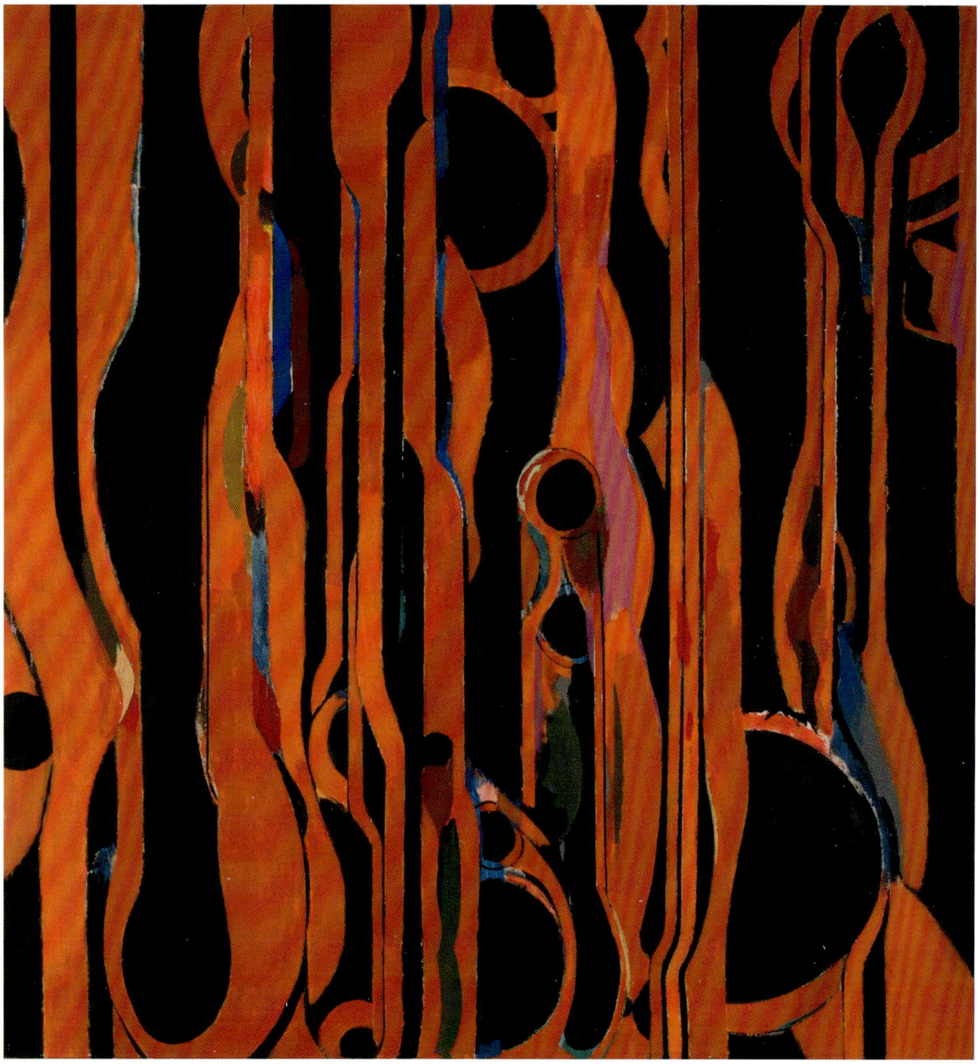

41

***G. P. 3-73*, 1973**

Oil on canvas, 71 7/8 x 69"

Mildred Lane Kemper Art Museum, Washington University in St. Louis, Gift of Eugene F. Williams Jr., 1989

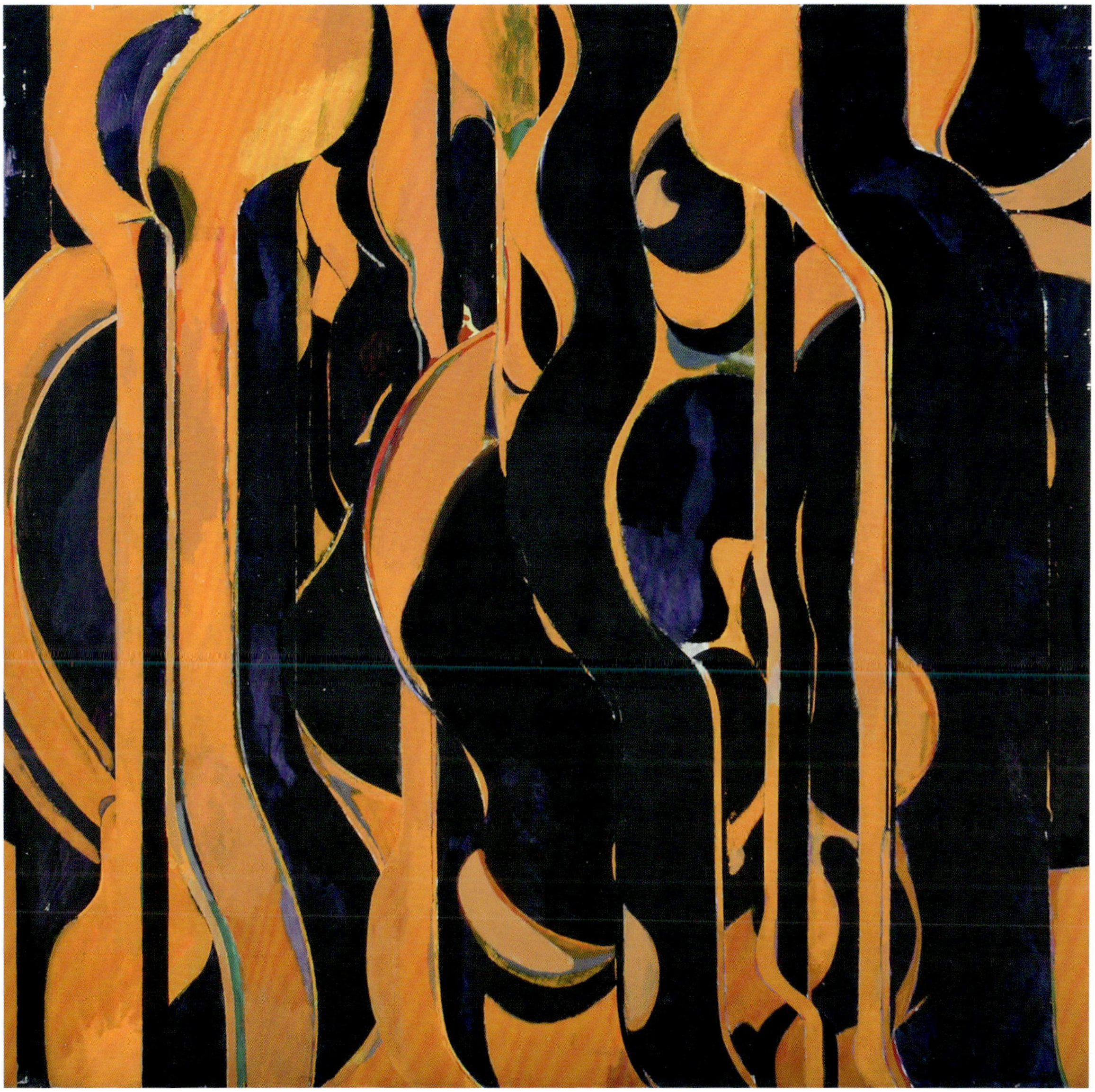

42
***G. P. 3-74*, 1974**
Oil on canvas, 79 x 84"
Estate of Arthur Osver and Ernestine Betsberg

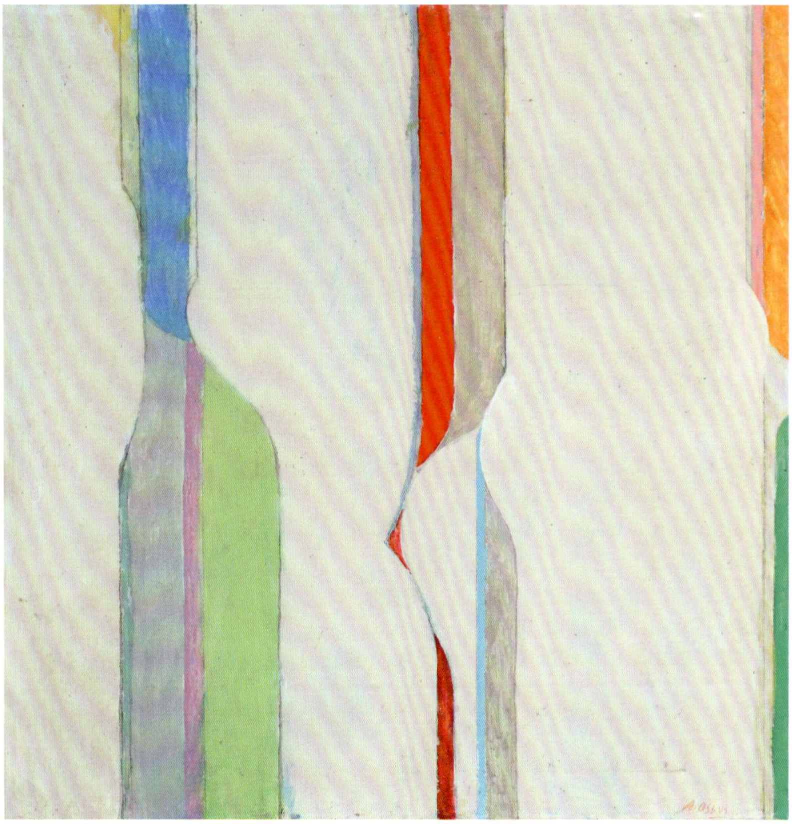

43
***Zenith*, 1981**
Oil on canvas, 25 x 25"
Courtesy of Philip Slein Gallery, St. Louis

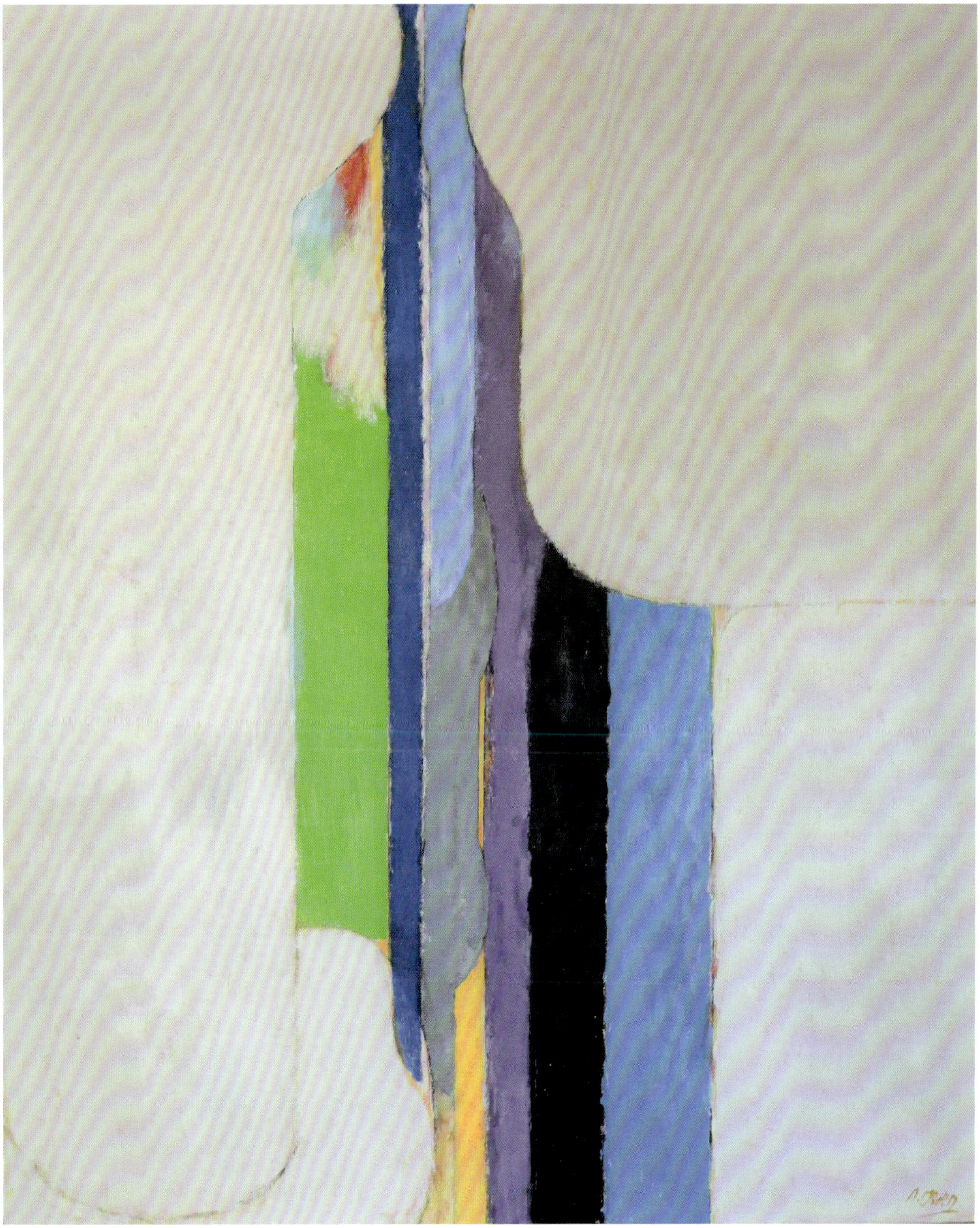

44

***Verticalities*, 1983**

Mixed media on canvas, 73 x 44"

Collection of James Costos and Michael S. Smith

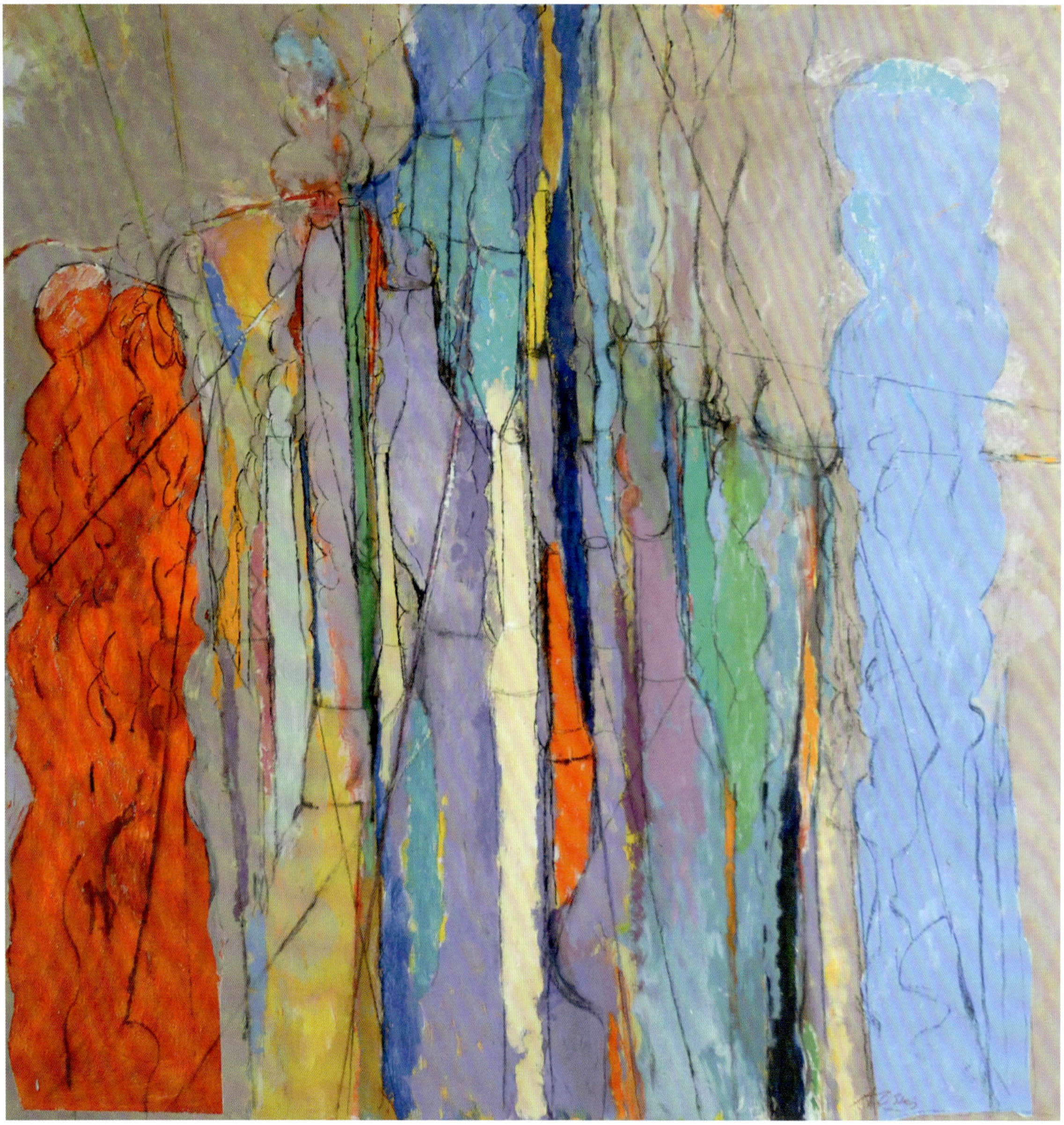

45

***Festoon*, 1985**

Oil on canvas, 68 x 67"

Collection of Dr. Valerie Ratts and Dr. Matthew Gornet

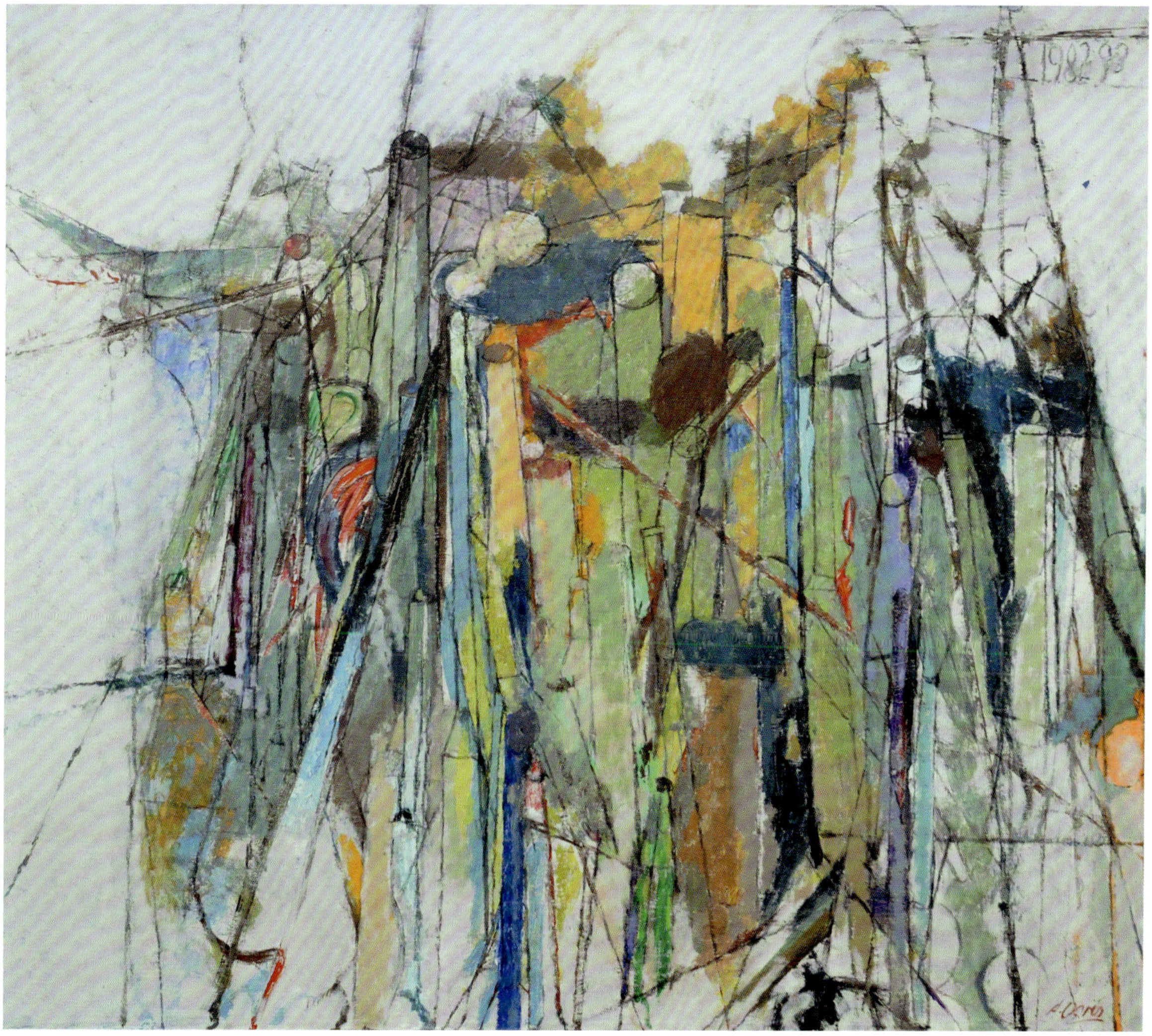

46
***Fly Away*, 1988**
Mixed media on canvas, 60 x 70"
Collection of Karen and Tom Stern

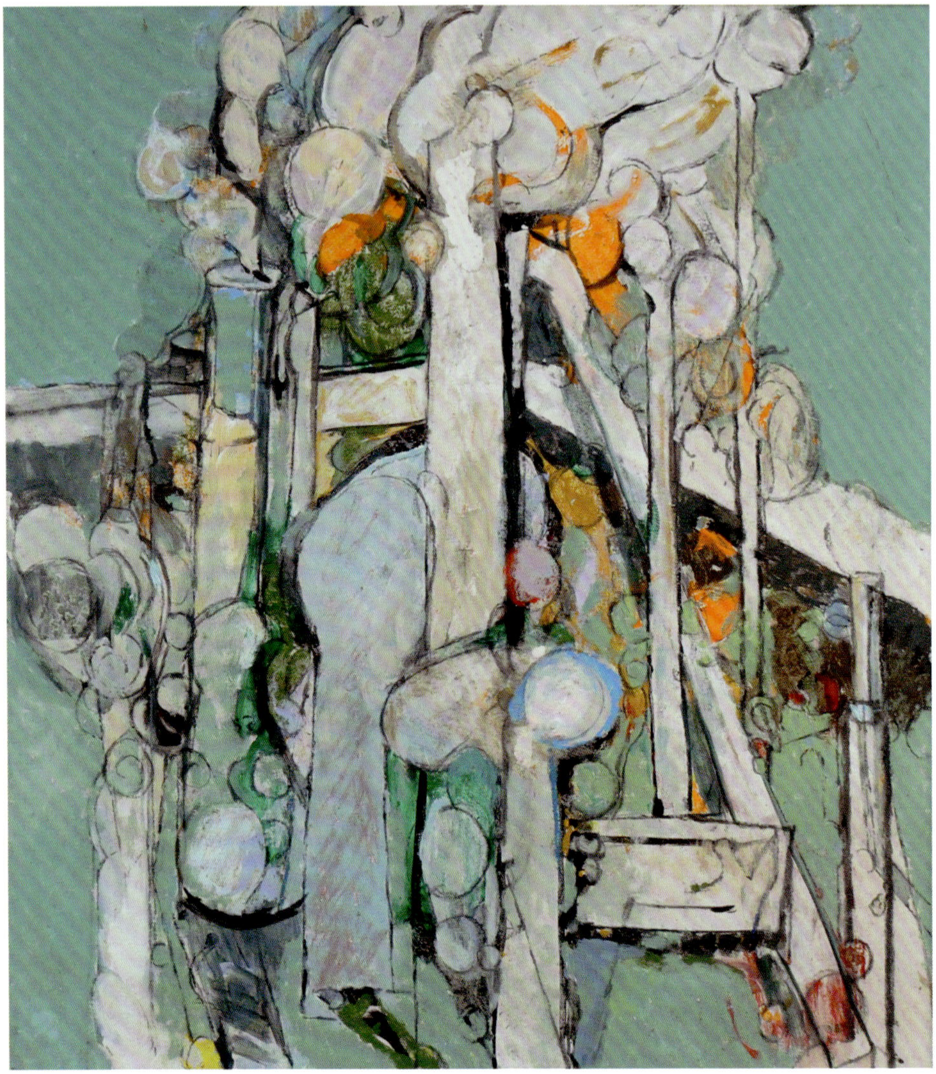

47

***Mondoverde*, 1990**

Oil on canvas, 49 x 44"

Estate of Arthur Osver and Ernestine Betsberg

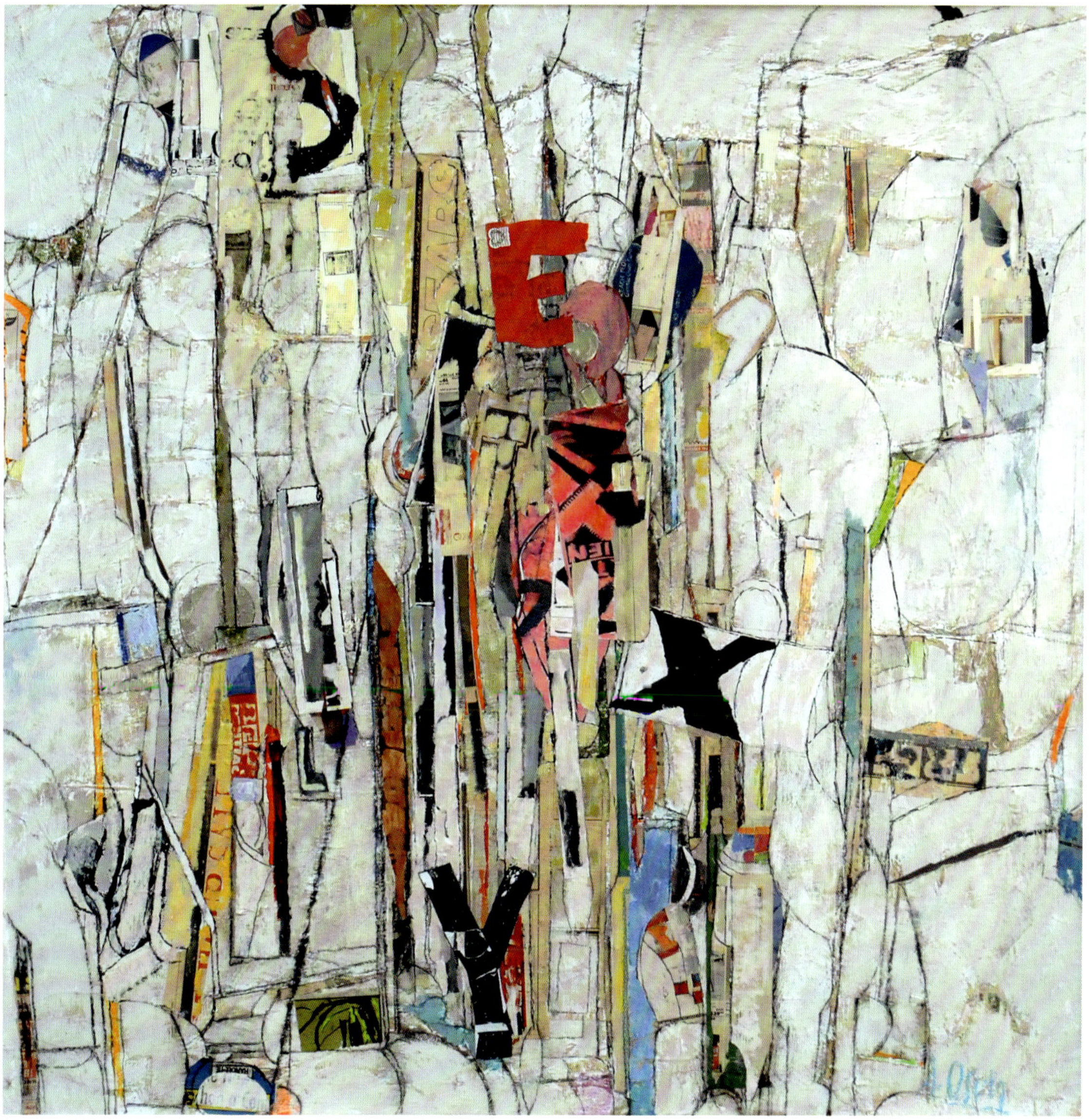

48
***S.E.X.Y.*, 1995**
Collage and oil on canvas, 53 x 54"
Estate of Arthur Osver and Ernestine Betsberg

CHRONOLOGY

Chronology

Compiled by Jennifer Padgett

Unless otherwise indicated, all biographical information is taken from Arthur Osver Papers, the Estate of Arthur Osver and Ernestine Betsberg, St. Louis; hereafter cited as Osver Papers, St. Louis. The papers include correspondence, biographical material, photographs, writings, sketches, exhibition catalogs, clippings, and ephemeral printed material.

1912
Arthur Osver is born in Chicago on July 25 to Herschel (Harry) and Yetta Osver, both Russian immigrants.

1930
Graduates from Proviso High School, Maywood, Illinois.

1930–31
Studies journalism at Northwestern University, Evanston, Illinois.

1931–36
Transfers to School of the Art Institute of Chicago to study painting with Russian émigré Boris Anisfeld. Included in 14th International Watercolor Exhibition, Art Institute of Chicago, while a student.

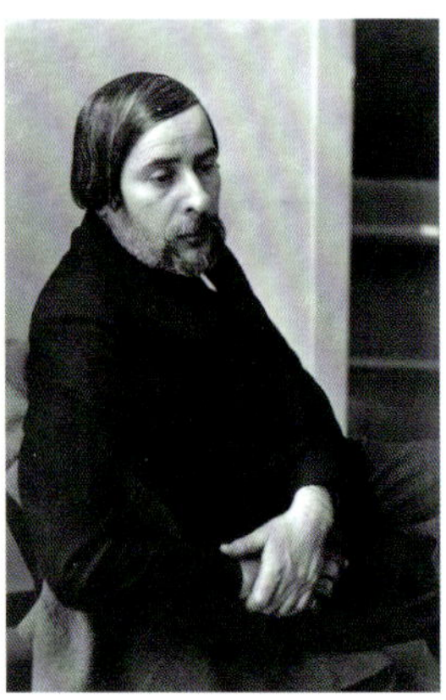

Boris Anisfeld, Osver's teacher at the School of the Art Institute of Chicago

1936
Travels to France on a James Nelson Raymond Traveling Fellowship, awarded by School of the Art Institute of Chicago.

1937
In Paris marries fellow student and painter Ernestine Betsberg, who also receives a traveling fellowship. They travel through France and Italy, settling on the Riviera in Cagnes-sur-Mer, France. Galerie des Beaux Arts, Cagnes, hosts his first solo exhibition.

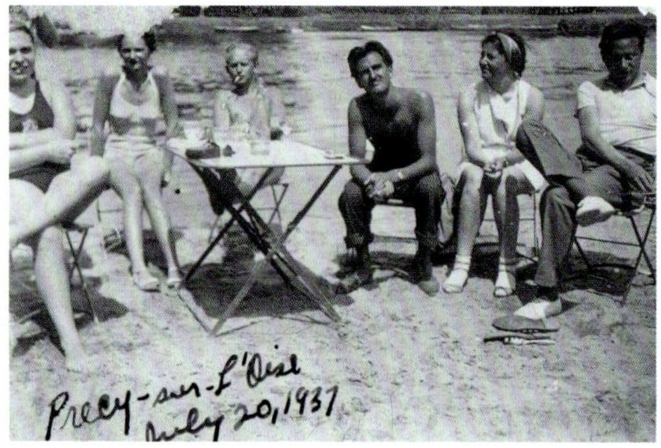

Osver (center right) with friends along the banks of the Oise River, north of Paris, 1937

1938
On his return to Chicago, Osver works making paints at the factory of Spanish-born artist Ramon Shiva, developer of oil and casein paints for artists as well as for wartime use.[1] Is supported by the Federal Art Project for eighteen months.[2] Participates in 42nd Annual Exhibition by Artists of Chicago and Vicinity, Art Institute of Chicago, and in group exhibition with Betsberg at Gallery House, Chicago.

1939
Exhibits at Pennsylvania Academy of the Fine Arts 134th Annual Exhibition in Philadelphia (also in 1944, 1947–51, 1953, 1954, 1956, 1962, 1966, and 1968).

1940
Settles in Greenwich Village, New York. First US solo exhibition at Gallery House, Chicago. Exhibits in 19th International Exhibition of Watercolors, Art Institute of Chicago, and at Golden Gate International Exposition in San Francisco.

1942
The Studio (1941–42; pl. 2) included in 46th Annual Exhibition by Artists of Chicago and Vicinity, Art Institute of Chicago, and acquired by Earle Ludgin of Chicago. *Melancholy of a Rooftop* (1942; pl. 3) acquired by Museum of Modern Art, New York, where it is included the following year in the exhibition *Romantic Painting in America.*

1943

Moves to Long Island City in Queens, New York. First solo exhibition in New York at Mortimer Brandt Gallery.

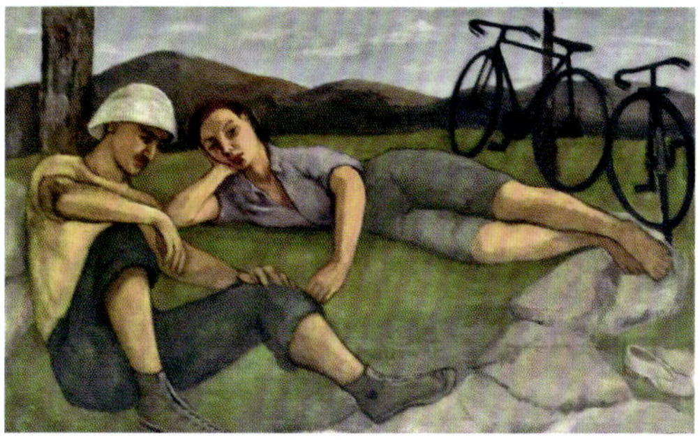

Ernestine Betsberg (1909–2007), *Self-Portrait with Arthur* (c. 1943), oil on canvas, 28 x 43", Collection of Peter Shank

1944

Receives John Barton Payne Award at American Painting Today, 4th Biennial Exhibition of Contemporary American Painting, Virginia Museum of Fine Arts, Richmond. *The Big Billboard* (1944; pl. 5) exhibited in *Art Panorama*, Boston, and in Annual Exhibition of Contemporary American Painting, Whitney Museum of American Art, New York (works also included in 1945–50, 1955, 1959, 1960, and 1963). Included in Carnegie Annual Exhibition, Pittsburgh (later Pittsburgh International and Carnegie International; also in 1945–50, 1955, 1958, and 1963). *Bridal Bouquet* (1944) awarded a prize in inaugural Pepsi-Cola art competition in conjunction with its touring exhibition *Portrait of America*; later purchased for Pepsi-Cola collection and illustrated on August cover of *Art News*.

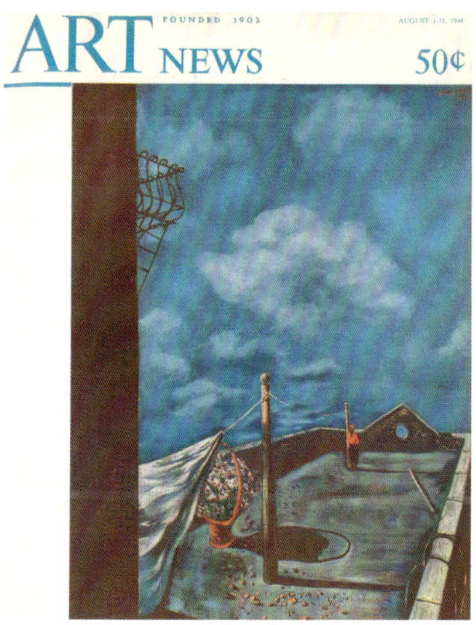

Bridal Bouquet (1944) on the cover of *Art News*, August 1944

1945

Red Ventilator (1945; pl. 9) exhibited in Carnegie Annual Exhibition. Exhibits in 4th Annual Audubon Artists Exhibition, National Academy Galleries, New York (also in 1946–48).

1946

Monday Morning (1946; pl. 11) exhibited in Carnegie Annual Exhibition. *Green Ventilator* (1946; fig. 4) included in Annual Exhibition of Contemporary American Painting, Whitney Museum of American Art. *The Majestic Tenement* (1946; fig. 19) awarded Hubbard Prize in Critics' Show, Grand Central Art Galleries, New York. *Forest of Chimneys* (1945; pl. 7) among works by thirteen artists—including Alexander Calder, Max Ernst, and Jacob Lawrence—purchased by Nelson A. Rockefeller for donation to nascent modern art museums in Rio de Janiero and São Paulo.

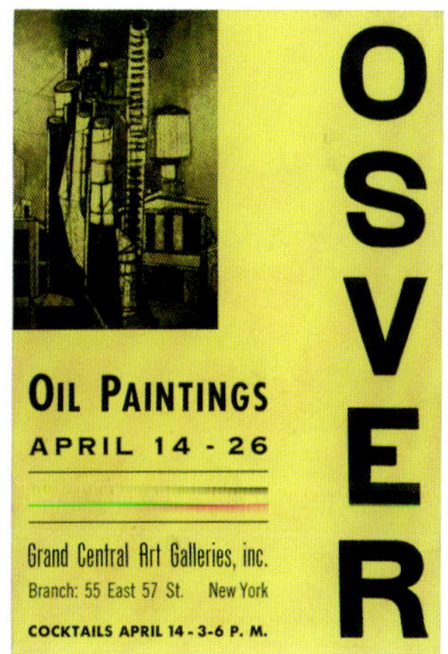

Brochure from Osver's first solo exhibition at Grand Central Art Galleries, 1947, featuring *The Cluster* (1947; pl. 16)

1947

Teaches at Brooklyn Museum Art School. *The Majestic Tenement* awarded Temple Gold Medal and purchase prize in Pennsylvania Academy of the Fine Arts 142nd Annual Exhibition. Solo exhibition at Grand Central Art Galleries (later Grand Central Moderns), New York (also in 1948, 1949, 1951, and 1957). *Queens Elevated Highway* (1946; pl. 12) exhibited in Carnegie Annual Exhibition and illustrated in Alfred M. Frankfurter's *Art News* review of the exhibition as one of the "outstanding" abstract works.[3] *Ice House* (1947; pl. 17) exhibited in Annual Exhibition of Contemporary American Painting, Whitney Museum of American Art. *Steam Jet* (1946; pl. 13) awarded purchase prize in Contemporary American Art, Toledo Museum of Art, and exhibited in Biennial Exhibition of Contemporary American Painting, Corcoran Gallery of Art, Washington, DC (works also included in 1951, 1953, 1957, and 1959). In *Magazine of Art*, John D. Morse describes Osver as "a happy product of our increasingly urban society, a city landscape painter."[4]

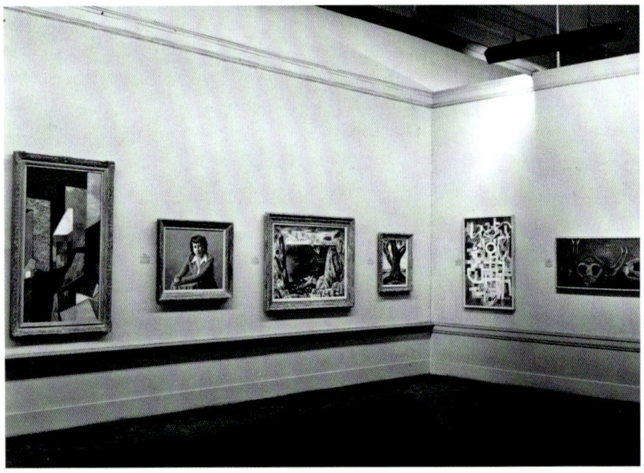

Installation view of the Carnegie Annual Exhibition, 1947, showing, from left, *Queens Elevated Highway* (1946; pl. 12) and works by H. S. Maurer, B. J. O. Nordfeldt, Audrey Buller, Bradley Walker Tomlin, and Howard Warshaw

1948

Reviewing the previous year, *Art News* names Osver's Grand Central solo exhibition as one of the year's ten best (along with those of Max Beckmann, Joan Miró, Pablo Picasso, and Ben Shahn).[5] Solo exhibition at University of Chattanooga. *The Cluster* (1947; pl. 16) exhibited in 5th annual Pepsi-Cola art competition. Included in annual exhibition of Contemporary American Painting and Sculpture, University of Illinois, Urbana (also in 1949–52, 1955, 1957, and 1959–61); and 24th Venice Biennale.

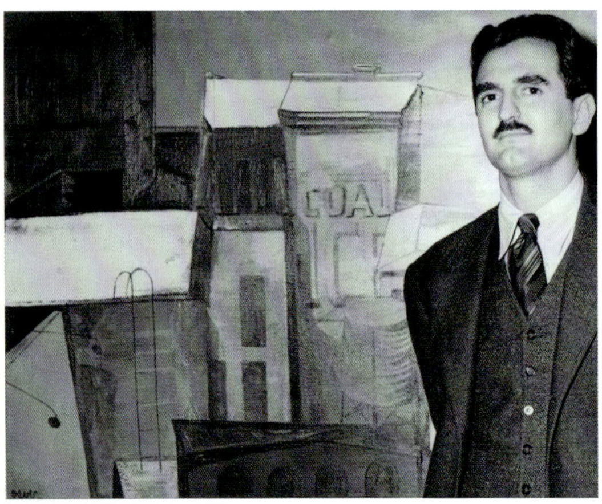

Osver at his solo exhibition at Grand Central Art Galleries, 1948

1949

Receives Guggenheim Fellowship. Solo exhibition at Syracuse University. *Chimneys and Buildings* (1947; pl. 15) awarded purchase prize by University of Illinois. *Smokestack and Tank* (1948; pl. 25) included in Biennial Exhibition of Contemporary American Painting, Corcoran Gallery of Art. After seeing Henri Matisse exhibition at Pierre Matisse Gallery, New York, Osver writes to his longtime friend and correspondent Al Leindecker that he is impressed by the power of the recent work of the nearly eighty-year-old Matisse.[6]

1950

Teaches at Columbia University, New York. Untitled painting (1949) appears on cover of March 1950 issue of *Fortune* magazine. Two-person exhibition at Drew Fine Arts Center, Hamline University, St. Paul (with Murray Turnbull). *Cranes* (1950; pl. 27) included in Metropolitan Museum of Art's *American Painting Today* exhibition and catalog, and later featured in *Life* magazine's review of the exhibition.[7] *Two Ventilators* (1947; pl. 19) included in Contemporary American Painting and Sculpture, University of Illinois, and acquired by Metropolitan Museum of Art, New York.

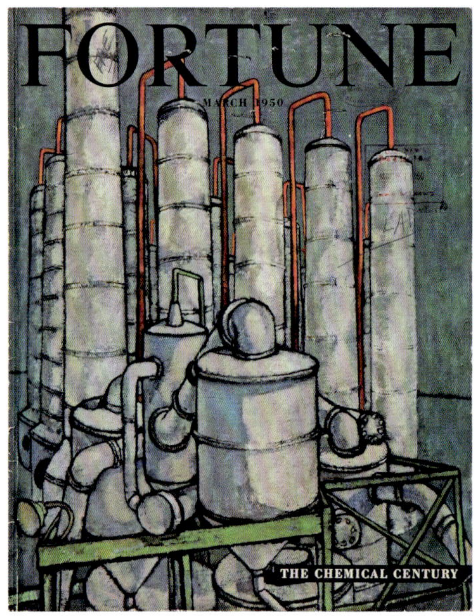

Untitled (1949) on the cover of *Fortune* magazine, March 1950

1951

Awarded second Guggenheim Fellowship. Solo exhibition at University of Florida, Gainesville (also in 1954). Osver and Betsberg have a joint exhibition at Queens Borough Public Library, Astoria Branch. Included in 3rd Tokyo Independent Art Exhibition and 60th Annual American Exhibition, Art Institute of Chicago (also in 1954). *Under the Tracks* (1951; pl. 29) acquired by City Art Museum, St. Louis (now Saint Louis Art Museum) after it is shown there in Contemporary American Painting and Sculpture exhibition.

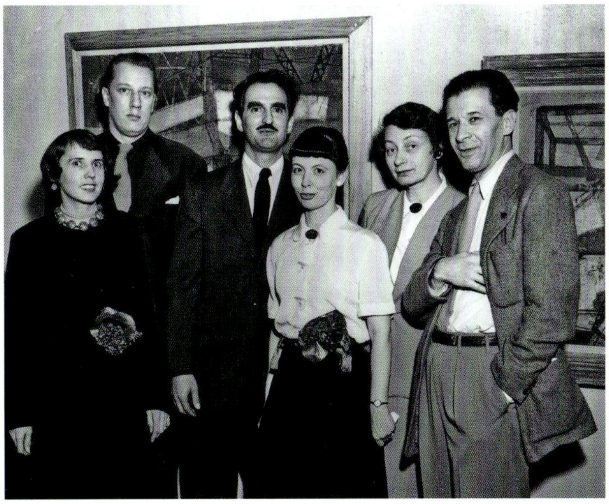

From left: Lynn Lagerstrom, Byron Browne, Osver, Betsberg, Clara Candell, and Victor Candell, at the opening of Osver's solo exhibition at Grand Central Moderns, 1951

1952

Awarded Rome Prize Fellowship in Painting (Prix de Rome) by American Academy in Rome. Included in *I pittori americani a Roma*, Galleria Nazionale, Rome. Serves on jury for Pennsylvania Academy of the Fine Arts 147th Annual Exhibition. Declines offer to teach at University of Florida.[8] Writes about Cézanne, whom he calls "the master of Aix," and observes how his "slow, almost painful growth gives one a wonderful perspective on our own 'à la mode' manner of painting today."[9]

1953

American Academy in Rome fellowship renewed. Two works by Osver exhibited in Bordighera, Italy, and included in Italian newsreels about the exhibition.[10] Osver's work reproduced in *New York Times Magazine* alongside paintings by Stuart Davis, John Marin, and others.[11] Refuses to add his comments to a pamphlet titled *Reality*—which includes statements to counter the rise of the abstract school by Milton Avery, Philip Evergood, Edward Hopper, Jacob Lawrence, Reginald Marsh, Ben Shahn, Raphael Soyer, and other painters whom Osver refers to as "realist, or humanist"—due to his belief that it is a threat to freedom of expression.[12] Experiments with using pastels in his paintings.[13] Purchases Rolleiflex camera and uses it to photograph the Colosseum in Rome and later the Grand Palais in Paris.[14]

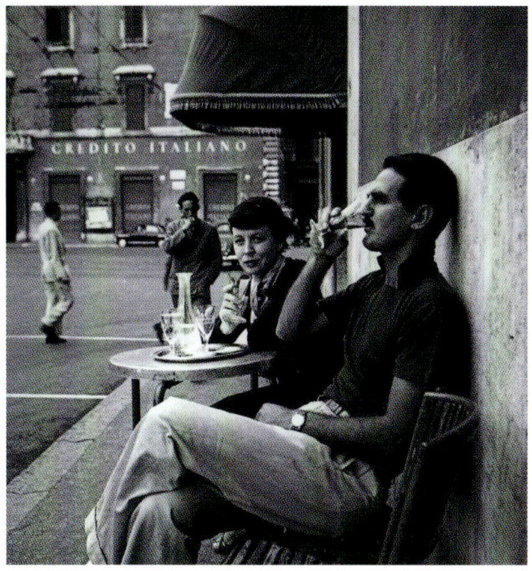

Betsberg and Osver in Rome, 1953

1954

Solo exhibition at American Academy in Rome, including a painting of the Siena cathedral, *Siena Interior* (1953; pl. 32). Works with oils on paper while also doing watercolors and drawings.[15] Tours Europe for five weeks. First of many solo exhibitions at Fairweather-Garnett Gallery, Evanston, Illinois (later Fairweather-Hardin Gallery, Chicago [also in 1955, 1957, 1962, 1964, 1966, 1969, 1981, 1982, 1985, and 1988]); nearly all works sell.[16] Appointed artist-in-residence at University of Florida, Gainesville; enrolls in courses toward his BFA.[17] *Gray Night* (1952; pl. 30) acquired by Phillips Collection, Washington, DC.

1955

Returns to New York and begins teaching at Cooper Union. Creates first plein air work since France in 1937.[18] *Big Withalacoochee* (1953–55; pl. 33) exhibited in Annual Exhibition of Contemporary American Painting, Whitney Museum of American Art, which subsequently purchases the painting. Included in *Italy Rediscovered*, Munson-Williams-Proctor Institute, Utica, New York (later circulated by Smithsonian Institution). Participates in symposium "Art: The Past Fifty Years," in Sarasota, Florida. Declines offer from School of the Art Institute of Chicago to become head of painting department.[19]

1956

Becomes member of International Fulbright Commission. Travels to Italy in summer. Exhibits a painting at 28th Venice Biennale. Hired by Josef Albers as visiting critic at Yale University for one day a week; notes, "I'm going into the lair of square." Likes Albers for his direct manner; appreciates discipline and intellectual rigor of the Yale classroom.[20]

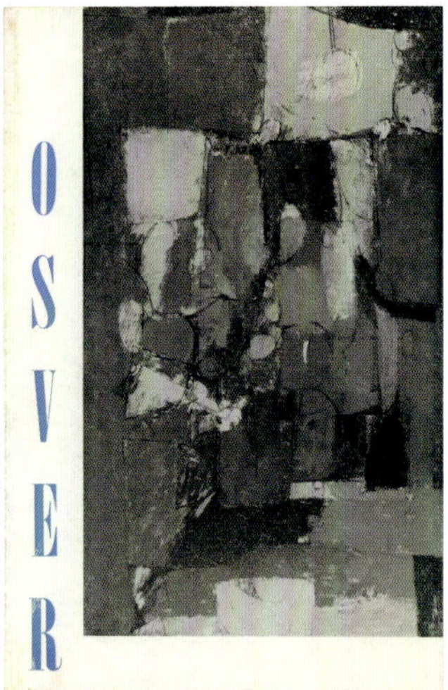

Brochure from Osver's solo exhibition at Grand Central Moderns, 1957, featuring *The Tall Green* (1956; pl. 36)

1957

Juries 62nd American Exhibition of Painting and Sculpture, Art Institute of Chicago. Solo exhibition at Grand Central Moderns, his first in New York since 1951. Included in exhibition *New York Artists Paint Staten Island*, Staten Island Museum. *The Tall Green* (1956; pl. 36) acquired by Washington University in St. Louis. Painter-in-residence at American Academy in Rome.

1958

Assists in selection of paintings by young American artists in Italy to be included in inaugural Festival of Two Worlds at Spoleto. Returns from Rome to teach at Cooper Union. Receives Emily Lowe Award from Audubon Artists (also in 1961).

1959

Becomes a member of Guggenheim Foundation Advisory Board (1959–70). Included in group exhibition at School of Architecture, Rensselaer Polytechnic Institute, Troy, New York. Listed in *Who's Who in American Art* (every year until his death in 2006).

1960

Accepts offer to teach at Washington University and is hired by Dean Kenneth Hudson, who previously hired Max Beckmann, Paul Burlin, Werner Drewes, Stephen Greene, and Philip Guston. Teaches summer school at Syracuse University. Included in Whitney Museum of American Art exhibition *Business Buys American Art*. Appointed to advisory board of American Academy in Rome (1960–72). Returns to rooftop theme in his painting.[21]

1961

Purchases one of the oldest houses in Webster Groves, a suburb of St. Louis, with studio space for him and Betsberg; house becomes a meeting place for friends and students. Included in 21st International Watercolor Biennial, Brooklyn Museum. Serves on Guggenheim and Rome Prize juries in New York. Osver and Betsberg begin spending summers in Southampton, Long Island, at the cottage of their close friends the modern dancers Alwin Nikolais and Murray Louis.

1962

Included in a roster of 102 leading American painters whose work was purchased by S. C. Johnson & Sons Inc.; *The Voyage* (1961; fig. 20) exhibited in *Art USA Now: The Johnson Collection of Contemporary American Paintings*, a national and international traveling exhibition circulated by United States Information Agency, and illustrated in its accompanying catalog. Two paintings selected as part of Vincent Price Collection of Fine Art to be sold by Sears, Roebuck and Company.[22] Included in Ravinia Festival Arts Exhibition, Highland Park, Illinois.

1963

Pleased by traces of figuration and promise shown in work he reviews as a member of Guggenheim committee.[23] Included in Kane Memorial Drawing Exhibition, Providence Art Club, Rhode Island; and *Drawings USA/63*, St. Paul Art Center.

1964

Solo exhibitions at St. Louis Artists' Guild and Milton College, Wisconsin. Included in exhibition *American Art Today*, New York World's Fair.

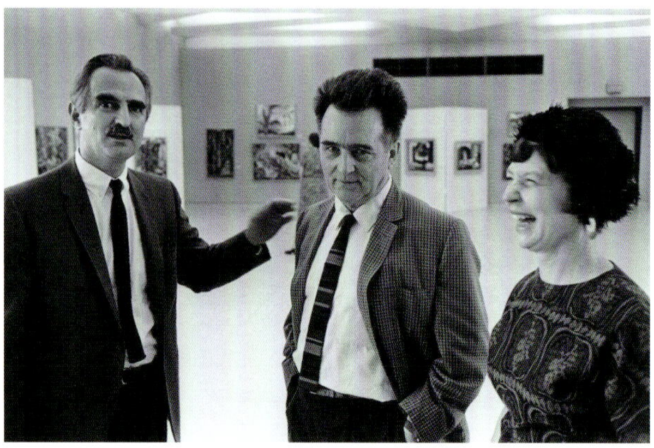

From left: Osver, Werner Drewes, and Betsberg at a retrospective exhibition of Drewes's work at the Washington University Gallery of Art, 1965, held on the occasion of Drewes's retirement after teaching at Washington University since 1946

1965
Serves on juries for Rome Prize and Guggenheim fellowships in New York.

1966
Blue Janus (1965) receives J. Henry Scheidt Memorial Prize at 161st Annual Exhibition of American Painting and Sculpture, Pennsylvania Academy of the Fine Arts. Solo exhibitions at Coe College, Cedar Rapids, Iowa; and Martin Schweig Gallery (also in 1969) and Maryville College, St. Louis. Included in National Mid-Year Show, Butler Institute of American Art, Youngstown, Ohio; Second Biennial Invitational Drawing Exhibition, Otis Art Institute, Los Angeles; *Art in Chicago Business*, Fairweather-Hardin Gallery, Chicago.

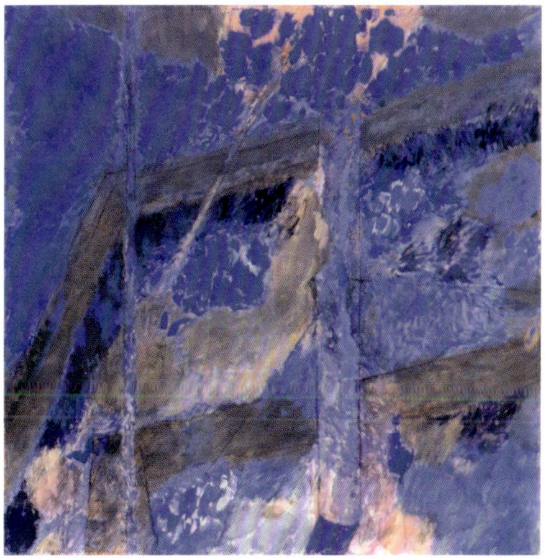

Blue Janus (1965), oil on canvas, 64 x 65", location unknown

1967
Two Ventilators (1947; pl. 19) included in American Federation of Arts traveling exhibition *American Painting: The 1940s*. Tries painting only in acrylic, but his techniques of glazing, scumbling, washes, and impasto prevent its exclusive use.[24] Receives a National Endowment for the Arts Grant awarded in 1966 and takes sabbatical leave; tours Europe; photographs the Grand Palais in Paris, which becomes the basis for later series. Writes about being filmed in his studio for CBS documentary *Local Accent on Art*.[25]

1968
First retrospective held at Gallery of Loretto-Hilton Center, Webster University, St. Louis. Solo exhibition at Iowa State FOCUS Art Festival, Ames. Included in exhibition *Ten Missouri Painters*, Missouri State Council on the Arts.

1969
Solo exhibition at St. Louis Artists' Guild. Chairs American Academy in Rome Committee on Fine Arts. Included in *A Collector's Choice*, Saint Louis Art Museum; *Draftsmen in Missouri*, Missouri State Council on the Arts; *1969–70 Printmaking in Missouri*, Missouri State Council on the Arts. St. Louis collector Morton May purchases six paintings from Osver's studio.[26]

1970
Donald S. Vogel of Dallas, Osver's friend from School of the Art Institute of Chicago, becomes one of his dealers.[27]

1971
Osver instrumental in nominating longtime friend and colleague Josef Albers for honorary degree at Washington University.[28]

1972
Included in *Mid-America 4*, Saint Louis Art Museum and Nelson Gallery–Atkins Museum, Kansas City (now Nelson–Atkins Museum).

1973
Mid-America Invitational, two-person exhibition with Howard Jones at Saint Louis Art Museum and Nelson Gallery–Atkins Museum. Awarded purchase prize in *Drawings: America*, Albrecht Gallery, St. Joseph, Missouri. Included in *Large Prints*, Missouri State Council on the Arts.

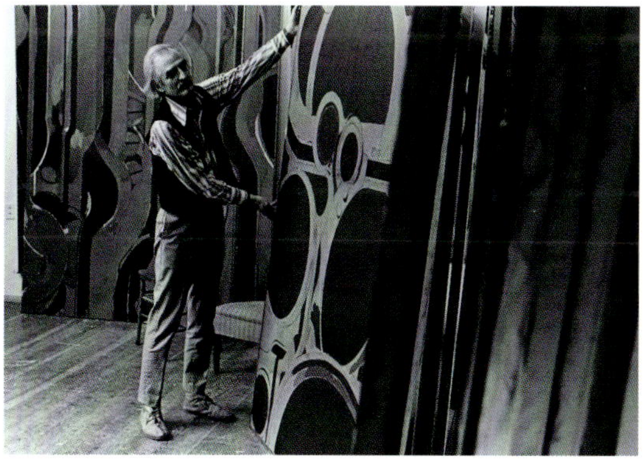

Osver in his studio, 1973, showing his Grand Palais paintings

1974
Serves as visiting critic for Portland School of Art, Maine.[29]

1975
Named a trustee of Saint Louis Art Museum (1975–78). Begins drawing on rice paper, also using collage techniques.[30] Solo exhibitions of drawings at Valley House Gallery, Dallas, and Terry Moore Gallery, St. Louis (also in 1977).

1976
Two-person exhibition at Johnson-Whitty Gallery, New Orleans (with James Butler).

1978
Returns to working with oil paints after a ten-year break; remarks, "how could I have stayed away for so long!"[31] Continues experimenting with different mediums, including commercial acrylic enamels.[32]

1981
Retires from teaching at Washington University; retrospective exhibition *Arthur Osver: The University Years* opens at Washington University Gallery of Art (now Mildred Lane Kemper Art Museum) and travels to University of Arkansas, Fayetteville; after retiring, accepts part-time position in MFA program. Solo exhibition at Timothy Burns Gallery, St. Louis (also in 1984).

1983
Visiting artist at Portland School of Art, Maine, where he experiments with color lithography.[33]

1984
Participates in exhibition at American Academy in Rome. Osver and Betsberg participate in *1 + 1 = 2*, an exhibition of the work of thirty couples at Brentwood Gallery, St. Louis.

1985
Receives Jewish Community Center Association Award for Artistic Excellence.

1986
Fairweather-Hardin Gallery features Osver works at Chicago Navy Pier Art Expo '86.

1987
Solo exhibition at B. Z. Wagman Gallery, St. Louis.

1989
Solo exhibition at University of Arkansas, Fayetteville. Exhibitions with Betsberg at Philip Samuels Fine Art, St. Louis, and Valley House Gallery, Dallas.

1991
Receives American Academy and Institute of Arts and Letters award. Solo exhibition at Randall Gallery, St. Louis.

1993
Named trustee emeritus, American Academy in Rome. Solo exhibition at Elliot Smith Contemporary Art, St. Louis (also in 1999 and 2004).

1997
Solo exhibition of recent collages at Dartmouth College, Hanover, New Hampshire.

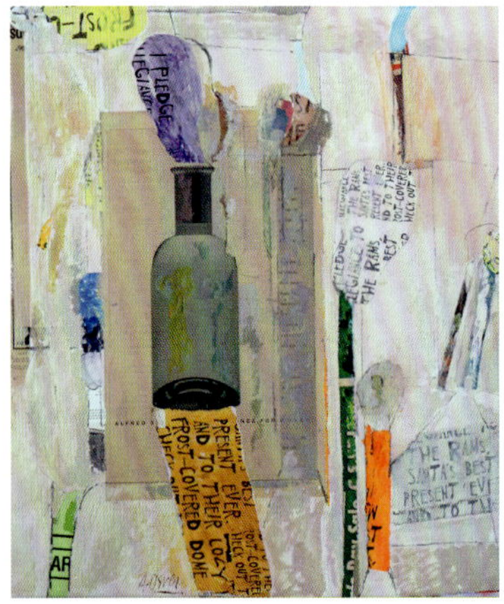

Metamorphosis (1995), collage on board, 43 x 36", Estate of Arthur Osver and Ernestine Betsberg

2000
Retrospective exhibition *Arthur Osver: The Saint Louis Years* at Saint Louis Art Museum. Two-person exhibition with Ellsworth Kelly at Dorothy Blau Gallery, Bal Harbour, Florida.

2002
Two-person exhibition with Betsberg at Elliot Smith Contemporary Art, St. Louis.

2006
Two-person exhibition with Betsberg at Philip Slein Gallery, St. Louis.

Dies on July 24 in St. Louis, age ninety-three. Memorial, "Arthur Osver, a Celebration of Life," held October 22, Graham Chapel, Washington University.

2007
Memorial exhibition at Philip Slein Gallery, St. Louis.

2008
Solo exhibition of works on paper at St. Louis Community College, Meramec.

2012
Arthur Osver: A Centennial Celebration at Philip Slein Gallery, St. Louis.

NOTES

1. Arthur Osver, in transcript of oral history interview conducted by Richard Gaugert, January 13–14, 1976, Archives of American Art, Smithsonian Institution, Washington, DC, 36; hereafter cited as AAA interview.
2. Ibid, 35–36.
3. Alfred M. Frankfurter, "Two States of the Union," *Art News* 46 (November 1947): 14–17.
4. John D. Morse, "Arthur Osver," *Magazine of Art* 40 (May 1947): 176.
5. Alfred M. Frankfurter, "The Year's Best: 1947," *Art News* 46 (January 1948): 36–37.
6. Arthur Osver to Henry A. (Al) Leindecker, March 1, 1949, correspondence between Henry A. (Al) Leindecker and Arthur Osver, 1949–64, microfilm reel 3948, Arthur Osver Papers 1943–1975, Archives of American Art, Smithsonian Institution, Washington, DC; hereafter cited as Osver Papers, AAA. Leindecker and Osver were students together at the School of the Art Institute of Chicago. Leindecker was a painter who also developed painting products, one of them called Eonite, a type of varnish used by Josef Albers and others. His correspondence with Osver lasted more than thirty years. Correspondence between Leindecker and Osver from April 1964 to January 1987 is in Osver Papers, St. Louis.
7. "The Metropolitan and Modern Art," *Life*, January 15, 1951, 35–38 (ill. p. 38).
8. Osver to Leindecker, February 14, 1952, Osver Papers, AAA.
9. Osver to Leindecker, May 26, 1952, Osver Papers, AAA.
10. Osver to Leindecker, April 30, 1954 Osver Papers, AAA.
11. A.B.L., "As the Artist Sees New York," *New York Times Magazine*, February 1, 1953.
12. Osver to Leindecker, June 22, 1953, Osver Papers, AAA. See *Reality: A Journal of Artists' Opinions* 1, no. 1 (Spring 1953).
13. Osver to Leindecker, June 22, 1953, Osver Papers, AAA.
14. Osver to Leindecker, August 8, 1953, Osver Papers, AAA.
15. Osver to Leindecker, February 26, 1954, Osver Papers, AAA.
16. Osver to Leindecker, June 16, 1954, Osver Papers, AAA.
17. Osver to Leindecker, September 30, 1954, Osver Papers, AAA.
18. Osver to Leindecker, February 5, 1955, Osver Papers, AAA.
19. Osver to Leindecker, April 9, 1955, Osver Papers, AAA.
20. Osver to Leindecker, September 6, 1956, Osver Papers, AAA.
21. Osver to Leindecker, January 1, 1960, Osver Papers, AAA.
22. Osver to Leindecker, July 14, 1962, Osver Papers, AAA.
23. Osver to Leindecker, March 31, 1963, Osver Papers, AAA.
24. Osver to Leindecker, January 9, 1967, Osver Papers, St. Louis.
25. Osver to Leindecker, August 24, 1967, Osver Papers, St. Louis.
26. Osver to Leindecker, February 21, 1969, Osver Papers, St. Louis.
27. Osver to Leindecker, June 30, 1970, Osver Papers, St. Louis.
28. Osver to Leindecker, July 6, 1971, Osver Papers, St. Louis.
29. Osver to Leindecker, March 19, 1974, Osver Papers, St. Louis.
30. Osver to Leindecker, May 22, 1975, Osver Papers, St. Louis.
31. Osver to Leindecker, March 24, 1978, Osver Papers, St. Louis.
32. Osver to Leindecker, December 28, 1978, Osver Papers, St. Louis.
33. Osver to Leindecker, November 2, 1983, Osver Papers, St. Louis.

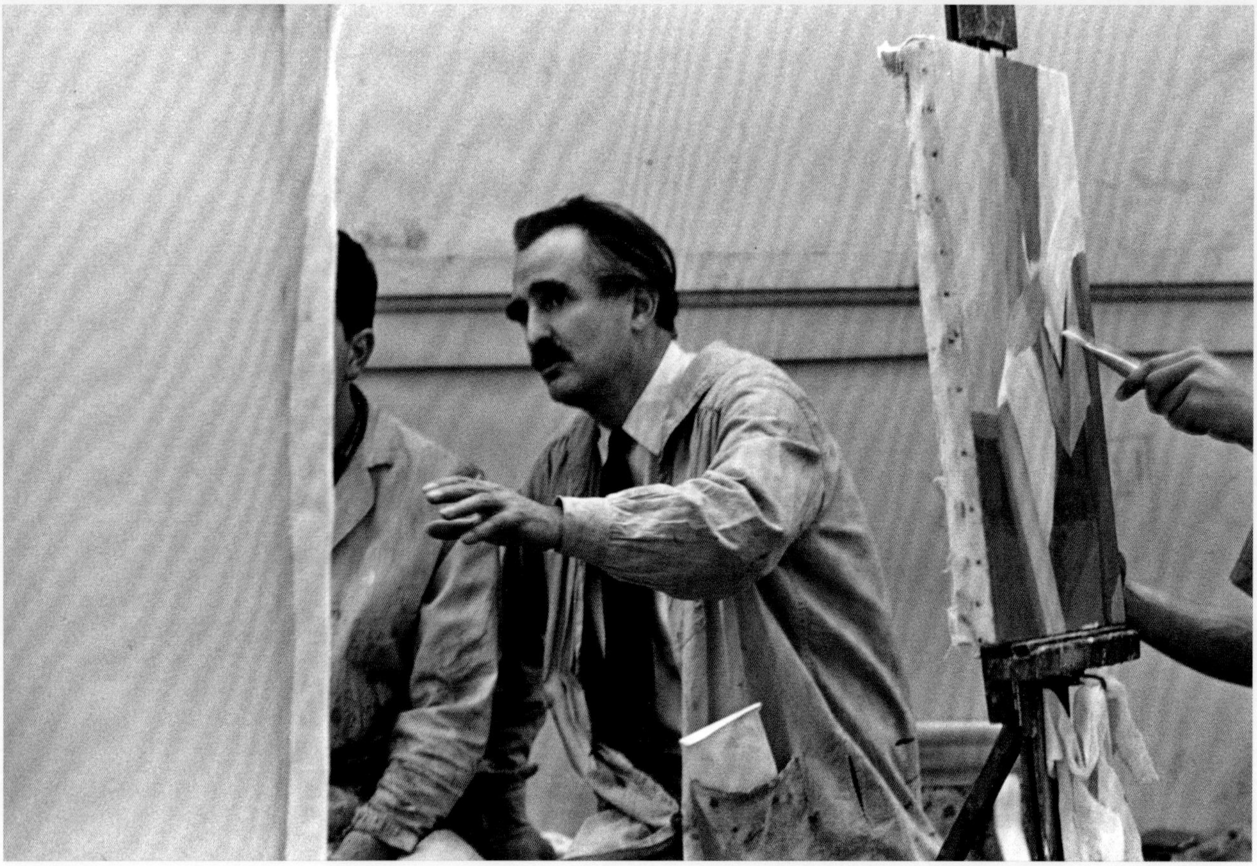

A REMEMBRANCE OF ARTHUR OSVER

As a former, and now retired, physician and scientist, I am hardly qualified to comment knowledgeably on the art of Arthur Osver, but as a longtime member and former chancellor of Washington University in St. Louis, I am honored to be asked to add a few thoughts about his role as an accomplished and gifted academic.

When Arthur joined Washington University in 1960, I had already been on the faculty for nine years, but as I spent almost all my working hours on the Medical Campus, we did not meet until after the summer of 1971, when I crossed the two miles of Forest Park to join what we then called the main campus as the new chancellor of our institution.

Arthur exemplified a model academic, very intelligent, with broad interests and great curiosity. This extended into writing, poetry, travel, his local and artistic communities, his friends, and what was happening in the world. He was, like other great academics I have admired, devoted to the calling that he had adopted as a young person. His studio, with its north light, was the center of his life. Even when ill in his nineties he remained eager to get back to it and the tools of his calling. His art evolved over time; it became more abstract and took in new objects, but it remained always true to how Arthur saw the world. He never lost faith in his artistic vision or his enthusiasm for getting it onto canvas.

His loyalties and central passions also remained constant. He married Ernestine Betsberg—also a gifted and dedicated painter—whom he met when they were both students at the School of the Art Institute of Chicago. As Arthur said, "We had the same ultimate goals—just to do our art." They agreed that her painting influenced his more than the other way around. They remained devoted partners until Arthur's death sixty-nine years after they joined their lives together, and Washington University and St. Louis remained their adopted home to the end of their days.

Arthur was an accomplished teacher and mentor with seemingly boundless enthusiasm for his students. He did not seek to turn them as artists into his imitators but rather to understand each student's aesthetics and emotions and to point out a way of achieving what he sensed the younger person was trying to do. Thus he passed on his enthusiasm and passion for painting along with knowledge of technical skills. And his students responded with admiration and with increased appreciation for art and for their own skills and ways of seeing.

I have had the good fortune to live in a university community and to know and observe talented academics, most of whom, like Arthur, had a special and often consuming passion. Among those who stand out in my memory, along with Arthur, are physicians, surgeons, pediatricians, biochemists, psychiatrists, poets, novelists, philosophers, physicists, chemists, historians, and architects—people who made unique contributions to the great store of human understanding and culture and form part of the great chain that passes on what humans have learned over the millennia to those coming after. Each of those lives has been, like Arthur's, a blessing.

WILLIAM H. DANFORTH
Chancellor Emeritus
Washington University in St. Louis

SELECTED COLLECTIONS

ArcelorMittal, Chicago

Art Institute of Chicago

Colorado Springs Fine Arts Center

Delaware Art Museum, Wilmington

Des Moines Art Center

Figge Art Museum, Davenport, Iowa

The John and Susan Horseman Collection, St. Louis

John Burroughs School, St. Louis

Krannert Art Museum and Kinkead Pavilion, University of Illinois at Urbana–Champaign

The Metropolitan Museum of Art, New York

Mildred Lane Kemper Art Museum, Washington University in St. Louis

Museu de Arte Contemporânea, Universidade de São Paulo

The Museum of Fine Arts, Houston

The Museum of Modern Art, New York

New Orleans Museum of Art

Pennsylvania Academy of the Fine Arts, Philadelphia

The Phillips Collection, Washington, DC

Saint Louis Art Museum

Saint Louis University Museum of Art

The Jason Schoen Collection, Miami

Sheldon Museum of Art, University of Nebraska–Lincoln

Smithsonian American Art Museum, Washington, DC

Syracuse University Art Galleries, New York

University of Michigan Museum of Art, Ann Arbor

Walker Art Center, Minneapolis

Whitney Museum of American Art, New York

SELECTED BIBLIOGRAPHY

"12 Americans Hit the Spot." *Art News* 43 (August 1944): 14.

A. B. L. "As the Artist Sees New York." *New York Times Magazine*, February 1, 1953.

American Artists Paint the City. Chicago: Art Institute of Chicago, 1956. 28th Venice Biennale exhibition catalog, with an essay by Katharine Kuh.

Arb, Renée. "Spotlight on: Osver." *Art News* 47 (November 1948): 19.

Arthur Osver: New Paintings from Italy. Evanston, IL: Fairweather-Garnett Gallery, 1954. Exhibition brochure, with "A Comment on the Exhibition" by Daniel Catton Rich.

Arthur Osver: The Saint Louis Years. St. Louis: Saint Louis Art Museum, 2000. Exhibition catalog, with the essay "Arthur Osver: Mondo Mio" by Alexandra Bellos Goldsand.

Arthur Osver: The University Years: 1960–1981. St. Louis: Washington University, 1981. Exhibition catalog, with the essay "The University Years: 1960–1981" by Mary King.

Art in Chicago Business. Chicago: Fairweather-Hardin Gallery, 1966. Exhibition brochure.

Burrows, Carlyle. "Art: Mainly Subjective." *New York Herald Tribune*, April 15, 1951.

Business Buys American Art, March 17–April 24, 1960: Third Loan Exhibition by the Friends of the Whitney Museum of American Art. New York: Whitney Museum of American Art, 1960. Exhibition catalog.

Cole, Mary. "Girders in the Sky." *Art Digest* 25 (April 15, 1951): 16.

Coming Home: American Paintings, 1930–1950, from the Schoen Collection. Athens: Georgia Museum of Art, 2003. Exhibition catalog, with illustrations and catalog entries by Drew Kane for *Red Ventilator* and *The Big Billboard*.

Devree, Howard. "Americans in Venice." *New York Times*, July 18, 1948.

———. "By Groups and Singly: The Whitney and Others—Kuhn and Osver." *New York Times*, November 14, 1948.

———. "Individual Modern: The Work of Modigliani—De Kooning—Osver." *New York Times*, April 15, 1951.

Duffy, Robert W. "'I Am Going to Miss the Students.'" *St. Louis Post-Dispatch*, April 26, 1981.

Fabri, Ralph. *Painting Cityscapes*. New York: Watson-Guptill, 1969.

Frankfurter, Alfred M. "Two States of the Union." *Art News* 46 (November 1947): 14–17.

———. "The Year's Best: 1947." *Art News* 46 (January 1948): 36–37.

Genauer, Emily. "Arthur Osver." *New York World-Telegram*, November 16, 1948.

———. "U.S. Art at Spoleto." *St. Louis Post-Dispatch*, June 29, 1958.

Gibbs, Jo. "Osver Overdue." *Art Digest* 21 (April 15, 1947): 13.

Hess, Thomas B. "Spotlight on: Osver." *Art News* 46 (April 1947): 26, 57–58.

Italy Rediscovered: An Exhibition of Work by American Painters in Italy since World War II. Utica, NY: Munson-Williams-Proctor Institute, 1955. Exhibition catalog.

Jewell, Edward Alden. "Collections in New Homes." *New York Times*, May 23, 1943.

———. "Divergent Abstractionists." *New York Times*, April 20, 1947.

Jones, Barbara L., with Judith Hansen O'Toole. *Painting in the United States 2008*. Greensburg, PA: Westmoreland Museum of American Art, 2008. Exhibition catalog on Carnegie Annual Exhibitions in the 1940s.

Keating, Micheline. "The Art of Abstraction." *Tucson Daily Citizen*, April 1, 1961.

"L. I. City Painter Wins Art Award." *New York Times*, January 26, 1947.

McCue, George. D. "Arthur Osver Comes to St. Louis." *St. Louis Post-Dispatch*, June 5, 1960.

"The Metropolitan and Modern Art." *Life*, January 15, 1951, 35–38.

Mid-America Invitational: Howard Jones and Arthur Osver. St. Louis: Saint Louis Art Museum, 1973. Exhibition catalog, with an essay by Emily S. Rauh.

Morse, John D. "Arthur Osver." *Magazine of Art* 40 (May 1947): 176–77.

Osver. St. Louis: Gallery of Loretto-Hilton Center, 1968. Exhibition catalog, with an essay by Kenneth E. Hudson.

Pease, Roland F., Jr. "Arthur Osver." In *Art USA Now*, edited by Lee Nordness, vol. 2, 264–67. New York: Viking, 1963.

Shopen, Kenneth. "Osver's Paintings Exhibited." *Chicago Daily News*, April 4, 1954.

Soby, James Thrall, and Dorothy C. Miller. *Romantic Painting in America*. New York: Museum of Modern Art, 1943. Exhibition catalog.

Trier, Marilyn Robb. "Osvers from Italy." *Art News* 53 (May 1954): 46.

CONTRIBUTORS

Matthew Bailey teaches at St. Louis Community College–Meramec. He received his PhD from the Department of Art History & Archaeology at Washington University in St. Louis.

Richard Gaugert served as a regional interviewer for the Archives of American Art Oral History Program at the Smithsonian Institution. He developed and coordinated public programs at the Saint Louis Art Museum from the 1970s until his death in 1990.

Angela Miller is professor in the Department of Art History & Archaeology at Washington University in St. Louis, where she teaches American art and visual culture. She has published and lectured extensively on the cultural history of nineteenth- and twentieth-century American arts throughout the United States and abroad. She is the author of *Empire of the Eye: Landscape Representations and American Cultural Politics, 1825–1875* (1993) and coauthor of *American Encounters: Art, History, and Cultural Identity* (2009), a comprehensive historical survey of the arts from pre-encounter to the present.

Jennifer Padgett is assistant curator at Crystal Bridges Museum of American Art in Bentonville, Arkansas. She received her PhD from the Department of Art History & Archaeology at Washington University in St. Louis.

Photography Credits

Reproductions of artworks by Arthur Osver appear courtesy of the Estate of Arthur Osver and Ernestine Betsberg. Additional credits are listed below. Images are referenced by page number.

Addison Gallery of American Art, Phillips Academy, Andover, MA / Art Resource, New York; © 2018 Artists Rights Society (ARS), New York: 23 (top)
Courtesy of Demuth Museum, Lancaster, PA: 17
© 2018 Succession H. Matisse / Artists Rights Society (ARS), New York: 41
Digital image © The Museum of Modern Art / Licensed by SCALA / Art Resource, New York: 26, 41, 66
Photo by Rich Sanders, Des Moines: 81
Photo © Sheldon Museum of Art: 86
Washington University Photographic Services, courtesy University Archives, Washington University Libraries, St. Louis: 118 (bottom), 119 (bottom), 122
Digital image © Whitney Museum of American Art: 96

Cover:
Red Ventilator, 1945
Oil on Masonite, 30 x 23"
The John and Susan Horseman Collection, St. Louis

Frontispiece:
Stop Light, 1943
Oil on canvas, 32 x 23"
Collection of Paul Shank

Pages 4–5:
West Side, 1944
Oil on board, 22 x 28"
Collection of Jeannine and Kent Kalkwarf

Pages 6, 52, 122, 128:
Photographs of Arthur Osver, 1953, c. 1940, 1962, and c. 1968, respectively. Estate of Arthur Osver and Ernestine Betsberg.

Support for this publication was provided by the Estate of Arthur Osver and Ernestine Betsberg.

PUBLISHED BY
Mildred Lane Kemper Art Museum
Sam Fox School of Design & Visual Arts
Washington University in St. Louis
One Brookings Drive
St. Louis, Missouri 63130
kemperartmuseum.wustl.edu

Managing editor: Jane E. Neidhardt
Copy editor: Karen Jacobson
Research assistants: Jennifer Padgett, Holly Tasker
Photo editor: Holly Tasker
Designer: Michael Worthington, Counterspace
Printer: Conti Tipocolor, Florence

DISTRIBUTED BY
The University of Chicago Press
11030 S. Langley Avenue
Chicago, IL 60628
Domestic:
Tel: 1-800-621-2736
Fax: 1-800-621-8476
International:
Tel: 1-773-702-7000
Fax: 1-773-702-7212

Library of Congress Control Number: 2017932502
ISBN: 978-0-936316-44-4

Limited Edition
Library of Congress Control Number: 2018957362
ISBN: 978-0-936316-45-1

Washington University in St. Louis
Sam Fox School of Design & Visual Arts

Mildred Lane Kemper Art Museum

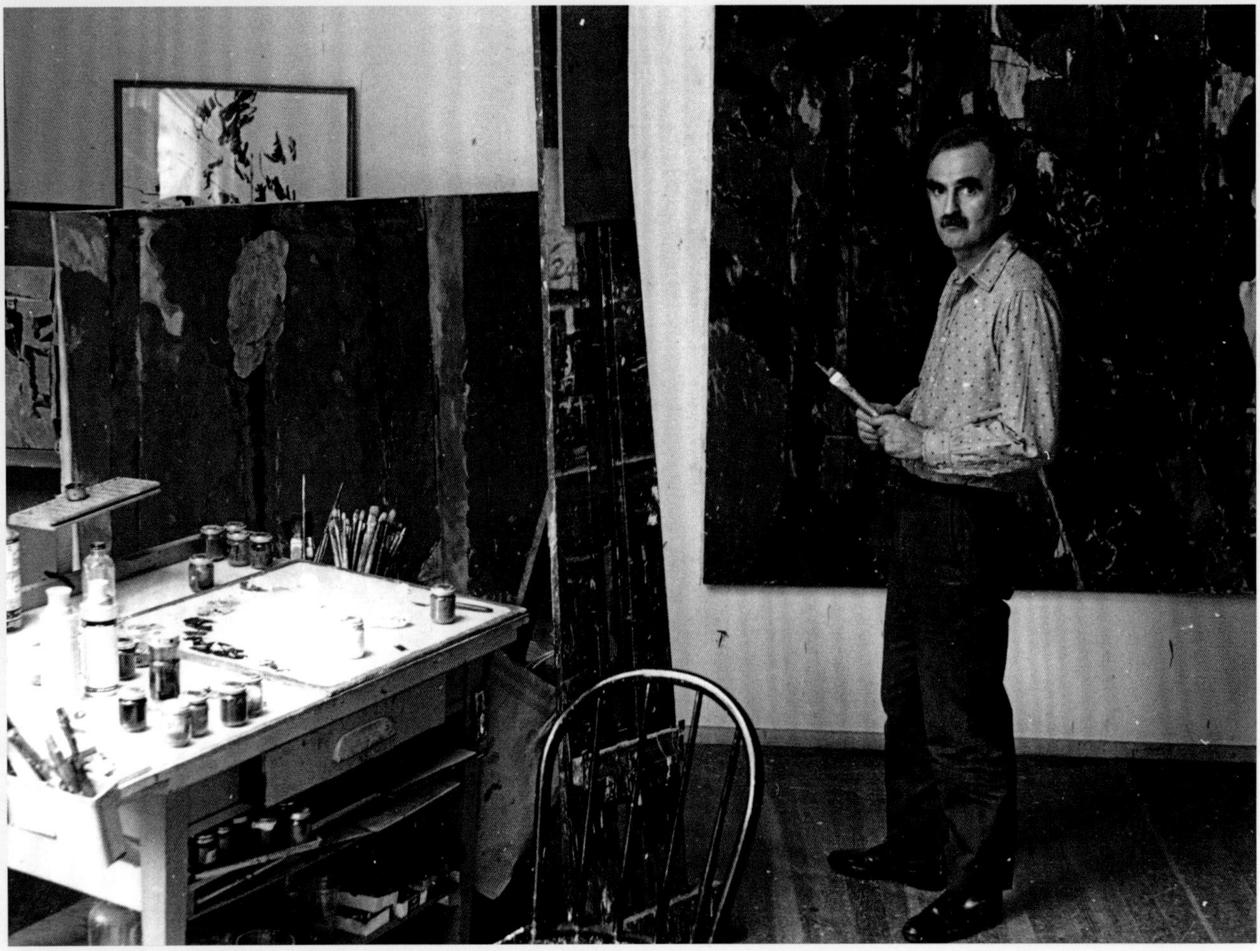